An Introduction to Political Philosophy

Ten Essays by
LEO STRAUSS

THE CULTURE OF JEWISH MODERNITY

General Editor
ALAN UDOFF, BALTIMORE HEBREW UNIVERSITY

Associate Editors
David Patterson, Oxford University
Sander Gilman, Cornell University
Amy Colin, University of Washington
Paul Mendes-Flohr, Hebrew University
Stephane Moses, Hebrew University
Saul Friedlander, University of Tel Aviv
Gillian Rose, University of Sussex

An Introduction to Political Philosophy

Ten Essays by LEO STRAUSS

edited with an introduction by

Hilail Gildin

 Wayne State University Press
Detroit

An earlier, shorter version of this book was published as *Political Philosophy: Six Essays by Leo Strauss* by Bobbs-Merrill in 1975. Copyright © 1975 by Hilail Gildin. Copyright © 1989 by Wayne State University Press, Detroit, Michigan 48201. All rights are reserved. No part of this book may be reproduced without formal permission.

09 08   10 9 8 7

Library of Congress Cataloging-in-Publication Data

Strauss, Leo.
    An introduction to political philosophy : ten essays / by Leo Strauss ; edited with an introduction by Hilail Gildin.
      p. cm. — (Culture of Jewish modernity)
    Bibliography: p.
    Includes index.
    ISBN 0–8143–1901–7 (alk. paper).—ISBN 0–8143–1902–5 (pbk. : alk. paper)
    1. Political science—Philosophy. 2. Political science—History.
I. Gildin, Hilail. II. Title. III. Series.
JA71.S7935   1989
320′.01—dc19   89–30367
                                                  CIP

Grateful acknowledgment is made for permission to reprint from the following sources:

"What Is Political Philosophy?" reprinted with permission of The Free Press, a Division of Macmillan, Inc., from *What Is Political Philosophy and Other Studies* by Leo Strauss. Copyright © 1959 by The Free Press.

"On Classical Political Philosophy" reprinted with permission from *Social Research*, February 1945.

"Natural Right and the Historical Approach" reprinted with permission from Leo Strauss, *Natural Right and History*. Copyright © 1950, 1953 by The University of Chicago. All rights reserved.

"An Epilogue" from *Essays in the Scientific Study of Politics* by Herbert Storing, copyright © 1962 by Holt, Rinehart and Winston, Inc., reprinted by permission of the publisher.

"Introduction" reprinted with permission from Leo Strauss and Joseph Cropsey, *History of Political Philosophy*, 3rd ed., The University of Chicago Press, 1987. Copyright © 1963, 1972 by Joseph Cropsey and Mirian Strauss. Copyright © 1987 by The University of Chicago. All rights reserved.

"Plato" reprinted with permission from Leo Strauss and Joseph Cropsey, *History of Political Philosophy*, 3rd ed., The University of Chicago Press, 1987. Copyright © 1963, 1972 by Joseph Cropsey and Miriam Strauss. Copyright © 1987 by The University of Chicago. All rights reserved.

"Progress or Return? The Contemporary Crisis in Western Civilization" reprinted with permission of Johns Hopkins University Press from *Modern Judaism* 1 (1981): 17–45.

"The Mutual Influence of Theology and Philosophy," published here as part three of "Progress or Return? The Contemporary Crisis in Western Civilization," reprinted with permission from *The Independent Journal of Philosophy* 3 (1979): 111–18.

"What Is Liberal Education?" from *Education for Public Responsibility*, edited by C. Scott Fletcher (New York: W. W. Norton, 1961), 43–51. Reprinted with permission of the author's estate.

"Liberal Education and Responsibility" from *Education: The Challenge Ahead*, edited by C. Scott Fletcher (New York: W. W. Norton, 1962), 49–70. Reprinted with permission of the author's estate.

ISBN-13: 978-0-8143-1902-4

ISBN-10: 0-8143-1902-5

Contents

Preface

A shorter version of this book of introductory essays by Strauss was published in 1975 under the title *Political Philosophy: Six Essays by Leo Strauss.* The present edition contains four important additional essays. Its title better reflects the intended design of the collection. All articles in this collection are printed in their entirety.

Several helpful suggestions for additions to the present collection were made by Laurence Berns and by the anonymous referees. Gisela Berns, William Elton and Stanley Corngold gave useful advice concerning some of the translations that appear in the editorial notes. The assistance of all is gratefully acknowledged.

Another welcome feature of this edition is the index, prepared by Marilyn Flaig. Footnotes preceded by an asterisk as well as all translations in brackets have been inserted by the editor.

Introduction

Leo Strauss can be described as the only important philosopher of our time who sought to revive political philosophy as it was practiced by thinkers like Plato, Machiavelli, Hobbes, and Montesquieu. Strauss is best known to scholars for his pathbreaking and solid studies of the great political philosophers of the past. Yet the thoughtful reader of Strauss finds in his works something in addition to the recovery of important insights of famous past thinkers. The more such a reader becomes aware of these insights, the more the suspicion dawns on him that the great political philosophers of the past possessed an understanding of political life, and therewith of human life, superior to that of, say, Marx, Freud, or T. S. Eliot. He begins to experience, perhaps with some astonishment, what it means to understand human affairs. In a word, the intelligent reader begins to realize that what at first glance seemed to be "merely historical" interpretations by Strauss are, in fact, at the very same time, Strauss' arguments for the revival of political philosophy. More will be said below about why Strauss chose to argue his case in this manner. Before proceeding any further, however, it is important to dispose of a possible misunderstanding.

In recent years, influential adherents of the analytic persuasion in philosophy, having noiselessly freed themselves from the tabu against believing that value-judgments can be true, began to exhibit an interest in normative political philosophy. The most impressive result of this emancipation is generally held to be John Rawls' *A Theory of Justice*.[1] Rawls' book can serve as an example of the essential differences between the political philosophy Strauss seeks to revive and what has been accomplished by the analytic school. Even those who most admire Rawls would have to admit the following: his is not the book one would recommend to someone who wished to gain an understanding of the inner workings of political life. In fairness to Rawls, it should be added that his work is not intended to supply such an understanding. Apparently, Rawls thought that it was possible to establish the norms by which political life should be governed in the absence of such an understanding. In any case, the attempt to achieve a comprehensive understanding of political things is essential to what Strauss means by political philosophy, while according to the approach represented by Rawls such an understanding can be dispensed with. When speaking of political philosophy in what follows, we will be referring to political philosophy in Strauss' sense of the term.

There would have been no need to revive political philosophy if it had not undergone a demise. The causes of that demise are reflected in the power of two different and incompatible schools of contemporary thought. To the adherents of these schools, it is no longer possible to accept as true the teaching of any political philosopher of the past without willfully disregarding something that should be obvious to every competent person today. According to one of these schools, the defect shared by all political philosophers finds expression in the manifestly "unscientific" character of their work, owing to which the conclusions of one political philosopher have never agreed with the conclusions of another. The adherents of the other school, which is called historicism, would raise a different objection. They would say that

1. *A Theory of Justice* (Cambridge, Mass.: Belknap Press, 1971).

no contemporary whose sense of history is still intact could possibly accept the claim of the great political philosophers of the past that their teachings were permanently valid, however much he might find to admire in the authors who advanced it. It will be clear from the essays that follow that Strauss did not think these objections to be equal in value, even though he found it necessary to devote a great deal of attention to each of them.

The objections to political philosophy in the name of science presuppose a distinction between philosophy and science that was unknown before the nineteenth century. Until that time, natural philosophy and natural science, political philosophy and political science, moral philosophy and moral science were equivalent expressions. In the third part of "What Is Political Philosophy?" and in the essay entitled "The Three Waves of Modernity," both of which are included in this collection, Strauss outlines the development of modern political philosophy, a development which can help one understand why that distinction came to be drawn. Strauss traces the origin of modern political philosophy to Machiavelli. The closing pages of his *Thoughts on Machiavelli* raise the question of the extent to which *all* modern philosophy or science found a congenial home on the new continent Machiavelli claimed to have discovered. Hobbes is described as having been the first great modern political philosopher to develop a new political science containing a moral teaching which was not exposed to the objection of ignoring men as they are that Machiavelli had leveled at his predecessors. Hobbes' criticism of what had been accomplished by political philosophers before his time reminds one of the kinds of objections one hears today. After listing various branches of human knowledge, Hobbes proceeds to comment on their achievements as follows:

> And truly the geometricians have very admirably performed their part. For whatsoever assistance doth accrue to the life of man, whether from the observation of the heavens or from the description of the earth, from the notation of times, or

from the remotest experiments of navigation; finally, whatsoever things they are in which this present age doth differ from the rude simpleness of antiquity, we must acknowledge to be a debt which we owe merely to geometry. If the moral philosophers had as happily discharged their duty, I know not what could have been added by human industry to the completion of that happiness, which is consistent with human life. For were the nature of human actions as distinctly known as the nature of quantity in geometrical figures, the strength of avarice and ambition, which is sustained by the erroneous opinions of the vulgar as touching the nature of right and wrong, would presently faint and languish; and mankind should enjoy such an immortal peace, that unless it were for habitation, on supposition that the earth should grow too narrow for her inhabitants, there would hardly be left any pretence for war. But now on the contrary, that neither the sword nor the pen should be allowed any cessation; that the knowledge of the law of nature should lose its growth, not advancing a whit beyond its ancient stature; that there should still be such siding with the several factions of philosophers, that the very same action should be decried by some, and as much elevated by others; that the very same man should at several times embrace his several opinions, and esteem his own actions far otherwise in himself than he does in others: these, I say, are so many signs, so many manifest arguments, that what hath hitherto been written by moral philosophers, hath not made any progress in the knowledge of the truth. . . .[2]

In another writing, Hobbes declares the need for a science of politics that would deserve a place alongside the achievements of Copernicus, Kepler, and Galileo, and he proclaims his political philosophy to be that very science. Because, as Hobbes thought, he had supplied men with their first distinct understanding of the evils besetting the human condition and with clear knowledge of what society can do to remedy them, he believed his philosophy made possible a political life that is based on knowledge of the political truth and is capable of being guided by such knowledge. The changes that Hobbes' political philosophy were later

2. *De cive,* Ep. ded. The translation is by Hobbes.

made to undergo are described by Strauss, who shows how indebted the philosophers who made them—and particularly Locke—were to the innovations of Hobbes. Strauss also reveals the extent to which these changes were based on an acceptance of Hobbes' premises and can therefore be described as the product of an internal criticism and development of Hobbes' teaching. The later versions of the new political science, at least in their popular form, were characterized, no less than was Hobbes' version, by confidence in the solidity of that science and in the beneficent social effects that would result from its widespread diffusion. The best-known expression of that confidence was the belief in Progress. Strauss shows how, at the very moment at which modern political philosophy began to exert practical influence, it was confronted with a crisis within its own ranks. He labels that crisis, which he associates with Rousseau, the first crisis of modernity. Rousseau's views too, according to Strauss, can be understood in large part as resulting from Rousseau's internal criticism of his great modern predecessors. Rousseau's criticism, however, tends as much to the destruction of the principles of his predecessors as it does to the further development of those principles. Rousseau therefore opens a new epoch in modern political philosophy, an epoch whose most easily recognizable feature is the replacement of nature by history as the key to understanding man. For a while it was believed that such a replacement was compatible with a knowledge of human affairs that is capable of supplying men with rational guidance. Nietzsche attacked the belief in this compatibility and argued that the insight into the historicity of man necessitated the abandonment of the traditional belief in reason. With Nietzsche began what Strauss calls the second and present-day crisis of modernity. While the criticisms of Rousseau and Nietzsche did not nullify the influence of early modern political philosophy, they did much to undermine confidence in its principles and tenets. After reading Strauss' account of modern political philosophy, one is led to wonder whether the sequence of transformations he describes is not, at least, understandable, or whether the "disgraceful diversity" of modern political philosophies does not, given the existence of modern philosophy, reflect more credit on the human spirit than would the absence of that diversity. Strauss certainly makes it difficult to adopt the superficial view that the bewildering variety of modern political philosophies represents so many alternatives from which one might be tempted to choose if one were not deterred from doing so by an uneasiness which their diversity reasonably arouses. In any event, modern philosophy or science was originally inspired by the hope of achieving indisputable success in all its branches, including political philosophy. During the nineteenth century, and contemporaneously with what Strauss called the first crisis of modernity, a distinction came to be drawn between the branches of modern philosophy that had, in a way, fulfilled that promise and those that had not. The successful parts of modern philosophy—modern natural science, physics in particular—came to be known as "science" while its less successful parts came to be known as "philosophy."[3] Those for whom the development of modern political philosophy demonstrated its failure to fulfill its original promise began to seek its fulfillment in an understanding of human affairs that would be part of "science" in the new sense of the term, and hence, it was hoped, free of the endless controversies which philosophy seemed to be doomed to generate and powerless to resolve. Those, on the other hand, for whom the development of modern political philosophy had culminated not in its self-destruction but in the discovery of a new dimension of reality, the "historical" dimension, ultimately sought to understand "science" itself in the light of that discovery.

The efforts to found a new science of politics are continuing today. These efforts are distinguished from those of Hobbes in that the new science is meant to be a branch of

3. Leo Strauss, *Natural Right and History* (Chicago: Univ. of Chicago Press, 1953), pp. 78–79.

science rather than a branch of philosophy. Since the existing sciences, through no fault of their own, supply no clear guidelines for the proper study of elections, revolutions, civil wars, and other political activities, the projected new science of politics must be preceded by reflections regarding the nature of science. The purpose of such reflections is to determine why the natural sciences have been successful so that one can proceed to achieve comparable success elsewhere. Unfortunately, these reflections have the character of philosophy rather than of science. The attempt to achieve an understanding of politics which is independent of philosophy thus proves to be itself dependent on philosophy to a degree which is far from negligible.

One well-known feature which is common to almost all present-day attempts to make the study of politics scientific is the distinction between facts and values. The effect of that distinction is to prohibit political science from either making value judgments or seeking to validate them, although political science remains free to study those who make value judgments and the causes that prompt them to do so. At times, the distinction between facts and values is propounded as if it were an obvious truth which even the most superficial familiarity with science should enable one to accept. Neither the distinction in question nor the arguments intended to enhance its plausibility appeared sound to Strauss. It did not seem obvious to him that it was impossible to conclude, on the basis of objective evidence, that someone was a coward or a fool. Nor was he persuaded by the contention that men could be compelled to agree about facts whereas values were always controversial. It seemed to him that there were cases in which agreement regarding the fact that someone was a "cheapskate" or a "sourpuss"—presumably value judgments—could be achieved with relative ease. On the other hand, agreement about the causes of the French Revolution—presumably a fact—seemed nowhere in sight. Despite his belief that the fact-value distinction was untenable, Strauss studied the arguments advanced on its behalf with great patience and care, and he made the effort to meet each one of them. The essay in this collection entitled "An Epilogue" as well as Part I of "What is Political Philosophy?" will introduce the reader to this portion of Strauss' work. Strauss did not base his arguments against the fact-value distinction on the claim that he had solved the riddle of knowledge. He did, however, criticize the theories of knowledge advanced in support of that distinction. However difficult it may be to give an adequate account of how "values" come to be known, or, for that matter, of how facts come to be known, or of the obstacle that stands in the way of effecting a separation between facts and values, that such an obstacle exists can be experienced without difficulty. One need only make the attempt to combine the "values" of Trotsky with Hitler's factual beliefs regarding human affairs, or the "values" of Hitler with Trotsky's factual beliefs regarding human affairs, something that it should be possible to do if the fact-value distinction were sound.

The contemporary attempt to make the study of politics into a modern science is largely inspired by a positivist or neo-positivist repudiation of traditional philosophy in general and of traditional political philosophy in particular. At the same time, that attempt is dependent upon reflections regarding the nature of modern science. According to Strauss, if those reflections were carried far enough the result would be the replacement of a positivist understanding of science by a historicist understanding of science. On one occasion,[4] Strauss used Ernest Nagel's *The Structure of Science*[5] to illustrate what he meant by affirming that if positivism understood itself, it would necessarily transform into historicism. Nagel opens his work by discussing the relation of science to common sense. Without denying the genuineness of the knowledge of the world that can be acquired by

4. A course entitled "Natural Right" given at the University of Chicago in the Autumn Quarter, 1962.
5. *The Structure of Science* (New York: Harcourt, Brace and World, 1961).

common sense, Nagel easily shows how superior the scientific knowledge of, say, health and disease is to the common sense knowledge of health and disease and, more generally, how superior scientific knowledge is to common sense knowledge. The conclusion of Nagel's discussion is that modern science is clearly the best way to achieve knowledge that is superior to common sense knowledge.[6] Later in the same work, Nagel pauses to consider certain difficulties connected with the principle of causality.[7] He dismisses the view that this principle is "a priori and necessary," and for various reasons he rejects the contention that the principle of causality can be understood as an empirical generalization. According to him, the principle of causality is a *"maxim* for inquiry" or a "methodological rule"[8] or, most interestingly of all, "the expression of a resolution."[9] The purpose of this maxim or rule is to formulate one of the goals pursued by theoretical science in modern times.[10] This maxim is of no small importance for modern science according to Nagel. Modern science as we know it stands or falls by its acceptance.[11] Yet one cannot be required to accept it either on grounds of its evident necessity or on factual grounds. The question therefore arises whether according to Nagel modern science rests on an arbitrary foundation. It is to Nagel's credit that he does not refuse to discuss this issue, even though his discussion of it is rather brief.

But if the principle [of causality] is a maxim, is it a rule that may be followed or ignored at will? Is it merely an arbitrary matter what general goals are pursued by theoretical

6. Nagel, *Structure*, p. 13, last paragraph.
7. Nagel, *Structure*, pp. 316–324.
8. Nagel, *Structure*, p. 320.
9. Nagel, *Structure*, p. 317.
10. Nagel, *Structure*, p. 322.
11. Nagel, *Structure*, p. 324: ". . . [I]t is difficult to understand how it would be possible for modern theoretical science to surrender the general ideal expressed by the principle [of causality] without becoming thereby transformed into something incomparably different from what that enterprise actually is."

> science in its development? It is undoubtedly only a con-
> tingent historical fact that the enterprise known as "science"
> does aim at achieving the type of explanations prescribed by
> the principle; for it is logically possible that in their efforts
> at mastering their environments men might have aimed at
> something quite different. Accordingly, the goals men adopt
> in the pursuit of knowledge are *logically* arbitrary.[12]

The fact that Nagel italicizes "logically" in this passage may
lead one to wonder whether according to him the principle
of causality possesses some powers of persuasion based
neither on logic nor on fact. Does he hold, for example, that
one is somehow compelled to accept this principle by a law
of human nature? Apparently not, since Nagel describes the
acceptance of the principle of causality as "undoubtedly
only a contingent historical fact." He further suggests that
what is true of the goal enunciated by that principle is true
of all the goals by whose pursuit modern science is defined.

The view of modern science that emerges from Nagel's
discussion of the principle of causality contradicts the view
he expressed earlier when he spoke of the relation between
science and common sense. Earlier, modern science seemed
to be *the* rational way to rise above common sense in the
pursuit of knowledge. Now it appears to be only one of a
number of ways of pursuing knowledge and to be no more
defensible rationally than any of the other ways. We may be
told that the earlier discussion was only introductory in
character and that it must be understood in the light of
Nagel's later remarks. If this step is taken, then the last bar-
rier to a historicist understanding of science is removed.

The historicist will have no difficulty in accepting Nagel's
view regarding the unevident character of the principle by
which science as we know it stands or falls. He will also
welcome the view that this principle is the expression of a
resolution and that its acceptance is due not to insight but
to a decision. That decision, he will point out, would not

12. Nagel, *Structure,* p. 324.

have been the epoch-making or "historic" decision that it proved to be if it had not been made by several generations of great minds in succession. The great men who made that decision believed themselves to be assenting to an evidently necessary truth and, in that belief, they often were willing to make that decision at great personal risk to themselves. Nevertheless, in retrospect their belief can be seen to have been a delusion. The power exerted by that delusion over generations of great minds is one example of what the historicist means when he speaks of the dependence of thought on history or time. In making these observations, the historicist is not recommending the abandonment of the scientific pursuit of knowledge. He would be the first to affirm that modern science is part of the historical destiny of modern man. He would only contend that a proper appreciation of the arbitrary decisions that lie at the foundation of modern science should dispel the temptation to regard all human thought that does not form part of modern science as somehow inferior in cognitive rank to scientific thought. In particular, the historicist would regard the understanding of the historicity of modern science as more fundamental in character than any result of scientific inquiry. He would further claim that what is true of science as a "historic event" is equally true of the great religious, political, and philosophic events of the past. All were based on unevident assumptions that belonged to a definite historical situation, even though the great men responsible for these events believed themselves to be giving their free assent to something that transcended history.

Certain experiences of modern Western man seem to lend plausibility to the historicist contention. Among these is the perceived loss in the compelling power of the beliefs in Reason, in Nature, and in the revealed word of God by which previous generations had taken their bearings when they made history. The experience of this loss, combined with the alleged insight into the arbitrary character of those beliefs, lends support to the view that those beliefs were themselves the work of history. History, by depriving modern Western man of the beliefs by which the great thoughts and actions of the past were sheltered and inspired—perhaps thereby endangering the possibility of great thoughts and actions in the future—has for the first time laid bare the true matrix of those beliefs, actions, and thoughts: it has laid bare the historicity of man.

In the essay of this collection entitled "Natural Right and the Historical Approach" Strauss discusses the various stages through which historicism passed before assuming its contemporary form. His analysis brings out the distrust of philosophical reason that characterized historicism from the start as well as the steps through which that distrust turned into a theoretical denial of the very possibility of insights that are universally valid and hence not historically relative. Strauss proceeds to point out the self-contradictory character of this position: In the very act of proclaiming that no human thought can be universally valid because all human thought is historically relative, historicism advances a thesis regarding all human thought for which thesis it claims universal validity. It would be a serious misunderstanding of Strauss to think that, according to him, this objection suffices to dispose of historicism. On the contrary, Strauss proceeds to show how the attempt to meet this objection gave rise to the most thoughtful and powerful version of historicism, a version which he labels radical historicism. In speaking of radical historicism, the thinker whom Strauss has in mind primarily is Martin Heidegger. The radical historicist faces the objection Strauss raises by ascribing his insight into the historicity of human existence to the unique and unprecedented historical situation of modern man. He claims that the manner in which his insight is achieved confirms the content of that insight. This claim is accompanied by an analysis that is meant to lay bare the ultimate assumptions which formerly guided and were thought to justify philosophy as the attempt to achieve comprehensive knowledge of the eternal order. This analysis attempts to show that those assumptions are by no means ultimate in character, that they are derived from a deeper root to which earlier thought had no access, that their validity is derivative and severely limited, and that they lack the power to justify philosophy in the traditional sense of the term. A fundamental part of this analysis is a wholly new account of human existence. That new account is held to be superior to all previous accounts precisely because it is not based on the questionable assumptions which all previous philosophers are alleged to have taken for granted.

Strauss wishes to encourage his readers to honestly face the challenge of historicism, at its intellectually most powerful, both to philosophy simply and to political philosophy in particular. For him this means facing the challenge of Heidegger. Strauss refrains from speaking of Heidegger in a way that could lead to an unthinking dismissal of him. At the same time, Strauss leaves his reader in no doubt concerning his rejection, for what he is convinced are solid reasons, of Heidegger's views. "Heidegger, who surpasses in speculative intelligence all his contemporaries and is at the same time intellectually the counterpart of what Hitler was politically, attempts to go a way not yet trodden by anyone, or rather to think in a way in which philosophers at any rate have never thought before. Certain it is that no one has questioned the premises of philosophy as radically as Heidegger."[13] The thinker of his own generation to whom Strauss was closer than to any other, despite their differences, Jacob Klein, studied with Heidegger. Klein, who was well versed in mathematics and the natural sciences at the time, found that Aristotle, as elucidated by Heidegger in Heidegger's attempt to overcome the philosophical tradition, was sounder and made more sense than Heidegger's own views did. Klein was led by this to further studies of classical philosophy and mathematics, as well as of their relation to modern philosophy, modern natural

13. Leo Strauss, "An Unspoken Prologue to a Public Lecture at St. John's," *The College* 30, no. 2 (January 1979): 31.

science, and modern mathematics. Some of the results of his studies appeared in a work he published on Greek mathematics and the origin of algebra,[14] a work Strauss praised as "unrivalled in the whole field of intellectual history, at least in our generation."[15] Strauss credited Klein with convincing him that "first, the one thing needed philosophically is in the first place a return to, a recovery of, classical philosophy; second, the way in which Plato is read, especially by professors of philosophy and by men who do philosophy, is wholly inadequate because it does not take into account the dramatic character of the dialogues, also and especially of those of their parts which look almost like philosophic treatises."[16] The effort by Klein and by Strauss to revive classical philosophy was somehow made possible by Heidegger, contrary to his own intention.

Strauss had reservations of his own, dating back to the same period, regarding Heidegger's views. The soundness of these reservations became apparent during the Hitler revolution of 1933 when Heidegger, as Strauss expresses it, proceeded to "submit to, or rather to welcome, as a dispensation of fate, the verdict of the least wise and least moderate part of his nation, while it was in its least wise and least moderate mood, and at the same time to speak of wisdom and moderation."[17] Strauss goes on to draw the conclusion that what history in 1933 "proved" was the untenability of historicism, including that of Heidegger: "The biggest event of 1933 would rather seem to have proved, if such proof was necessary, that man cannot abandon the question of the good society, and that he cannot

14. Jacob Klein, "Die griechische Logistik und die Entstehung der modernen Algebra," *Quellen und Studien zur Geschichte der Mathematik, Astronomie und Physik*, Abteilung B: *Studien*, 3, no. 1 (1934): 18–105; no. 2 (1936): 122–235. This work has been translated into English by Eva Brann: *Greek Mathematical Thought and the Origin of Algebra* (Cambridge: M.I.T. Press, 1968).

15. Jacob Klein and Leo Strauss, "A Giving of Accounts," *The College* 22, no. 1 (April 1970): 31.

16. Klein and Strauss, "A Giving of Accounts," p. 31.

17. See below, pp. 23–24.

free himself from the responsibility for answering it by deferring to History or to any other power different from his own reason."[18] Strauss is by no means suggesting that all historicists are fascists. There have been Marxists who became supporters of Stalin not because they were attracted to him but because they regarded his victory over his rivals for the leadership of the communist movement as the verdict of History. There are American and British conservatives and liberals who support the American or the British Constitution on historicist grounds. Even Burke, whom Strauss admired greatly as a statesman, and whose defense of practical wisdom against the "speculatist" approach to politics he considered an enduring contribution to political philosophy, is criticized by Strauss for the concluding paragraph of *Thoughts on French Affairs*. There Burke can at least be understood to be saying that his refutation of the "speculatist" political doctrinairism which animated the French Revolution could be rendered invalid by the triumph of that Revolution. "Burke comes close to suggesting that to oppose [what he himself regards as] a thoroughly evil current in human affairs is perverse if that current is sufficiently powerful; he is oblivious of the nobility of last-ditch resistance. . . . It is only a short step from this thought of Burke to the supersession of the distinction between good and bad by the distinction between the progressive and the retrograde, or between what is and what is not in harmony with the historical process."[19] To Burke's credit, he did not take this step, according to Strauss.

To return to Heidegger, Strauss declares that the National Socialist episodes in his career cannot and should not be ignored. Moreover, he asserts that "one is bound to misunderstand Heidegger's thought radically if one does not see their intimate connection with the core of his philosophic thought." However, this is not the end of the mat-

18. See below, p. 24.
19. Strauss, *Natural Right and History*, pp. 317–318.

ter. Strauss goes on to add that "nevertheless" these episodes "afford too small a basis for the proper understanding of his thought."[20] Strauss believed that there simply was a good deal one could still learn from Heidegger in spite of his grave errors. To give only one example, Strauss admired the interpretation of the thought of Kant found in Heidegger's *Die Frage nach dem Ding*.

Strauss' comments on Heidegger's relation to Husserl shed additional light on Strauss' understanding of Heidegger. According to Strauss, "Husserl . . . had realized more profoundly than anybody else that the scientific understanding of the world, far from being the perfection of our natural understanding, is derivative from the latter in such a way as to make us oblivious of the very foundations of the scientific understanding: all philosophic understanding must start from our common understanding of the world, from our understanding of the world as sensibly perceived prior to all theorizing. Heidegger went much further than Husserl in the same direction. . . ."[21] Elsewhere, Strauss explains what he means by going much further: "what is primary is not the object of sense-perception but the things we handle and with which we are concerned, *pragmata*."[22] What is primary is the pre-scientific world of human concern. Interestingly, the transition from Weberian social science to Socratic political philosophy is described by Strauss in almost the same terms.[23] The all-important difference is that Heidegger's pre-scientific world of human concern is understood in the light of the experience of History, whereas the pre-scientific world of Socratic political philosophy is understood as the work of nature and law. For "according to Socrates the things which are 'first in themselves' are somehow 'first for us'; the things which are 'first

20. Leo Strauss, *Studies in Platonic Political Philosophy* (Chicago: Univ. of Chicago Press, 1983), p. 30.
21. Strauss, *Studies in Platonic Political Philosophy*, p. 31.
22. Klein and Strauss, "A Giving of Accounts," p. 3.
23. Strauss, *Natural Right and History*, pp. 79–83, 120–125.

in themselves' are in a manner, but necessarily, revealed in men's opinions."[24] In Socratic political philosophy, man's natural understanding of the world is somehow natural in the literal sense, and makes possible an ascent to the pursuit of comprehensive and universally valid understanding, which Husserl regarded as the true goal of philosophy. Strauss and Klein affirm that Heidegger surpasses all his contemporaries in speculative intelligence. But they do not think that he surpasses Socrates, Plato or Aristotle in speculative intelligence, or that his new account of human existence rivals that of those classical thinkers.

In conclusion, something should be said about how Strauss understood the practical implications for political life today of his attempt to return to classical political philosophy. Although the following passage has been quoted more than once by other writers, it would seem that enough attention has still not been paid to it by some critics of Strauss:

> We cannot reasonably expect that a fresh understanding of classical political philosophy will supply us with recipes for today's use. For the relative success of modern political philosophy has brought into being a kind of society wholly unknown to the classics, a kind of society to which the classical principles as stated and elaborated by the classics are not immediately applicable. Only we living today can possibly find a solution to the problems of today. But an adequate understanding of the principles as elaborated by the classics may be the indispensable starting point for an adequate analysis, to be achieved by us, of present-day society in its peculiar character, and for the wise application, to be achieved by us, of these principles to our task.[25]

While he defended the validity of the classical solution for the kind of society for which it was elaborated, he thought that "liberal or constitutional democracy comes closer to

24. Leo Strauss, *The City and Man* (Chicago: Rand McNally & Company, 1964), p. 19.
25. Strauss, *The City and the Man*, p. 11.

what the classics demanded that any alternative that is viable in our age."[26] He was no less sincere an ally of constitutional democracy than Winston Churchill and Alexis de Tocqueville, even though, like them, he was not a doctrinaire democrat. Nor did he think, any more than they did, that modern constitutional democracy was somehow a disguised aristocracy. He was immune to the appeal of grandiose and extravagant promises to create a higher and better humanity, however conceived, and fully awake to the evils of tyranny. He therefore saw through communism and fascism without difficulty. He thought that there was a human nature and that it could not be changed but his understanding of it and of the standards implied in it was loftier and more comprehensive than that of Hobbes and did not omit the things with which Hobbes dealt. The reader is referred to the essays in this collection entitled "What Is Liberal Education?" and "Liberal Education and Responsibility" for more light on how Strauss understands the gravest problems of the present.

26. Leo Strauss, *What Is Political Philosophy and Other Studies* (Glencoe, Ill.: Free Press, 1959), p.113.

Part One

Editor's Note: This essay is a revised version of the Judah L. Magnes Lectures, which were delivered at the Hebrew University, Jerusalem, in December 1954 and January 1955, and published in 1959 in *What Is Political Philosophy and Other Studies* (Glencoe: The Free Press). When the essay was reprinted in the earlier edition of this volume (Hilail Gildin, ed., *Political Philosophy: Six Essays by Leo Strauss* [Indianapolis: Bobbs-Merrill, 1975]), the initial paragraph was omitted on the insistence of the publisher and with the permission of Leo Strauss. The paragraph is here restored.

It is a great honor, and at the same time a challenge to accept a task of particular difficulty, to be asked to speak about political philosophy in Jerusalem. In this city, and in this land, the theme of political philosophy—"the city of righteousness, the faithful city"—has been taken more seriously than anywhere else on earth. Nowhere else has the longing for justice and the just city filled the purest hearts and the loftiest souls with such zeal as on this sacred soil. I know all too well that I am utterly unable to convey to you what in the best possible case, in the case of any man, would be no more than a faint reproduction or a weak imitation of our prophets' vision. I shall even be compelled to lead you into a region where the dimmest recollection of that vision is on the point of vanishing altogether—where the Kingdom of God is derisively called an imagined principality—to say here nothing of the region which was never illumined by it. But while being compelled, or compelling myself, to wander far away from our sacred heritage, or to be silent about it, I shall not for a moment forget what Jerusalem stands for.

What Is Political Philosophy?

1 The Problem of Political Philosophy

The meaning of political philosophy and its meaningful character is as evident today as it always has been since the time when political philosophy came to light in Athens. All political action aims at either preservation or change. When desiring to preserve, we wish to prevent a change to the worse; when desiring to change, we wish to bring about something better. All political action is then guided by some thought of better and worse. But thought of better or worse implies thought of the good. The awareness of the good which guides all our actions has the character of opinion: it is no longer questioned but, on reflection, it proves to be questionable. The very fact that we can question it directs us towards such a thought of the good as is no longer questionable—towards a thought which is no longer opinion but knowledge. All political action has then in itself a directedness towards knowledge of the good: of the good life, or of the good society. For the good society is the complete political good.

If this directedness becomes explicit, if men make it their explicit goal to acquire knowledge of the good life and of the good society, political philosophy emerges. By calling this pursuit political philosophy, we imply that it forms a part of a larger whole: of philosophy; or that political philosophy is a branch of philosophy. In the expression "political philosophy," "philosophy" indicates the manner of treatment: a treatment which both goes to the roots and is comprehensive; "political" indicates both the subject matter and the function: political philosophy deals with political matters in a manner that is meant to be relevant for political life; therefore its subject must be identical with the goal, the ultimate goal of political action. The theme of political philosophy is mankind's great objectives, freedom and government or empire—objectives which are capable of lifting all men beyond their poor selves. Political philosophy is that branch of philosophy which is closest to political life, to nonphilosophic life, to human life. Only in his *Politics* does Aristotle make use of oaths—the almost inevitable accompaniment of passionate speech.

Since political philosophy is a branch of philosophy, even the most provisional explanation of what political philosophy is cannot dispense with an explanation, however provisional, of what philosophy is. Philosophy, as quest for wisdom, is quest for universal knowledge, for knowledge of the whole. The quest would not be necessary if such knowledge were immediately available. The absence of knowledge of the whole does not mean, however, that men do not have thoughts about the whole: philosophy is necessarily preceded by opinions about the whole. It is, therefore, the attempt to replace opinions about the whole by knowledge of the whole. Instead of "the whole," the philosophers also say "all things": the whole is not a pure ether or an unrelieved darkness in which one cannot distinguish one part from the other, or in which one cannot discern anything. Quest for knowledge of "all things" means quest for knowledge of God, the world, and man—or rather quest for knowledge of the natures of all things: the natures in their totality are "the whole."

Philosophy is essentially not possession of the truth, but quest for the truth. The distinctive trait of the philosopher is that "he knows that he knows nothing," and that his insight into our ignorance concerning the most important things induces him to strive with all his power for knowledge. He would cease to be a philosopher by evading the questions concerning these things or by disregarding them because they cannot be answered. It may be that as regards the possible answers to these questions, the pros and cons will always be in a more or less even balance, and therefore that philosophy will never go beyond the stage of discussion or disputation and will never reach the stage of decision. This would not make philosophy futile. For the clear grasp of a fundamental question requires understanding of the nature of the subject matter with which the question is concerned. Genuine knowledge of a fundamental question, thorough understanding of it, is better than blindness to it, or indifference to it, be that indifference or blindness accompanied by knowledge of the answers to a vast number of peripheral or ephemeral questions or not. *Minimum quod potest haberi de cognitione rerum altissimarum, desiderabilius est quam certissima cognitio quae habetur de minimis rebus.** (Thomas Aquinas, *Summa Theologica*, I, qu. 1a.5)

Of philosophy thus understood, political philosophy is a branch. Political philosophy will then be the attempt to replace opinion about the nature of political things by knowledge of the nature of political things. Political things are by their nature subject to approval and disapproval, to choice and rejection, to praise and blame. It is of their essence not to be neutral but to raise a claim to men's obedience, allegiance, decision, or judgment. One does not understand them as what they are, as political things, if one does not

* "The least knowledge one can have of the highest things is more desirable than the most certain knowledge one has of the lowest things."

take seriously their explicit or implicit claim to be judged in terms of goodness or badness, of justice or injustice, i.e., if one does not measure them by some standard of goodness or justice. To judge soundly one must know the true standards. If political philosophy wishes to do justice to its subject matter, it must strive for genuine knowledge of these standards. Political philosophy is the attempt truly to know both the nature of political things and the right, or the good, political order.

Political philosophy ought to be distinguished from political thought in general. In our times, they are frequently identified. People have gone so far in debasing the name of philosophy as to speak of the philosophies of vulgar impostors. By political thought we understand the reflection on, or the exposition of, political ideas; and by a political idea we may understand any politically significant "phantasm, notion, species, or whatever it is about which the mind can be employed in thinking" concerning the political fundamentals. Hence, all political philosophy is political thought but not all political thought is political philosophy. Political thought is, as such, indifferent to the distinction between opinion and knowledge; but political philosophy is the conscious, coherent, and relentless effort to replace opinions about the political fundamentals by knowledge regarding them. Political thought may not be more, and may not even intend to be more, than the expounding or the defense of a firmly held conviction or of an invigorating myth; but it is essential to political philosophy to be set in motion, and be kept in motion, by the disquieting awareness of the fundamental difference between conviction, or belief, and knowledge. A political thinker who is not a philosopher is primarily interested in, or attached to, a specific order or policy; the political philosopher is primarily interested in, or attached to, the truth. Political thought which is not political philosophy finds its adequate expression in laws and codes, in poems and stories, in tracts and public speeches *inter alia;* the proper form of presenting political philosophy is the treatise. Political thought is as old as the human race; the first man who uttered a word like "father" or an expression like "thou shalt not . . ." was the first political thinker; but political philosophy appeared at a knowable time in the recorded past.

By political theory, people frequently understand today comprehensive reflections on the political situation which lead up to the suggestion of a broad policy. Such reflections appeal in the last resort to principles accepted by public opinion or a considerable part of it; i.e., they dogmatically assume principles which can well be questioned. Works of political theory in this sense would be Pinsker's *Autoemancipation* and Herzl's *Judenstaat.* Pinsker's *Autoemancipation* carries as its motto the words: "If I am not for myself, who will be for me? And if not now, when?" It omits the words: "And if I am only for myself, what am I?" Pinsker's silent rejection of the thought expressed in the omitted words is a crucial premise of the argument developed in his tract. Pinsker does not justify this rejection. For a justification, one would have to turn to the 3rd and 16th chapters of Spinoza's *Tractatus theologico-politicus,* to a work of a political philosopher.

We are compelled to distinguish political philosophy from political theology. By political theology we understand political teachings which are based on divine revelation. Political philosophy is limited to what is accessible to the unassisted human mind. As regards social philosophy, it has the same subject matter as political philosophy, but it regards it from a different point of view. Political philosophy rests on the premise that the political association—one's country or one's nation—is the most comprehensive or the most authoritative association, whereas social philosophy conceives of the political association as a part of a larger whole which it designates by the term "society."

Finally, we must discuss the relation of political philosophy to political science. "Political science" is an ambiguous term: it designates such investigations of political things as are guided by the model of natural science, and it designates the work which is being done by the members of political science departments. As regards the former, or what we may call "scientific" political science, it conceives of itself as *the* way towards genuine knowledge of political things. Just as genuine knowledge of natural things began when people turned from sterile and vain speculation to empirical and experimental study, the genuine knowledge of political things will begin when political philosophy will have given way completely to the scientific study of politics. Just as natural science stands on its own feet, and at most supplies unintentionally materials for the speculations of natural philosophers, political science stands on its own feet, and at most supplies unintentionally materials for the speculations of political philosophers. Considering the contrast between the solidity of the one pursuit and the pitiful pretentiousness characteristic of the other, it is however more reasonable to dismiss the vague and inane speculations of political philosophy altogether than to go on paying lip service to a wholly discredited and decrepit tradition. The sciences, both natural and political, are frankly nonphilosophic. They need philosophy of a kind: methodology or logic. But these philosophic disciplines have obviously nothing in common with political philosophy. "Scientific" political science is in fact incompatible with political philosophy.

The useful work done by the men called political scientists is independent of any aspiration towards "scientific" political science. It consists of careful and judicious collections and analyses of politically relevant data. To understand the meaning of this work, we remind ourselves of our provisional definition of political philosophy. Political philosophy is the attempt to understand the nature of political things. Before one can even think of attempting to understand the nature of political things, one must know political things: one must possess political knowledge. At least every sane adult possesses political knowledge to some degree. Everyone knows something of taxes, police, law, jails, war, peace, armistice. Everyone knows that the aim of war is victory, that war demands the supreme sacrifice and many other deprivations, that bravery deserves praise and cowardice deserves blame. Everyone knows that buying a shirt, as distinguished from casting a vote, is not in itself a political action. The man in the street is supposed to possess less political knowledge than the men who make it their business to supply him with information and guidance regarding political things. He certainly possesses less political knowledge than very intelligent men of long and varied political experience. At the top of the ladder we find the great statesman who possesses political knowledge, political understanding, political wisdom, political skill in the highest degree: political science (*politikē epistēmē*) in the original meaning of the term.

All political knowledge is surrounded by political opinion and interspersed with it. By political opinion we understand here opinion as distinguished from knowledge of political things: errors, guesses, beliefs, prejudices, forecasts, and so on. It is of the essence of political life to be guided by a mixture of political knowledge and political opinion. Hence, all political life is accompanied by more or less coherent and more or less strenuous efforts to replace political opinion by political knowledge. Even governments which lay claim to more than human knowledge are known to employ spies.

The character of political knowledge and of the demands made on it has been profoundly affected by a fairly recent change in the character of society. In former epochs, intelligent men could acquire the political knowledge, the political understanding they needed, by listening to wise old men or, which is the same thing, by reading good historians, as well as by looking around and by devoting themselves to public affairs. These ways of acquiring political knowledge are no longer sufficient because we live in "dynamic mass societies," i.e., in societies which are characterized by both immense complexity and rapid change. Political knowledge is more difficult to come by and it becomes obsolete more rapidly than in former times. Under these conditions it becomes necessary that a number of men should devote themselves entirely to the task of collecting and digesting knowledge of political things. It is this activity which today is frequently called political science. It does not emerge if it has not been realized among other things that even such political matters as have no bearing on the situation of the day deserve to be studied, and that their study must be carried on with the greatest possible care: a specific care which is designed to counteract the specific fallacies to which our judgment on political things is exposed. Furthermore, the men we speak of invest much toil in giving political knowledge the form of teachings which can be transmitted in classrooms. Moreover, while even the most unscrupulous politician must constantly try to replace in his own mind political opinion by political knowledge in order to be successful, the scholarly student of political things will go beyond this by trying to state the results of his investigations in public without any concealment and without any partisanship: he will act the part of the enlightened and patriotic citizen who has no axe of his own to grind. Or, differently expressed, the scholarly quest for political knowledge is essentially animated by a moral impulse, the love of truth. But however one may conceive of the difference between the scholarly and the nonscholarly quest for political knowledge, and however important these differences may be, the scholarly and the nonscholarly quest for political knowledge are identical in the decisive respect: their center of reference is the given political situation, and even in most cases the given political situation in the individual's own country. It is true that a botanist in Israel pays special attention to the flora of Israel, whereas the botanist in Canada pays special attention to the flora of

Canada. But this difference, which is not more than the outcome of a convenient and even indispensable division of labor, has an entirely different character than the only apparently similar difference between the preoccupation of the Israeli political scientist and the Canadian political scientist. It is only when the Here and Now ceases to be the center of reference that a philosophic or scientific approach to politics can emerge.

All knowledge of political things implies assumptions concerning the nature of political things; i.e., assumptions which concern not merely the given political situation, but political life or human life as such. One cannot know anything about a war going on at a given time without having some notion, however dim and hazy, of war as such and its place within human life as such. One cannot see a policeman as a policeman without having made an assumption about law and government as such. The assumptions concerning the nature of political things, which are implied in all knowledge of political things, have the character of opinions. It is only when these assumptions are made the theme of critical and coherent analysis that a philosophic or scientific approach to politics emerges.

The cognitive status of political knowledge is not different from that of the knowledge possessed by the shepherd, the husband, the general, or the cook. Yet the pursuits of these types of man do not give rise to a pastoral, marital, military, or culinary philosophy because their ultimate goals are sufficiently clear and unambiguous. The ultimate political goal, on the other hand, urgently calls for coherent reflection. The goal of the general is victory, whereas the goal of the statesman is the common good. What victory means is not essentially controversial, but the meaning of the common good is essentially controversial. The ambiguity of the political goal is due to its comprehensive character. Thus the temptation arises to deny, or to evade, the comprehensive character of politics and to treat politics as one compartment among many. But this temptation must be resisted if it is necessary to face our situation as human beings, i.e., the whole situation.

Political philosophy as we have tried to circumscribe it has been cultivated since its beginnings almost without any interruption until a relatively short time ago. Today, political philosophy is in a state of decay and perhaps of putrefaction, if it has not vanished altogether. Not only is there complete disagreement regarding its subject matter, its methods, and its function; its very possibility in any form has become questionable. The only point regarding which academic teachers of political science still agree concerns the usefulness of studying the history of political philosophy. As regards the philosophers, it is sufficient to contrast the work of the four greatest philosophers of the last forty years—Bergson, Whitehead, Husserl, and Heidegger—with the work of Hermann Cohen in order to see how rapidly and thoroughly political philosophy has become discredited. We may describe the present situation as follows. Originally political philosophy was identical with political science, and it was the all-embracing study of human affairs. Today, we find it cut into pieces which behave as if they were parts of a worm. In the first place, one has applied the distinction between philosophy and science to the study of human affairs, and accordingly one makes a distinction between a nonphilosophic political science and a nonscientific political philosophy, a distinction which under present conditions takes away all dignity, all honesty from political philosophy. Furthermore, large segments of what formerly belonged to political philosophy or political science have become emancipated under the names of economics, sociology, and social psychology. The pitiable rump for which honest social scientists do not care is left as prey to philosophers of history and to people who amuse themselves more than others with professions of faith. We hardly exaggerate when we say that today political philosophy does not exist any more, except as matter for burial, i.e., for historical research, or else as a theme of weak and unconvincing protestations.

If we inquire into the reasons for this great change, we receive these answers: political philosophy is unscientific, or it is unhistorical, or it is both. Science and History, those two great powers of the modern world, have finally succeeded in destroying the very possibility of political philosophy.

The rejection of political philosophy as unscientific is characteristic of present-day positivism. Positivism is no longer what it desired to be when Auguste Comte originated it. It still agrees with Comte by maintaining that modern science is the highest form of knowledge, precisely because it aims no longer, as theology and metaphysics did, at absolute knowledge of the Why, but only at relative knowledge of the How. But after having been modified by utilitarianism, evolutionism and neo-Kantianism, it has abandoned completely Comte's hope that a social science modeled on modern natural science would be able to overcome the intellectual anarchy of modern society. In about the last decade of the nineteenth century, social science positivism reached its final form by realizing or decreeing that there is a fundamental difference between facts and values, and that only factual judgments are within the competence of science: scientific social science is incompetent to pronounce value judgments, and must avoid value judgments altogether. As for the meaning of the term "value" in statements of this kind, we can hardly say more than that "values" mean both things preferred and principles of preference.

A discussion of the tenets of social science positivism is today indispensable for explaining the meaning of political philosophy. We reconsider especially the practical consequences of this positivism. Positivistic social science is "value-free" or "ethically neutral": it is neutral in the conflict between good and evil, however good and evil may be understood. This means that the ground which is com-

mon to all social scientists, the ground on which they carry
on their investigations and discussions, can only be reached
through a process of emancipation from moral judgments,
or of abstracting from moral judgments: moral obtuseness
is the necessary condition for scientific analysis. For to the
extent to which we are not yet completely insensitive to
moral distinctions, we are forced to make value judgments.
The habit of looking at social or human phenomena without making value judgments has a corroding influence on
any preferences. The more serious we are as social scientists,
the more completely we develop within ourselves a state
of indifference to any goal, or of aimlessness and drifting, a
state which may be called nihilism. The social scientist is
not immune to preferences; his activity is a constant fight
against the preferences he has as a human being and a
citizen and which threaten to overcome his scientific de-
tachment. He derives the power to counteract these dangerous influences by his dedication to one and only one value
—to truth. But according to his principles, truth is not a
value which it is necessary to choose: one may reject it as
well as choose it. The scientist as scientist must indeed have
chosen it. But neither scientists nor science are simply necessary. Social science cannot pronounce on the question of
whether social science itself is good. It is then compelled
to teach that society can with equal right and with equal
reason favor social science as well as suppress it as disturbing, subversive, corrosive, nihilistic. But strangely enough
we find social scientists very anxious to "sell" social science,
i.e., to prove that social science is necessary. They will argue
as follows. Regardless of what our preferences or ends may
be, we wish to achieve our ends; to achieve our ends, we
must know which means are conducive to our ends; but
adequate knowledge of the means conducive to any social
ends is the sole function of social science and only of social
science; hence social science is necessary for any society or
any social movement; social science is then simply necessary; it is a value from every point of view. But once we

grant this we are seriously tempted to wonder if there are not a few other things which must be values from every point of view or for every thinking human being. To avoid this inconvenience the social scientist will scorn all considerations of public relations or of private advancement, and take refuge in the virtuous contention that he does not know, but merely believes that quest for truth is good: other men may believe with equal right that quest for truth is bad. But what does he mean by this contention? Either he makes a distinction between noble and ignoble objectives or he refuses to make such a distinction. If he makes a distinction between noble and ignoble objectives, he will say there is a variety of noble objectives or of ideals, and that there is no ideal which is compatible with all other ideals: if one chooses truth as one's ideal, one necessarily rejects other ideals; this being the case, there cannot be a necessity, an evident necessity for noble men to choose truth in preference to other ideals. But as long as the social scientist speaks of ideals, and thus makes a distinction between noble and not noble objectives, or between idealistic integrity and petty egoism, he makes a value judgment which according to his fundamental contention is, as such, no longer necessary. He must then say that it is as legitimate to make the pursuit of safety, income, deference one's sole aim in life as it is to make the quest for truth one's chief aim. He thus lays himself open to the suspicion that his activity as a social scientist serves no other purpose than to increase his safety, his income, and his prestige, or that his competence as a social scientist is a skill which he is prepared to sell to the highest bidder. Honest citizens will begin to wonder whether such a man can be trusted, or whether he can be loyal, especially since he must maintain that it is as defensible to choose loyalty as one's value as it is to reject it. In a word, he will get entangled in the predicament which leads to the downfall of Thrasymachus and his taming by Socrates in the first book of Plato's *Republic*.

It goes without saying that while our social scientist may

be confused, he is very far from being disloyal and from lacking integrity. His assertion that integrity and quest for truth are values which one can with equal right choose or reject is a mere movement of his lips and his tongue, to which nothing corresponds in his heart or mind. I have never met any scientific social scientist who apart from being dedicated to truth and integrity was not also wholeheartedly devoted to democracy. When he says that democracy is a value which is not evidently superior to the opposite value, he does not mean that he is impressed by the alternative which he rejects, or that his heart or his mind is torn between alternatives which in themselves are equally attractive. His "ethical neutrality" is so far from being nihilism or a road to nihilism that it is not more than an alibi for thoughtlessness and vulgarity: by saying that democracy and truth are values, he says in effect that one does not have to think about the reasons why these things are good, and that he may bow as well as anyone else to the values that are adopted and respected by his society. Social science positivism fosters not so much nihilism as conformism and philistinism.

It is not necessary to enter here and now into a discussion of the theoretical weaknesses of social science positivism. It suffices to allude to the considerations which speak decisively against this school.

1. It is impossible to study social phenomena, i.e., all important social phenomena, without making value judgments. A man who sees no reason for not despising people whose horizon is limited to their consumption of food and their digestion may be a tolerable econometrist; he cannot say anything relevant about the character of a human society. A man who refuses to distinguish between great statesmen, mediocrities, and insane impostors may be a good bibliographer; he cannot say anything relevant about politics and political history. A man who cannot distinguish between a profound religious thought and a languishing superstition may be a good statistician; he cannot say any-

thing relevant about the sociology of religion. Generally speaking, it is impossible to understand thought or action or work without evaluating it. If we are unable to evaluate adequately, as we very frequently are, we have not yet succeeded in understanding adequately. The value judgments which are forbidden to enter through the front door of political science, sociology, or economics enter these disciplines through the back door; they come from that annex of present-day social science which is called psychopathology. Social scientists see themselves compelled to speak of unbalanced, neurotic, maladjusted people. But these value judgments are distinguished from those used by the great historians, not by greater clarity or certainty, but merely by their poverty: a slick operator is as well adjusted as—he may be better adjusted than—a good man or a good citizen. Finally, we must not overlook the invisible value judgments which are concealed from undiscerning eyes but nevertheless most powerfully present in allegedly purely descriptive concepts. For example, when social scientists distinguish between democratic and authoritarian habits or types of human beings, what they call "authoritarian" is in all cases known to me a caricature of everything of which they, as good democrats of a certain kind, disapprove. Or when they speak of three principles of legitimacy—rational, traditional, and charismatic—their very expression "routinization of charisma" betrays a Protestant or liberal preference which no conservative Jew and no Catholic would accept: in the light of the notion of "routinization of charisma," the genesis of the Halakah out of biblical prophesy on the one hand, and the genesis of the Catholic Church out of the New Testament teaching, necessarily appear as cases of "routinization of charisma." If the objection should be made that value judgments are indeed inevitable in social science but have a merely conditional character, I would reply as follows: Are the conditions in question not necessarily fulfilled when we are interested in social phenomena? Must the social scientist not necessarily make the assumption that a healthy social life in this world is good, just as medicine necessarily makes the assumption that health and a healthy long life are good? And also are not all factual assertions based on conditions, or assumptions, which however do not become questionable as long as we deal with facts qua facts (e.g., that there are "facts," that events have causes)?

The impossibility of a "value-free" political science can be shown most simply as follows. Political science presupposes a distinction between political things and things which are not political; it presupposes therefore some answer to the question "what is political?" In order to be truly scientific, political science would have to raise this question and to answer it explicitly and adequately. But it is impossible to define the political, i.e., that which is related in a relevant way to the *polis,* the "country" or the "state," without answering the question of what constitutes this kind of society. Now, a society cannot be defined without reference to its purpose. The most well-known attempt to define "the state" without regard to its purpose admittedly led to a definition which was derived from "the modern type of state" and which is fully applicable only to that type; it was an attempt to define the modern state without having first defined the state. But by defining the state, or rather civil society, with reference to its purpose, one admits a standard in the light of which one must judge political actions and institutions: the purpose of civil society necessarily functions as a standard for judging of civil societies.

2. The rejection of value judgments is based on the assumption that the conflicts between different values or value-systems are essentially insoluble for human reason. But this assumption, while generally taken to be sufficiently established, has never been proven. Its proof would require an effort of the magnitude of that which went into the conception and elaboration of the *Critique of Pure Reason;* it would require a comprehensive critique of evaluating

reason. What we find in fact are sketchy observations which pretend to prove that this or that specific value conflict is insoluble. It is prudent to grant that there are value conflicts which cannot in fact be settled by human reason. But if we cannot decide which of two mountains whose peaks are hidden by clouds is higher than the other, cannot we decide that a mountain is higher than a molehill? If we cannot decide, regarding a war between two neighboring nations which have been fighting each other for centuries, which nation's cause is more just, cannot we decide that Jezebel's action against Naboth was inexcusable? The greatest representative of social science positivism, Max Weber, has postulated the insolubility of all value conflicts, because his soul craved a universe in which failure, that bastard of forceful sinning accompanied by still more forceful faith, instead of felicity and serenity, was to be the mark of human nobility. The belief that value judgments are not subject, in the last analysis, to rational control encourages the inclination to make irresponsible assertions regarding right and wrong or good and bad. One evades serious discussion of serious issues by the simple device of passing them off as value problems. One even creates the impression that all important human conflicts are value conflicts, whereas, to say the least, many of these conflicts arise out of men's very agreement regarding values.

3. The belief that scientific knowledge, i.e., the kind of knowledge possessed or aspired to by modern science, is the highest form of human knowledge, implies a depreciation of prescientific knowledge. If one takes into consideration the contrast between scientific knowledge of the world and prescientific knowledge of the world, one realizes that positivism preserves in a scarcely disguised manner Descartes' universal doubt of prescientific knowledge and his radical break with it. It certainly distrusts prescientific knowledge, which it likes to compare to folklore. This superstition fosters all sorts of sterile investigations or complicated idiocies. Things which every ten-year-old child of normal in-

telligence knows are regarded as being in need of scientific proof in order to become acceptable as facts. And this scientific proof, which is not only not necessary, is not even possible. To illustrate this by the simplest example: all studies in social science presuppose that its devotees can tell human beings from other beings; this most fundamental knowledge was not acquired by them in classrooms; and this knowledge is not transformed by social science into scientific knowledge, but retains its initial status without any modification throughout. If this prescientific knowledge is not knowledge, all scientific studies, which stand or fall with it, lack the character of knowledge. The preoccupation with scientific proof of things which everyone knows well enough, and better, without scientific proof, leads to the neglect of that thinking, or that reflection, which must precede all scientific studies if these studies are to be relevant. The scientific study of politics is often presented as ascending from the ascertainment of political "facts," i.e., of what has happened hitherto in politics, to the formulation of "laws" whose knowledge would permit the prediction of future political events. This goal is taken as a matter of course without a previous investigation as to whether the subject matter with which political science deals admits of adequate understanding in terms of "laws" or whether the universals through which political things can be understood as what they are must not be conceived of in entirely different terms. Scientific concern with political facts, relations of political facts, recurrent relations of political facts, or laws of political behavior, requires isolation of the phenomena which it is studying. But if this isolation is not to lead to irrelevant or misleading results, one must see the phenomena in question within the whole to which they belong, and one must clarify that whole, i.e., the whole political or politico-social order. One cannot arrive, e.g., at a kind of knowledge of "group politics" which deserves to be called scientific if one does not reflect on what genus of political orders is presupposed if there is to be "group politics" at all, and what kind of political order is presupposed by the specific "group politics" which one is studying. But one cannot clarify the character of a specific democracy, e.g., or of democracy in general, without having a clear understanding of the alternatives to democracy. Scientific political scientists are inclined to leave it at the distinction between democracy and authoritarianism, i.e., they absolutize the given political order by remaining within a horizon which is defined by the given political order and its opposite. The scientific approach tends to lead to the neglect of the primary or fundamental questions and therewith to thoughtless acceptance of received opinion. As regards these fundamental questions our friends of scientific exactness are strangely unexacting. To refer again to the most simple and at the same time decisive example, political science requires clarification of what distinguishes political things from things which are not political; it requires that the question be raised and answered "What is political?" This question cannot be dealt with scientifically but only dialectically. And dialectical treatment necessarily begins from prescientific knowledge and takes it most seriously. Prescientific knowledge, or "common sense" knowledge, is thought to be discredited by Copernicus and the succeeding natural science. But the fact that what we may call telescopic-microscopic knowledge is very fruitful in certain areas does not entitle one to deny that there are things which can only be seen as what they are if they are seen with the unarmed eye; or, more precisely, if they are seen in the perspective of the citizen, as distinguished from the perspective of the scientific observer. If one denies this, one will repeat the experience of Gulliver with the nurse in Brobdingnag and become entangled in the kind of research projects by which he was amazed in Laputa.

4. Positivism necessarily transforms itself into historicism. By virtue of its orientation by the model of natural science, social science is in danger of mistaking peculiarities of, say, mid-twentieth century United States, or more generally of

modern Western society, for the essential character of human society. To avoid this danger, it is compelled to engage in "cross-cultural research," in the study of other cultures, both present and past. But in making this effort, it misses the meaning of those other cultures, because it interprets them through a conceptual scheme which originates in modern Western society, which reflects that particular society, and which fits at best only that particular society. To avoid this danger, social science must attempt to understand those cultures as they understand or understood themselves: the understanding primarily required of the social scientist is historical understanding. Historical understanding becomes the basis of a truly empirical science of society. But if one considers the infinity of the task of historical understanding, one begins to wonder whether historical understanding does not take the place of the scientific study of society. Furthermore, social science is said to be a body of true propositions about social phenomena. The propositions are answers to questions. What valid answers, objectively valid answers, are, may be determined by the rules or principles of logic. But the questions depend on one's direction of interest, and hence on one's values, i.e., on subjective principles. Now it is the direction of interests, and not logic, which supplies the fundamental concepts. It is therefore not possible to divorce from each other the subjective and objective elements of social science: the objective answers receive their meaning from the subjective questions. If one does not relapse into the decayed Platonism which is underlying the notion of timeless values, one must conceive of the values embodied in a given social science as dependent on the society to which the social science in question belongs, i.e., on history. Not only is social science superseded by historical studies; social science itself proves to be "historical." Reflection on social science as a historical phenomenon leads to the relativization of social science and ultimately of modern science generally. As a consequence, modern science comes to be viewed as one historically relative way of understanding things which is not in principle superior to alternative ways of understanding.

It is only at this point that we come face to face with the serious antagonist of political philosophy: historicism. After having reached its full growth, historicism is distinguished from positivism by the following characteristics: (1) It abandons the distinction between facts and values, because every understanding, however theoretical, implies specific evaluations. (2) It denies the authoritative character of modern science, which appears as only one form among many of man's thinking orientation in the world. (3) It refuses to regard the historical process as fundamentally progressive, or, more generally stated, as reasonable. (4) It denies the relevance of the evolutionist thesis by contending that the evolution of man out of nonman cannot make intelligible man's humanity. Historicism rejects the question of the good society, that is to say, of *the* good society, because of the essentially historical character of society and of human thought: there is no essential necessity for raising the question of the good society; this question is not in principle coeval with man; its very possibility is the outcome of a mysterious dispensation of fate. The crucial issue concerns the status of those permanent characteristics of humanity, such as the distinction between the noble and the base, which are admitted by the thoughtful historicists: can these permanencies be used as criteria for distinguishing between good and bad dispensations of fate? The historicist answers this question in the negative. He looks down on the permanencies in question because of their objective, common, superficial, and rudimentary character: to become relevant, they would have to be completed, and their completion is no longer common but historical. It was the contempt for these permanencies which permitted the most radical historicist in 1933 to submit to, or rather to welcome, as a dispensation of fate, the verdict of the least wise and least moderate part of his nation while it was in its least wise and least moderate mood, and at the same time to speak of wisdom and moderation. The biggest event of 1933 would rather seem to have proved, if such proof was necessary, that man cannot abandon the question of the good society, and that he cannot free himself from the responsibility for answering it by deferring to History or to any other power different from his own reason.

2   *The Classical Solution*

When we describe the political philosophy of Plato and of Aristotle as classical political philosophy, we imply that it is the classic form of political philosophy. The classic was once said to be characterized by noble simplicity and quiet grandeur. This suggestion guides us in the right direction. It is an attempt to articulate what was formerly also called the "natural" character of classical thought. "Natural" is here understood in contradistinction to what is merely human, all too human. A human being is said to be natural if he is guided by nature rather than by convention, or by inherited opinion, or by tradition, to say nothing of mere whims. Classical political philosophy is nontraditional, because it belongs to the fertile moment when all political traditions were shaken, and there was not yet in existence a tradition of political philosophy. In all later epochs, the philosophers' study of political things was mediated by a tradition of political philosophy which acted like a screen between the philosopher and political things, regardless of whether the individual philosopher cherished or rejected that tradition. From this it follows that the classical philosophers see the political things with a freshness and directness which have never been equaled. They look at political things in the perspective of the enlightened citizen or statesman. They see things clearly which the enlightened citizens or statesmen do not see clearly, or do not see at all. But this has no other reason but the fact that they look further afield in the same direction as the enlightened citizens or statesmen. They do not look at political things from the outside, as spectators of political life. They speak the language of the citizens or statesmen: they hardly use a single term which is not familiar to the market place. Hence their political philosophy is comprehensive; it is both political theory and political skill; it is as open-minded to the legal and institutional aspects of political life as it is to that which transcends the legal and institutional; it is equally free from the narrowness of the lawyer, the brutality of the technician, the vagaries of the visionary, and the baseness of the opportunist. It reproduces, and raises to its perfection, the magnanimous flexibility of the true statesman, who crushes the insolent and spares the vanquished. It is free from all fanaticism because it knows that evil cannot be eradicated and therefore that one's expectations from politics must be moderate. The spirit which animates it may be described as serenity or sublime sobriety.

Compared with classical political philosophy, all later political thought, whatever else its merits may be, and in particular modern political thought, has a derivative character. This means that in later times there has occurred an estrangement from the simple and primary issues. This has given to political philosophy the character of "abstractness," and has therefore engendered the view that the philosophic movement must be a movement, not from opinion to knowledge, not from the here and now to what is always or eternal, but from the abstract towards the concrete. It was thought that by virtue of this movement towards the concrete, recent philosophy has overcome the limitations not only of modern political philosophy, but of classical political philosophy as well. It was overlooked, however, that this change of orientation perpetuated the original defect of modern philosophy because it accepted abstractions as its starting point, and that the concrete at which one eventually arrived was not at all the truly concrete, but still an abstraction.

One example must suffice here. Today it is held in certain

circles that the basic task of political or social science is to
understand the most concrete human relation, and that
relation is called the I–Thou–We relation. It is obvious that
the Thou and the We are supplements to Descartes' Ego;
the question is whether the fundamental inadequacy of
Descartes' Ego can be disposed of by any supplements, and
whether it is not necessary to return to a more fundamental
beginning, or to the natural beginning. The phenomenon
which is now called the I–Thou–We relation was known to
the classics by the name of friendship. When speaking to a
friend I address him in the second person. But philosophic
or scientific analysis is not speaking to a friend, i.e., to this
individual here and now, but speaking to anyone concerned
with such analysis. Such analysis cannot be meant to be a
substitute for living together as friends; it can at best only
point to such living together or arouse a desire for it. When
speaking about someone with whom I have a close relation
I call him my friend. I do not call him my Thou. Adequate
"speaking about" in analytical or objective speech must be
grounded in and continue the manner of "speaking about"
which is inherent in human life. By speaking of "the Thou"
instead of "the friend," I am trying to preserve in objective
speech what cannot be preserved in objective speech; I am
trying to objectify something that is incapable of being
objectified. I am trying to preserve in "speaking about"
what can be actual only in "speaking to." Hence I do injustice to the phenomena; I am untrue to the phenomena;
I miss the concrete. While attempting to lay a foundation
for genuine human communication, I preserve an inca-
pacity for genuine human communication.

The character of classical political philosophy appears
with the greatest clarity from Plato's *Laws,* which is his
political work par excellence. The *Laws* is a conversation
about law, and political things in general, between an old
Athenian stranger, an old Cretan, and an old Spartan. The
conversation takes place on the island of Crete. At the beginning one receives the impression that the Athenian has

come to Crete in order to study there the best laws. For if it is true that the good is identical with the ancestral, the best laws for a Greek would be the oldest Greek laws, and these are the Cretan laws. But the equation of the good with the ancestral is not tenable if the first ancestors were not gods, or sons of gods, or pupils of gods. Hence, the Cretans believed that their laws were originated by Zeus, who instructed his son Minos, the Cretan legislator. The *Laws* opens with an expression of this belief. It appears immediately afterwards that this belief has no other ground, no better ground, than a saying of Homer—and the poets are of questionable veracity—as well as what the Cretans say—and the Cretans were famous for their lack of veracity. However this may be, very shortly after its beginning, the conversation shifts from the question of the origins of the Cretan laws and the Spartan laws to the question of their intrinsic worth: a code given by a god, by a being of super-human excellence, must be unqualifiedly good. Very slowly, very circumspectly does the Athenian approach this grave question. To begin with he limits his criticism of the principle underlying the Cretan and the Spartan codes by criticizing not these codes, but a poet, a man without authority and, in addition, an expatriate, who had praised the same principle. In the sequel, the philosopher attacks not yet the Cretan and the Spartan codes, but the interpretation of these codes which had been set forth by his two interlocutors. He does not begin to criticize these venerable codes explicitly until he has appealed to a presumed Cretan and Spartan law which permits such criticism under certain conditions—under conditions which are fulfilled, to some extent, in the present conversation. According to that law, all must say with one voice and with one mouth that all the laws of Crete, or of Sparta, are good because they are god-given, and no one is suffered to say something different; but an old citizen may utter a criticism of an allegedly divine law before a magistrate of his own age if no young men are present. By this time it has become clear to the reader that the Athenian has not come to Crete in order to study there the best laws, but rather in order to introduce into Crete new laws and institutions, truly good laws and institutions. These laws and institutions will prove to be, to a considerable extent, of Athenian origin. It seems that the Athenian, being the son of a highly civilized society, has embarked on the venture of civilizing a rather uncivilized society. Therefore he has to apprehend that his suggestions will be odious, not only as innovations, but above all as foreign, as Athenian: deep-seated, old animosities and suspicions will be aroused by his recommendations. He begins his explicit criticism with a remark about the probable connection between certain Cretan and Spartan institutions and the practice of homosexuality in these cities. The Spartan, rising in defense of his fatherland, does not, indeed, defend homosexuality, but, turning to the offensive, rebukes the Athenians for their excessive drinking. The Athenian is thus given a perfect excuse for recommending the introduction of the Athenian institution of banquets: he is compelled to defend that institution; by defending it he acts the part, not of a civilizing philosopher who, being a philosopher, is a philanthropist, but of the patriot. He acts in a way which is perfectly understandable to his interlocutors and perfectly respectable in their opinion. He attempts to show that wine-drinking, and even drunkenness, if it is practiced in well-presided banquets, is conducive to education in temperance or moderation. This speech about wine forms the bulk of the first two books of the *Laws*. Only after the speech about wine has been brought to its conclusion does the Athenian turn to the question of the beginning of political life, to a question which is the true beginning of his political theme. The speech about wine appears to be *the* introduction to political philosophy.

Why does *the* Platonic dialogue about politics and laws begin with such an extensive conversation about wine? What is the artistic or logographic necessity demanding this?

The proper interlocutors in a conversation about laws are old citizens of communities famous for their laws, for their obedience and allegiance to their old laws. Such men understand best what living under laws, living in laws, means. They are the perfect incarnation of the spirit of laws: of lawfulness, of law-abidingness. But their very virtue becomes a defect if there is no longer a question of preserving old laws, but of seeking the best laws or introducing new and better ones. Their habits and their competence make these men impervious to suggestions for improvement. The Athenian induces them to participate in a conversation about wine-drinking, about a pleasure that is forbidden to them by their old laws. The talk about wine-drinking is a kind of vicarious enjoyment of wine, especially since wine-drinking is a forbidden pleasure. Perhaps the talk reminds the two old interlocutors of secret and pleasurable transgressions of their own. The effect of the talk about wine is therefore similar to the effect of actual wine-drinking; it loosens their tongues; it makes them young; it makes them bold, daring, willing to innovate. They must not actually drink wine, since this would impair their judgment. They must drink wine, not in deed, but in speech.

But this means that wine-drinking educates to boldness, to courage, and not to moderation, and yet wine-drinking was said to be conducive to moderation. Let us therefore consider the other partner in the conversation, the Athenian philosopher. To doubt the sacredness of the ancestral means to appeal from the ancestral to the natural. It means to transcend all human traditions, nay, the whole dimension of the merely human. It means to learn to look down on the human as something inferior or to leave the cave. But by leaving the cave one loses sight of the city, of the whole political sphere. If the philosopher is to give political guidance, he must return to the cave: from the light of the sun to the world of shadows; his perception must be dimmed; his mind must undergo an obfuscation. The vicarious enjoyment of wine through a conversation about wine, which enlarges the horizon of the law-bred old citizens, limits the horizon of the philosopher. But this obfuscation, this acceptance of the political perspective, this adoption of the language of political man, this achievement of harmony between the excellence of man and the excellence of the citizen, or between wisdom and law-abidingness is, it seems, the most noble exercise of the virtue of moderation: wine-drinking educates to moderation. For moderation is not a virtue of thought: Plato likens philosophy to madness, the very opposite of sobriety or moderation; thought must be not moderate, but fearless, not to say shameless. But moderation is a virtue controlling the philosopher's speech.

We have suggested that the Athenian stranger had gone to Crete in order to civilize an uncivilized society, and that he had done this out of philanthropy. But does not philanthropy begin at home? Did he not have more pressing duties to perform at home? What kind of man is the Athenian stranger? The *Laws* begins with the word "God": it is the only Platonic dialogue which begins in that manner. There is one and only one Platonic dialogue which ends with the word "God": the *Apology of Socrates*. In the *Apology of Socrates* an old Athenian philosopher, Socrates, defends himself against the charge of impiety, of not believing that the gods worshiped by the city of Athens exist. It seems that there is a conflict between philosophy and accepting the gods of the city. In the *Laws* an old Athenian philosopher recommends a law about impiety which renders impossible the conflict between philosophy and the city, or which brings about harmony between philosophy and the city. The gods whose existence is to be admitted by every citizen of the city of the *Laws* are beings whose existence can be demonstrated. That old Athenian philosopher of the *Apology of Socrates* was condemned to death by the city of Athens. He was given an opportunity to escape from prison: he refused to avail himself of this opportunity. His refusal was not based on an appeal to a categorical imperative demanding passive obedience, without if's and but's. His refusal was based on a deliberation, on a prudential consideration of what was the right thing to do in the circumstances. One of the circumstances was Socrates' old age: we are forced to wonder how Socrates would have decided if he had been 30 or 40 years old instead of 70. Another circumstance was the unavailability of a proper place of exile: where should he flee? He seems to have a choice between law-abiding cities nearby, where his life would be unbearable, since he would be known as a fugitive from justice, and a lawless country far away, where the prevailing lack of order would make his life miserable. The disjunction is obviously incomplete: there were law-abiding cities far away, for instance on Crete, which is mentioned as a law-abiding place in the very deliberation in question. We are entitled to infer that if Socrates had fled, he would have gone to Crete. The *Laws* tells us what he would have done in Crete after his arrival: he would have brought the blessings of Athens, Athenian laws, Athenian institutions, banquets, and philosophy to Crete. (When Aristotle speaks about Plato's *Laws,* he takes it for granted that the chief character of the *Laws* is Socrates.) Escaping to Crete, living in Crete, was the alternative to dying in Athens. But Socrates chose to die in Athens. Socrates preferred to sacrifice his life in order to preserve philosophy in Athens rather than to preserve his life in order to introduce philosophy into Crete. If the danger to the future of philosophy in Athens had been less great, he might have chosen to flee to Crete. His choice was a political choice of the highest order. It did not consist in the simple subsumption of his case under a simple, universal, and unalterable rule.

But let us return after this long story to the beginning of Plato's *Laws.* If the originator of the Cretan laws, or any other laws, is not a god, the cause of the laws must be human beings, the human legislator. There is a variety of types of human legislators: the legislator has a different character in a democracy, in an oligarchy, in a monarchy.

The legislator is the governing body, and the character of the governing body depends on the whole social and political order, the *politeia,* the regime. The cause of the laws is the regime. Therefore the guiding theme of political philosophy is the regime rather than the laws. Regime becomes the guiding theme of political thought when the derivative or questionable character of laws has been realized. There are a number of biblical terms which can be properly translated by "law"; there is no biblical equivalent to "regime."

Regime is the order, the form, which gives society its character. Regime is therefore a specific manner of life. Regime is the form of life as living together, the manner of living of society and in society, since this manner depends decisively on the predominance of human beings of a certain type, on the manifest domination of society by human beings of a certain type. Regime means that whole, which we today are in the habit of viewing primarily in a fragmentized form: regime means simultaneously the form of life of a society, its style of life, its moral taste, form of society, form of state, form of government, spirit of laws. We may try to articulate the simple and unitary thought that expresses itself in the term *politeia* as follows: life is activity which is directed towards some goal; social life is an activity which is directed towards such a goal as can be pursued only by society; but in order to pursue a specific goal, as its comprehensive goal, society must be organized, ordered, constructed, constituted in a manner which is in accordance with that goal; this, however, means that the authoritative human beings must be akin to that goal.

There is a variety of regimes. Each regime raises a claim, explicitly or implicitly, which extends beyond the boundaries of any given society. These claims conflict, therefore, with each other. There is a variety of conflicting regimes. Thus the regimes themselves, and not any preoccupation of mere bystanders, force us to wonder which of the given conflicting regimes is better, and ultimately, which regime is the best regime. Classical political philosophy is guided by the question of the best regime.

The actualization of the best regime depends on the coming together, on the coincidence of, things which have a natural tendency to move away from each other (e.g., on the coincidence of philosophy and political power); its actualization depends therefore on chance. Human nature is enslaved in so many ways that it is almost a miracle if an individual achieves the highest; what can one expect of society! The peculiar manner of being of the best regime—namely, its lacking actuality while being superior to all actual regimes—has its ultimate reason in the dual nature of man, in the fact that man is the in-between being: in between brutes and gods.

The practical meaning of the notion of the best regime appears most clearly when one considers the ambiguity of the term "good citizen." Aristotle suggests two entirely different definitions of the good citizen. In his more popular *Constitution of Athens* he suggests that the good citizen is a man who serves his country well, without any regard to the difference of regimes—who serves his country well in fundamental indifference to the change of regimes. The good citizen, in a word, is the patriotic citizen, the man whose loyalty belongs first and last to his fatherland. In his less popular *Politics,* Aristotle says that there is not *the* good citizen without qualification. For what it means to be a good citizen depends entirely on the regime. A good citizen in Hitler's Germany would be a bad citizen elsewhere. But whereas good citizen is relative to the regime, good man does not have such a relativity. The meaning of good man is always and everywhere the same. The good man is identical with the good citizen only in one case—in the case of the best regime. For only in the best regime is the good of the regime and the good of the good man identical, that goal being virtue. This amounts to saying that in his *Politics* Aristotle questions the proposition that patriotism is enough. From the point of view of the patriot, the fatherland is more important than any difference of regimes. From the point of view of the patriot, he who prefers any regime to the fatherland is a partisan, if not a traitor. Aristotle says in effect that the partisan sees deeper than the patriot but that only one kind of partisan is superior to the patriot; this is the partisan of virtue. One can express Aristotle's thought as follows: patriotism is not enough for the same reason that the most doting mother is happier if her child is good than if he is bad. A mother loves her child because he is her own; she loves what is her own. But she also loves the good. All human love is subject to the law that it be both love of one's own and love of the good, and there is necessarily a tension between one's own and the good, a tension which may well lead to a break, be it only the breaking of a heart. The relation between one's own and the good finds its political expression in the relation between the fatherland and the regime. In the language of classical metaphysics, the fatherland or the nation is the matter whereas the regime is the form. The classics held the view that the form is higher in dignity than the matter. One may call this view "idealism." The practical meaning of this idealism is that the good is of higher dignity than one's own, or that the best regime is a higher consideration than the fatherland. The Jewish equivalent of this relation might be said to be the relation between the Torah and Israel.

Classical political philosophy is today exposed to two very common objections, the raising of which requires neither originality nor intelligence, nor even erudition. The objections are these: (1) classical political philosophy is antidemocratic and hence bad; (2) classical political philosophy is based on classical natural philosophy or on classical cosmology, and this basis has been proven to be untrue by the success of modern natural science.

To speak first of the classics' attitude towards democracy, the premises: "the classics are good," and "democracy is good" do not validate the conclusion "hence the classics were good democrats." It would be silly to deny that the classics rejected democracy as an inferior kind of regime. They were not blind to its advantages. The severest indictment of democracy that ever was written occurs in the eighth book of Plato's *Republic*. But even there, and precisely there, Plato makes it clear—by coordinating his arrangement of regimes with Hesiod's arrangement of the ages of the world—that democracy is, in a very important respect, equal to the best regime, which corresponds to Hesiod's golden age: since the principle of democracy is freedom, all human types can develop freely in a democracy, and hence in particular the best human type. It is true that Socrates was killed by a democracy; but he was killed when he was 70; he was permitted to live for 70 long years. Yet Plato did not regard this consideration as decisive. For he was concerned not only with the possibility of philosophy, but likewise with a stable political order that would be congenial to moderate political courses; and such an order, he thought, depends on the predominance of old families. More generally, the classics rejected democracy because they thought that the aim of human life, and hence of social life, is not freedom but virtue. Freedom as a goal is ambiguous, because it is freedom for evil as well as for good. Virtue emerges normally only through education, that is to say, through the formation of character, through habituation, and this requires leisure on the part of both parents and children. But leisure in its turn requires some degree of wealth—more specifically a kind of wealth whose acquisition or administration is compatible with leisure. Now, as regards wealth, it so happens, as Aristotle observes, that there is always a minority of well-to-do people and a majority of the poor, and this strange coincidence will last forever because there is a kind of natural scarcity. "For the poor shall never cease out of the land." It is for this reason that democracy, or rule of the majority, is government by the uneducated. And no one in his senses would wish to live under such a government. This classical argument would not be stringent if men did not need education in order to acquire a firm adhesion to virtue. It is no accident that it was Jean-Jacques Rousseau who taught that all knowledge which men need in order to live virtuously is supplied by the conscience, the preserve of the simple souls rather than of other men: man is sufficiently equipped by nature for the good life; man is by nature good. But the same Rousseau was compelled to develop a scheme of education which very few people could financially afford. On the whole the view has prevailed that democracy must become rule by the educated, and this goal will be achieved by universal education. But universal education presupposes that the economy of scarcity has given way to an economy of plenty. And the economy of plenty presupposes the emancipation of technology from moral and political control. The essential difference between our view and the classical view consists then, not in a difference regarding moral principle, not in a different understanding of justice: we, too, even our communist coexistents, think that it is just to give equal things to equal people and unequal things to people of unequal merit. The difference between the classics and us with regard to democracy consists exclusively in a different estimate of the virtues of technology. But we are not entitled to say that the classical view has been refuted. Their implicit prophecy that the emancipation of technology, of the arts, from moral and political control would lead to disaster or to the dehumanization of man has not yet been refuted.

Nor can we say that democracy has found a solution to the problem of education. In the first place, what is today called education very frequently does not mean education proper, i.e., the formation of character, but rather instruction and training. Secondly, to the extent to which the formation of character is indeed intended, there exists a very dangerous tendency to identify the good man with the good sport, the cooperative fellow, the "regular guy," i.e., an overemphasis on a certain part of social virtue and a corresponding neglect of those virtues which mature, if they do not flourish, in privacy, not to say in solitude: by educating people to cooperate with each other in a friendly spirit, one does not yet educate nonconformists, people who are prepared to stand alone, to fight alone, "rugged individualists." Democracy has not yet found a defense against the creeping conformism and the ever-increasing invasion of privacy which it fosters. Beings who look down on us from a star might find that the difference between democracy and communism is not quite as great as it appears to be when one considers exclusively the doubtless very important question of civil and political liberties, although only people of exceptional levity or irresponsibility say that the difference between communism and democracy is negligible in the last analysis. Now to the extent to which democracy is aware of these dangers, to the same extent it sees itself compelled to think of elevating its level and its possibilities by a return to the classics' notions of education: a kind of education which can never be thought of as mass-education, but only as higher and highest education of those who are by nature fit for it. It would be an understatement to call it royal education.

Yet granted that there are no valid moral or political objections to classical political philosophy—is that political philosophy not bound up with an antiquated cosmology? Does not the very question of the nature of man point to the question of the nature of the whole, and therewith to one or the other specific cosmology? Whatever the significance of modern natural science may be, it cannot affect our understanding of what is human in man. To understand man in the light of the whole means for modern natural science to understand man in the light of the subhuman. But in that light man as man is wholly unintelligible. Classical political philosophy viewed man in a different light. It was originated by Socrates. And Socrates was so far from being committed to a specific cosmology that his knowledge was knowledge of ignorance. Knowledge of ignorance is not ignorance. It is knowledge of the elusive character of the truth, of the whole. Socrates, then, viewed man in the light of the mysterious character of the whole. He held therefore that we are more familiar with the situation of man as man than with the ultimate causes of that situation. We may also say he viewed man in the light of the unchangeable ideas, i.e., of the fundamental and permanent problems. For to articulate the situation of man means to articulate man's openness to the whole. This understanding of the situation of man which includes, then, the quest for cosmology rather than a solution to the cosmological problem, was the foundation of classical political philosophy.

To articulate the problem of cosmology means to answer the question of what philosophy is or what a philosopher is. Plato refrained from entrusting the thematic discussion of this question to Socrates. He entrusted it to a stranger from Elea. But even that stranger from Elea did not discuss explicitly what a philosopher is. He discussed explicitly two kinds of men which are easily mistaken for the philosopher—the sophist and the statesman: by understanding both sophistry (in its highest as well as in its lower meaning) and statesmanship, one will understand what philosophy is. Philosophy strives for knowledge of the whole. The whole is the totality of the parts. The whole eludes us but we know parts: we possess partial knowledge of parts. The knowledge which we possess is characterized by a fundamental dualism which has never been overcome. At one pole we find knowledge of homogeneity: above all in arithmetic, but also in the other branches of mathematics, and derivatively in all productive arts or crafts. At the opposite pole we find knowledge of heterogeneity, and in particular of heterogeneous ends; the highest form of this kind of knowledge is the art of the statesman and of the educator. The latter kind of knowledge is superior to the former for this reason. As knowledge of the ends of human life, it is knowledge of what makes human life complete or whole; it is therefore knowledge of a whole. Knowledge of the ends of man implies knowledge of the human soul; and the human soul is the only part of the whole which is open to the whole and therefore more. akin to the whole than anything else is. But this knowledge—the political art in the highest sense—is not knowledge of *the* whole. It seems that knowledge of the whole would have to combine somehow political knowledge in the highest sense with knowledge of homogeneity. And this combination is not at our disposal. Men are therefore constantly tempted to force the issue by imposing unity on the phenomena, by absolutizing either knowledge of homogeneity or knowledge of ends. Men are constantly attracted and deluded by two opposite charms: the charm of competence which is engendered by mathematics and everything akin to mathematics, and the charm of humble awe, which is engendered by meditation on the human soul and its experiences. Philosophy is characterized by the gentle, if firm, refusal to succumb to either charm. It is the highest form of the mating of courage and moderation. In spite of its highness or nobility, it could appear as Sisyphean or ugly, when one contrasts its achievement with its goal. Yet it is necessarily accompanied, sustained, and elevated by *eros*. It is graced by nature's grace.

3   The Modern Solutions

It was possible to speak of the classical solution to the problem of political philosophy because there is a fundamental and at the same time specific agreement among all classical political philosophers: the goal of political life is virtue, and the order most conducive to virtue is the aristocratic republic, or else the mixed regime. But in modern times, we find a great variety of fundamentally different political philosophies. Nevertheless, all modern political philosophies belong together because they have a fundamental principle in common. This principle can best be stated negatively: rejection of the classical scheme as unrealistic. The positive principle animating modern political philosophy has undergone a great variety of fundamental changes. This fact, and its reason, can be shown best if we proceed in a somewhat more narrative way than we have done hitherto.

The founder of modern political philosophy is Machiavelli. He tried to effect, and he did effect, a break with the whole tradition of political philosophy. He compared his achievement to that of men like Columbus. He claimed to have discovered a new moral continent. His claim is well founded; his political teaching is "wholly new." The only question is whether the new continent is fit for human habitation.

In his *Florentine Histories* he tells the following story: Cosimo de Medici once said that men cannot maintain power with paternosters in their hands. This gave occasion to Cosimo's enemies to slander him as a man who loved himself more than his fatherland and who loved this world more than the next. Cosimo was then said to be somewhat immoral and somewhat irreligious. Machiavelli himself is open to the same charge. His work is based on a critique of religion and a critique of morality.

His critique of religion, chiefly of biblical religion, but also of paganism, is not original. It amounts to a restatement of the teaching of pagan philosophers, as well as that medieval school which goes by the name of Averroism and which gave rise to the notion of the three impostors. Machiavelli's originality in this field is limited to the fact that he was a great master of blasphemy. The charm and gracefulness of his blasphemies will however be less strongly felt by us than their shocking character. Let us then keep them under the veil under which he has hidden them. I hasten to his critique of morality which is identical with his critique of classical political philosophy. One can state the main point as follows: there is something fundamentally wrong with an approach to politics which culminates in a utopia, in the description of a best regime whose actualization is highly improbable. Let us then cease to take our bearings by virtue, the highest objective which a society might choose; let us begin to take our bearings by the objectives which are actually pursued by all societies. Machiavelli consciously lowers the standards of social action. His lowering of the standards is meant to lead to a higher probability of actualization of that scheme which is constructed in accordance with the lowered standards. Thus, the dependence on chance is reduced: chance will be conquered.

The traditional approach was based on the assumption that morality is something substantial: that it is a force in the soul of man, however ineffective it may be especially in the affairs of states and kingdoms. Against this assumption Machiavelli argues as follows: virtue can be practiced only within society; man must be habituated to virtue by laws, customs and so forth. Men must be educated to virtue by human beings. But to quote that Machiavellian, Karl Marx, the educators themselves must be educated. The original educators, the founders of society, cannot have been educated to virtue: the founder of Rome was a fratricide. Morality is possible only within a context which cannot be created by morality, for morality cannot create itself. The context within which morality is possible is created by immorality. Morality rests on immorality, justice rests on injustice, just as all legitimacy ultimately rests on revolutionary foundations. Man is not by nature directed towards virtue. If he were, pangs of conscience would be the greatest evil for him; but in fact we find that the pangs of disappointment are at least as strong as the pangs of guilt. In other words, one cannot define the good of society, the common good, in terms of virtue, but one must define virtue in terms of the common good. It is this understanding of virtue which in fact determines the life of societies. By the common good we must understand the objectives actually pursued by all societies. These objectives are: freedom from foreign domination, stability or rule of law, prosperity, glory or empire. Virtue in the effectual sense of the

word is the sum of habits which are required for or conducive to this end. It is this end, and this end alone, which
makes our actions virtuous. Everything done effectively for
the sake of this end is good. This end justifies every means.
Virtue is nothing but civic virtue, patriotism, or devotion to
collective selfishness.

Machiavelli cannot leave it at this. Devotion to the
fatherland is itself dependent on education. This means
that patriotism is not natural. Just as man is not by nature
directed toward virtue, he is not by nature directed toward
society. By nature man is radically selfish. Yet while men
are by nature selfish, and nothing but selfish, hence bad,
they can become social, public spirited, or good. This transformation requires compulsion. The success of this compulsion is due to the fact that man is amazingly malleable:
much more so than had hitherto been thought. For if man
is not by nature ordered toward virtue or perfection, if
there is no natural end of man, man can set for himself
almost any end he desires: man is almost infinitely malleable. The power of man is much greater, and the power of
nature and chance is correspondingly much smaller, than
the ancients thought.

Men are bad; they must be compelled to be good. But
this compulsion must be the work of badness, of selfishness,
of selfish passion. Which passion will induce a bad man to
be passionately concerned with compelling other bad men
to become good and to remain good? Which passion will
educate the educator of men? The passion in question is the
desire for glory. The highest form of the desire for glory
is the desire to be a new prince in the fullest sense of the
term, a wholly new prince: a discoverer of a new type of
social order, a molder of many generations of men. The
founder of society has a selfish interest in the preservation
of society, of his work. He has therefore a selfish interest in
the members of his society being and remaining sociable,
and hence good. The desire for glory is the link between
badness and goodness. It makes possible the transformation

of badness into goodness. The wholly new prince of the highest kind is animated by nothing but selfish ambition. The great public tasks which he undertakes are for him only opportunities for coloring his design. He is distinguished from great criminals merely by the fact that the criminals lack a defensible opportunity; the moral motivation is the same.

It is not possible here to show how Machiavelli succeeds in building on this basis a political teaching which does full justice to all possible requirements of any policy of blood and iron, and which is at the same time most favorable to political liberty and the rule of law. I must limit myself to indicating how easy it is, after a few centuries of Machiavellianization of Western thought, to give Machiavelli's teaching an air of perfect respectability. He can be presented as arguing as follows: you want justice? I am going to show you how you can get it. You will not get it by preaching, by hortatory speeches. You will get it only by making injustice utterly unprofitable. What you need is not so much formation of character and moral appeal, as the right kind of institutions, institutions with teeth in them. The shift from formation of character to the trust in institutions is the characteristic corollary of the belief in the almost infinite malleability of man.

In Machiavelli's teaching we have the first example of a spectacle which has renewed itself in almost every generation since. A fearless thinker seems to have opened up a depth from which the classics, in their noble simplicity, recoiled. As a matter of fact, there is in the whole work of Machiavelli not a single true observation regarding the nature of man and of human affairs with which the classics were not thoroughly familiar. An amazing contraction of the horizon presents itself as an amazing enlargement of the horizon. How can we account for this delusion? By Machiavelli's time the classical tradition had undergone profound changes. The contemplative life had found its home in monasteries. Moral virtue had been transfigured into Chris-

tian charity. Through this, man's responsibility to his fellow
men and for his fellow men, his fellow creatures, had been
infinitely increased. Concern with the salvation of men's
immortal souls seemed to permit, nay, to require courses of
action which would have appeared to the classics, and
which did appear to Machiavelli, to be inhuman and cruel:
Machiavelli speaks of the pious cruelty of Ferdinand of
Aragon, and by implication of the Inquisition, in expelling
the Marranos from Spain. Machiavelli was the only non-
Jew of his age who expressed this view. He seems to have
diagnosed the great evils of religious persecution as a necessary consequence of the Christian principle, and ultimately
of the biblical principle. He tended to believe that a considerable increase in man's inhumanity was the unintended
but not surprising consequence of man's aiming too high.
Let us lower our goals so that we shall not be forced to
commit any bestialities which are not evidently required
for the preservation of society and of freedom. Let us replace charity by calculation, by a kind of utilitarianism
*avant la lettre.** Let us revise all traditional goals from this
point of view. I would then suggest that the narrowing of
the horizon which Machiavelli was the first to effect, was
caused, or at least facilitated, by antitheological ire—a passion which we can undertand but of which we cannot
approve.

Machiavelli radically changed, not only the substance of
the political teaching, but its mode as well. The substance
of his political teaching may be said to be the wholly new
teaching regarding the wholly new prince, i.e., regarding the
essential inherence of immorality in the foundation of society and hence in the structure of society. The discoverer of
such a teaching is necessarily a bringer of a new moral code,
of a new Decalogue. He is a wholly new prince in the
highest possible sense of the term, a new Moses, a prophet.
Concerning prophets, Machiavelli teaches that all armed

* i.e., a kind of utilitarianism that preceded the appearance of the
doctrine called by that name.

prophets have conquered and all unarmed prophets have failed. The greatest example of an armed prophet is Moses. The greatest example of an unarmed prophet is Jesus. But can Machiavelli reasonably say that Jesus has failed? Or to put the same question in a different form, is not Machiavelli himself an unarmed prophet? How can he possibly hope for the success of his more than daring venture if unarmed founders necessarily fail?

Jesus failed insofar as he was crucified. He did not fail insofar as the new modes and orders found by him have become accepted by many generations of many nations. This victory of Christianity was due to propaganda: the unarmed prophet conquered posthumously by virtue of propaganda. Machiavelli, being himself an unarmed prophet, has no other hope of conquest except through propaganda. The only element of Christianity which Machiavelli took over was the idea of propaganda. This idea is the only link between his thought and Christianity. He attempted to destroy Christianity by the same means by which Christianity was originally established. He desired to imitate, not Moses, the armed prophet, but Jesus. It goes without saying that Machiavelli's *imitatio Christi* is limited to this point. In particular, the author of *Mandragola* avoided the cross in more than one sense by not publishing his great works during his lifetime.

Machiavelli assumed that every religion or "sect" has a lifespan of between 1,666 and 3,000 years. He was then uncertain as to whether the end of Christianity would come about a century after his death or whether Christianity might still last for another millennium and a half. Machiavelli thought and wrote in this perspective: that he himself might be preparing a radical change of modes and orders, a change which would be consummated in a not too distant future, but that it is equally possible that his enterprise would fail completely. He certainly reckoned with the possibility that the destruction of the Christian Church was imminent. As for the way in which Christianity might be superseded by a new social order, he saw this alternative. One possibility was the irruption of barbarian hordes from the East, from what is now Russia: it was this region which he regarded as the pool from which the human race rejuvenates itself periodically. The alternative was a radical change within the civilized world. It was of course only the latter kind of change for which he was anxious, and which he did everything in his power to prepare. He conceived of this preparation as of a war, a spiritual war. He desired to bring about a change of opinion which in due time would precipitate a change in political power. He did not except more than the conversion of very few men, but he counted on influencing many. These many were those who, in case of conflict between their fatherland and their souls, the salvation of their souls, would prefer their fatherland; these many were the lukewarm Christians. He expected these many to be sympathetic to his enterprise, which was infinitely more favorable to the earthly fatherland than to the heavenly fatherland of the Christians. These many would not be able to understand the full meaning of his undertaking, but they could be counted upon to guarantee that his books would get some hearing. They would make his books publicly defensible. However, they would not be reliable allies in his war to the finish. His long-range success depended on the full conversion of some men, of very few. They would provide the vital center which would gradually inspire, in favorable circumstances, the formation of a new ruling class, a new kind of princes, comparable to the patriciate of ancient Rome. Machiavelli's warfare has the character of propaganda. No earlier philosopher had thought of guaranteeing the posthumous success of his teaching by developing a specific strategy and tactics for this purpose. The earlier philosophers of all persuasions were resigned to the fact that their teaching, the true teaching,

would never supersede what they regarded as false teachings, but would coexist with them. They offered their teachings to their contemporaries and above all to posterity,
without even dreaming of controlling the future fate of
human thought in general. And if they were political philosophers, and had arrived at definite conclusions regarding
the right political order, they would have been vicious, and
hence not philosophers, if they had not been willing to
help their fellow men in ordering their common affairs in
the best possible way. But they did not for one moment
believe that the true political teaching is, or is likely to be,
the political teaching of the future. Machiavelli is the first
philosopher who attempted to force chance, to control the
future by embarking on a campaign, a campaign of propaganda. This propaganda is at the opposite pole of what is
now called propaganda, high-pressure salesmanship and
holdup of captive audiences. Machiavelli desires to convince, not merely to persuade or to bully. He was the first
of a long series of modern thinkers who hoped to bring
about the establishment of new modes and orders by means
of enlightenment. The enlightenment—*lucus a non lu-
cendo**—begins with Machiavelli.

In order to realize the magnitude of Machiavelli's success
it is necessary that one should have a clear grasp of his
principle. This principle, to repeat, is this: one must lower
the standards in order to make probable, if not certain, the
actualization of the right or desirable social order or in
order to conquer chance; one must effect a shift of emphasis
from moral character to institutions. The right order, as
Machiavelli himself conceived of it, was the hard-headed
republic, which was modelled on ancient Rome, but which
was meant to be an improvement on ancient Rome. For
what the Romans had done haphazardly or instinctively can
now be done consciously and deliberately: now—after Ma-

---

* A Latin phrase which literally means "bush from not being light."
It is employed to point out the absurdity of an etymological derivation.
In the text, the phrase is used to question the enlightenment's right to
its name.

chiavelli has understood the reasons of the success of the Romans. Republicanism in the Roman style, as interpreted by Machiavelli, became one of the most powerful trends of modern political thought. We observe its presence in the works of Harrington, Spinoza, Algernon Sydney, Montesquieu, Rousseau, and in *The Federalist,* and among those upper-class Frenchmen who favored the French revolution out of concern for the status of France as a great power. But this posthumous success of Machiavelli is not comparable in importance to that which came about through the transformation of his scheme—a transformation which was inspired by his own principle.

Machiavelli's scheme was open to serious theoretical difficulties. The theoretical or cosmological basis of his political teaching was a kind of decayed Aristotelianism. This means that he assumed, but did not demonstrate, the untenable character of teleological natural science. He rejected the view that man must take his bearings by virtue, by his perfection, by his natural end; but this rejection required a criticism of the notion of natural ends. This proof was supplied, or was thought to be supplied, by the new natural science of the seventeenth century. There is a hidden kinship between Machiavelli's political science and the new natural science. The classics had taken their bearings by the normal case as distinguished from the exception; Machiavelli effects his radical change in the understanding of political things by taking his bearings by the exception, by the extreme case. As appears from Bacon, there is a close connection between Machiavelli's orientation and the notion of torturing nature, i.e, of the controlled experiment.

But the main reason why Machiavelli's scheme had to be modified was its revolting character. The man who mitigated Machiavelli's scheme in a manner which was almost sufficient to guarantee the success of Machiavelli's primary intention was Hobbes. One could think for a moment that Hobbes's correction of Machiavelli consists in a masterpiece of prestidigitation. Machiavelli wrote a book called *On The*

Prince; Hobbes wrote a book called *On The Citizen;* i.e., Hobbes chose as his theme, not the practices of kingdoms and states, but rather the duties of subjects; hence what Hobbes did teach sounds much more innocent than what Machiavelli had taught, without necessarily contradicting Machiavelli's teaching. But it is both more charitable and more correct to say that Hobbes was an honest and plain-spoken Englishman who lacked the fine Italian hand of his master. Or if you wish, you may compare Hobbes to Sherlock Holmes and Machiavelli to Professor Moriarty. For certainly Hobbes took justice much more seriously than Machiavelli had done. He may even be said to have defended the cause of justice: he denies that it is of the essence of civil society to be founded on crime. To refute Machiavelli's fundamental contention may be said to be the chief purpose of Hobbes's famous doctrine about the state of nature. He accepted the traditional notion that justice is not merely the work of society but that there is a natural right. But he also accepted Machiavelli's critique of traditional political philosophy: traditional political philosophy aimed too high. Hence he demanded that natural right be derived from the beginnings: the elementary wants or urges, which effectively determine all men most of the time and not from man's perfection or end, the desire for which effectively determines only a few men, and by no means most of the time. These primary urges are of course selfish; they can be reduced to one principle: the desire for self-preservation, or negatively expressed, the fear of violent death. This means that not the glitter and glamor of glory —or pride—but the terror of fear of death stands at the cradle of civil society: not heroes, if fratricidal and incestuous heroes, but naked, shivering poor devils were the founders of civilization. The appearance of the diabolical vanishes completely. But let us not be too rash. Once government has been established, the fear of violent death turns into fear of government. And the desire for self-preservation expands into the desire for comfortable self-preservation. Machiavelli's glory is indeed deflated; it stands now revealed as mere, unsubstantial, petty, ridiculous vanity. That glory does not however give way to justice or human excellence, but to concern with solid comfort, with practical, pedestrian hedonism. Glory survives only in the form of competition. In other words, whereas the pivot of Machiavelli's political teaching was glory, the pivot of Hobbes's political teaching is power. Power is infinitely more businesslike than glory. Far from being the goal of a lofty or demonic longing, it is required by, or the expression of, a cold objective necessity. Power is morally neutral. Or, what is the same thing, it is ambiguous if of concealed ambiguity. Power, and the concern with power, lack the direct human appeal of glory and the concern with glory. It emerges through an estrangement from man's primary motivation. It has an air of senility. It becomes visible in gray eminences rather than in Scipios and Hannibals. Respectable, pedestrian hedonism, sobriety without sublimity and subtlety, protected or made possible by "power politics"—this is the meaning of Hobbes's correction of Machiavelli.

Hobbes's teaching was still much too bold to be acceptable. It, too, was in need of mitigation. The mitigation was the work of Locke. Locke took over the fundamental scheme of Hobbes and changed it only in one point. He realized that what man primarily needs for his self-preservation is less a gun than food, or more generally, property. Thus the desire for self-preservation turns into the desire for property, for acquisition, and the right to self-preservation becomes the right to unlimited acquisition. The practical consequences of this small change are enormous. Locke's political teaching is the prosaic version of what in Hobbes still had a certain poetic quality. It is, precisely on Hobbes's premises, more reasonable than Hobbes's own political teaching. With a view to the resounding success of Locke, as contrasted with the apparent failure of Hobbes, especially in the Anglo-Saxon world, we can say that Machiavelli's discovery or invention of the need for an immoral or amoral substitute for morality became victorious through Locke's discovery or invention that that substitute is acquisitiveness. Here we have an utterly selfish passion whose satisfaction does not require the spilling of any blood and whose effect is the improvement of the lot of all. In other words, the solution of the political problem by economic means is the most elegant solution, once one accepts Machiavelli's premise: economism is Machiavellianism come of age. No one understood this more profoundly than Montesquieu. His *Esprit des Lois* reads as if it were nothing but the document of an incessant fight, an unresolved conflict, between two social or political ideals: the Roman republic, whose principle is virtue, and England, whose principle is political liberty. But in fact Montesquieu decides eventually in favor of England. The superiority of England is based in his view on the fact that the English had found a substitute for stern, republican, Roman virtue; that substitute is trade and finance. The ancient republics based on virtue needed pure manners; the modern system, which replaces virtue by trade, is productive of gentle manners, of *humanité*. In Montesquieu's work we observe a last resurgence of the poetry underlying modern prose. There are only two books of the *Esprit des Lois* which are prefaced with poems: the book dealing with population is prefaced with Lucretius' verses in praise of Venus; the first book dealing with commerce is prefaced with a prose poem which is the work of Montesquieu himself.

This serpentine wisdom, which corrupted by charming and charmed by corrupting, this degradation of man, called forth Jean-Jacques Rousseau's passionate and still unforgettable protest. With Rousseau there begins what we may call the second wave of modernity: the wave which bore both German idealistic philosophy and the romanticism of all ranks in all countries. This great and complex countermovement consisted in the first place in a return from the world of modernity to premodern ways of thinking. Rousseau returned from the world of finance, from what he was the first to call the world of the *bourgeois,* to the world of virtue and the city, to the world of the *citoyen.* Kant returned from Descartes' and Locke's notion of ideas to the Platonic notion. Hegel returned from the philosophy of reflection to the "higher vitality" of Plato and Aristotle. And romanticism as a whole is primarily a movement of return to the origins. Yet in all these cases, the return to premodern thought was only the initial step of a movement which led, consciously or unconsciously, to a much more radical form of modernity—to a form of modernity which was still more alien to classical thought than the thought of the seventeenth and eighteenth centuries had been.

Rousseau returned from the modern state as it had developed by his time to the classical city. But he interpreted the classical city in the light of Hobbes's scheme. For according to Rousseau too, the root of civil society is the right of self-preservation. But deviating from Hobbes and from Locke, he declares that this fundamental right points to a social order which is closely akin to the classical city. The reason for this deviation from Hobbes and Locke is identical with the primary motivation of modern political philosophy in general. In Hobbes's and Locke's schemes, the fundamental right of man had retained its original status even within civil society: natural law remained the standard for positive law; there remained the possibility of appealing from positive law to natural law. This appeal was of course, generally speaking, ineffective; it certainly did not carry with itself the guarantee of its being effective. Rousseau drew from this the conclusion that civil society must be so constructed as to make the appeal from positive law to natural law utterly superfluous; a civil society properly constructed in accordance with natural law will automatically produce just positive law. Rousseau expresses this thought as follows: the general will, the will of a society, in which everyone subject to the law must have had a say in the making of the law, cannot err. The general will, the will immanent in societies of a certain kind, replaces the transcendent natural right. One cannot emphasize too strongly that Rousseau would have abhorred the totalitarianism of our day. He favored, indeed, the totalitarianism of a free society, but he rejected in the clearest possible language any possible totalitarianism of government. The difficulty into which Rousseau leads us lies deeper. If the ultimate criterion of justice becomes the general will, i.e., the will of a free society, cannibalism is as just as its opposite. Every institution hallowed by a folk-mind has to be regarded as sacred.

Rousseau's thought marks a decisive step in the secular movement which tries to guarantee the actualization of the ideal, or to prove the necessary coincidence of the rational and the real, or to get rid of that which essentially transcends every possible human reality. The assumption of such a transcendence had permitted earlier men to make a tenable distinction between liberty and license. License consists in doing what one lists; liberty consists in doing in the right manner the good only; and our knowledge of the good must come from a higher principle, from above. These men acknowledged a limitation of license which comes from above, a vertical limitation. On the basis of Rousseau, the limitation of license is effected horizontally by the license of other men. I am just if I grant to every other man the same rights which I claim for myself, regardless of what these rights may be. The horizontal limitation is preferred to the vertical limitation because it seems to be more realistic: the horizontal limitation, the limitation of my claim by the claims of others is self-enforcing.

One might say that Rousseau's doctrine of the general will is a juridical, not a moral doctrine, and that the law is necessarily more lax than morality. One might illustrate this distinction by referring to Kant, who declared in his moral teaching that every lie, the saying of any untruth, is immoral, whereas he declared in his juridical teaching that the right of freedom of speech is as much the right to lie as the right to say the truth. But one may very well wonder whether the separation of law and morality, of which German legal philosophy was so proud, is in itself a sound suggestion. Above all, the moral teaching of Rousseau does not dispose of the difficulty indicated. The place occupied in his juridical teaching by the right of self-preservation is occupied in his moral teaching by the right or duty of self-legislation. "Material" ethics gives way to "formal" ethics with the result that it becomes impossible ever to establish clear substantive principles, and that one is compelled to borrow substantive principles from the "general will" or from what came to be called History.

Rousseau was not unaware of these difficulties. They had been caused by the exinanition of the notion of human nature and ultimately by the turn from man's end to man's beginning. Rousseau had accepted Hobbes's antiteleological principle. By following it more consistently than Hobbes himself had done, he was compelled to reject Hobbes's scheme or to demand that the state of nature—man's primitive and presocial condition—be understood as perfect, i.e., as not pointing beyond itself toward society. He was compelled to demand that the state of nature, man's beginning, become the goal for social man: only because man has drifted away from his beginnings, because he has thus become corrupted, does he need an end. That end is primarily the just society. The just society is distinguished from the unjust society by the fact that it comes as close to the state of nature as a society possibly can: the desire determining man in the state of nature, the desire for self-preservation, is the root of the just society and determines its end. This fundamental desire, which is at the same time the fundamental right, animates the juridical as distinguished from the moral: society is so far from being based on morality that it is the basis of morality; the end of society must therefore be defined in juridical, not in moral terms; and there cannot be an obligation to enter society (or the social contract cannot bind "the body of the people"). Whatever the meaning and the status of morality may be, it certainly presupposes society, and society, even the just society, is bondage or alienation from nature. Man ought therefore to transcend the whole social and moral dimension and to return to the wholeness and sincerity of the state of nature. Since the concern with self-preservation compels man to enter society, man ought to go back beyond self-preservation to the root of self-preservation. This root, the absolute beginning, is the feeling of existence, the feeling of the sweetness of mere existence. By giving himself to the sole feeling of his present existence without any thought of the future, by thus living in blessed oblivion of every care and fear, the individual senses the sweetness of all existence: he has returned to nature. It is the feeling of one's existence which gives rise to the desire for the preservation of one's existence. This desire compels man to devote himself entirely to action and thought, to a life of care and duty and misery, and therewith cuts him off from the bliss which is buried in his depth or origin. Only very few men are capable of finding the way back to nature. The tension between the desire for the preservation of existence and the feeling of existence expresses itself therefore in the insoluble antagonism between the large majority who in the best case will be good citizens and the minority of solitary dreamers who are the salt of the earth. Rousseau left it at that antagonism. The German philosophers who took up his problem thought that a reconciliation is possible, and that reconciliation can be brought about, or has already been brought about, by History.

German idealistic philosophy claimed to have restored, and more than restored, the high level of classical political philosophy while fighting against the debasement caused by the first wave of modernity. But to say nothing of the replacement of Virtue by Freedom, the political philosophy belonging to the second wave of modernity is inseparable from philosophy of history, and there is no philosophy of history in classical political philosophy. For what is the meaning of the philosophy of history? Philosophy of history shows the essential necessity of the actualization of the right order. There is no chance in the decisive respect, i.e., the same realistic tendency which led to the lowering of the standards in the first wave led to philosophy of history in the second wave. Nor was the introduction of philosophy of history a genuine remedy for the lowering of the standards. The actualization of the right order is achieved by blind selfish passion: the right order is the unintended by-product of human activities which are in no way directed toward the right order. The right order may have been as loftily conceived by Hegel as it was by Plato, which one may doubt. It certainly was thought by Hegel to be established in the Machiavellian way, not in the Platonic way: it was thought to be established in a manner which contradicts the right order itself. The delusions of communism are already the delusions of Hegel and even of Kant.

The difficulties to which German idealism was exposed gave rise to the third wave of modernity—of the wave that bears us today. This last epoch was inaugurated by Nietzsche. Nietzsche retained what appeared to him to be the insight due to the historical consciousness of the nineteenth century. But he rejected the view that the historical process is rational as well as the premise that a harmony between the genuine individual and the modern state is possible. He may be said to have returned, on the level of the historical consciousness, from Hegel's reconciliation to Rousseau's antinomy. He taught then that all human life and human thought ultimately rests on horizon-forming creations which are not susceptible of rational legitimization. The creators are great individuals. The solitary creator who gives a new law unto himself and who subjects himself to all its rigors takes the place of Rousseau's solitary dreamer. For Nature has ceased to appear as lawful and merciful. The fundamental experience of existence is therefore the experience, not of bliss, but of suffering, of emptiness, of an abyss. Nietzsche's creative call to creativity was addressed to individuals who should revolutionize their own lives, not to society or to his nation. But he expected or hoped that his call, at once stern and imploring, questioning and desirous to be questioned, would tempt the best men of the generations after him to become true selves and thus to form a new nobility which would be able to rule the planet. He opposed the possibility of a planetary aristocracy to the alleged necessity of a universal classless and stateless society. Being certain of the tameness of modern Western man, he preached the sacred right of "merciless extinction" of large masses of men with as little restraint as his great antagonist had done. He used much of his unsurpassable and inexhaustible power of passionate and fascinating speech for making his readers loathe, not only socialism and communism, but conservatism, nationalism, and democracy as well. After having taken upon himself this great political responsibility, he could not show his readers a way toward political responsibility. He left them no choice except that between irresponsible indifference to politics and irresponsible political options. He thus prepared a regime which, as long as it lasted, made discredited democracy look again like the golden age. He tried to articulate his understanding both of the modern situation and of human life as such by his doctrine of the will to power. The difficulty inherent in the philosophy of the will to power led after Nietzsche to the explicit renunciation of the very notion of eternity. Modern thought reaches its culmination, its highest self-consciousness, in the most radical historicism, i.e., in explicitly condemning to oblivion the notion of eternity. For oblivion of eternity, or, in other words, estrangement from man's deepest desire and therewith from the primary issues, is the price which modern man had to pay, from the very beginning, for attempting to be absolutely sovereign, to become the master and owner of nature, to conquer chance.

On Classical
Political Philosophy

The purpose of the following remarks is to discuss especially those characteristic features of classical political philosophy which are in particular danger of being overlooked
or insufficiently stressed by the schools that are most influential in our time. These remarks are not intended to
sketch the outlines of an adequate interpretation of classical
political philosophy. They will have fulfilled their purpose
if they point to the way which, as it seems to me, is the
only one whereby such an interpretation can eventually be
reached by us.

Classical political philosophy is characterized by the fact
that it was related to political life directly. It was only after
the classical philosophers had done their work that political
philosophy became definitely "established" and thus acquired a certain remoteness from political life. Since that
time the relationship of political philosophers to political
life, and their grasp of it, have been determined by the
existence of an inherited political philosophy: since then
political philosophy has been related to political life through
the medium of a tradition of political philosophy. The
tradition of political philosophy, being a tradition, took for
granted the necessity and possibility of political philosophy.
The tradition that originated in classical Greece was re-

jected in the sixteenth and seventeenth centuries in favor of a new political philosophy. But this "revolution" did not restore the direct relation to political life that had existed in the beginning: the new political philosophy was related to political life through the medium of the inherited general notion of political philosophy or political science, and through the medium of a new concept of science. The modern political philosophers tried to replace both the teaching and the method of traditional political philosophy by what they considered as the true teaching and the right method; they took it for granted that political philosophy as such is necessary and possible. Today, political science may believe that by rejecting, or by emancipating itself from, political philosophy it stands in the most direct relation to political life; actually it is related to political life through the medium of modern natural science, or of the reaction to modern natural science, and through a number of basic concepts inherited from the philosophic tradition, however despised or ignored.

It was its direct relation to political life which determined the orientation and scope of classical political philosophy. Accordingly, the tradition which was based on that philosophy, and which preserved its orientation and scope, preserved that direct relation to a certain extent. The fundamental change in this respect begins with the new political philosophy of the early modern period and reaches its climax in present-day political science. The most striking difference between classical political philosophy and present-day political science is that the latter is no longer concerned at all with what was the guiding question for the former: the question of the best political order. On the other hand, modern political science is greatly preoccupied with a type of question that was of much less importance to classical political philosophy: questions concerning method. Both differences must be traced to the same reason: to the different degree of directness in which classical political philosophy, on the one hand, and present-day political science, on the other, are related to political life.

Classical political philosophy attempted to reach its goal by accepting the basic distinctions made in political life exactly in the sense and with the orientation in which they are made in political life, and by thinking them through, by understanding them as perfectly as possible. It did not start from such basic distinctions as those between "the state of nature" and "the civil state," between "facts" and "values," between "reality" and "ideologies," between "the world" and "the worlds" of different societies, or between "the I, Me, Thou and We," distinctions which are alien, and even unknown, to political life as such and which originate only in philosophic or scientific reflection. Nor did it try to bring order into that chaos of political "facts" which exists only for those who approach political life from a point of view outside of political life, that is to say, from the point of view of a science that is not itself essentially an element of political life. Instead, it followed carefully and even scrupulously the articulation which is inherent in, and natural to, political life and its objectives.

The primary questions of classical political philosophy, and the terms in which it stated them, were not specifically philosophic or scientific; they were questions that are raised in assemblies, councils, clubs, and cabinets, and they were stated in terms intelligible and familiar, at least to all sane adults, from everyday experience and everyday usage. These questions have a natural hierarchy which supplies political life, and hence political philosophy, with its fundamental orientation. No one can help distinguishing among questions of smaller, of greater, and of paramount importance, and between questions of the moment and questions that are always present in political communities; and intelligent men apply these distinctions intelligently.

Similarly it can be said that the method, too, of classical political philosophy was presented by political life itself.

Political life is characterized by conflicts between men asserting opposed claims. Those who raise a claim usually believe that what they claim is good for them. In many cases they believe, and in most cases they say, that what they claim is good for the community at large. In practically all cases claims are raised, sometimes sincerely and sometimes insincerely, in the name of justice. The opposed claims are based, then, on opinions of what is good or just. To justify their claims, the opposed parties advance arguments. The conflict calls for arbitration, for an intelligent decision that will give each party what it truly deserves. Some of the material required for making such a decision is offered by the opposed parties themselves, and the very insufficiency of this partial material—an insufficiency obviously due to its partisan origin—points the way to its completion by the umpire. The umpire par excellence is the political philosopher.[1] He tries to settle those political controversies that are both of paramount and of permanent importance.

This view of the function of the political philosopher—that he must not be a "radical" partisan who prefers victory in civil war to arbitration—is also of political origin: it is the duty of the good citizen to make civil strife cease and to create, by persuasion, agreement among the citizens.[2] The political philosopher first comes into sight as a good citizen who can perform this function of the good citizen in the

1. Note the procedure of Aristotle in *Politics* 1280a7–1284b34 and 1297a6–7; also Plato, *Eighth Letter* 354a1–5 and 352c8 ff., and *Laws* 627d11–628a4.
2. See Xenophon, *Memorabilia* IV 6, 14–15 and context; also Aristotle, *Athenian Constitution* 28, 5; also the remark by Hume (in his essay "Of the Original Contract"): "But philosophers, who have embraced a party (if that be not a contradiction in terms) . . ." The difference between the classical political philosopher and the present day political scientist is illustrated by Macaulay's remark on Sir William Temple: "Temple was not a mediator. He was merely a neutral." Cf. de Tocqueville, *De la démocratie en Amérique*: "J'ai entrepris de voir, non pas autrement, mais plus loin que les partis." ["I have attempted to see, not differently, but farther than the parties."—Ed.]

best way and on the highest level. In order to perform his function he has to raise ulterior questions, questions that are never raised in the political arena; but in doing so he does not abandon his fundamental orientation, which is the orientation inherent in political life. Only if that orientation were abandoned, if the basic distinctions made by political life were considered merely "subjective" or "unscientific" and therefore disregarded, would the question of how to approach political things in order to understand them, that is to say, the question of method, become a fundamental question, and, indeed, *the* fundamental question.

It is true that political life is concerned primarily with the individual community to which the people happen to belong, and mostly even with individual situations, whereas political philosophy is concerned primarily with what is essential to all political communities. Yet there is a straight and almost continuous way leading from the prephilosophic to the philosophic approach. Political life requires various kinds of skills, and in particular that apparently highest skill which enables a man to manage well the affairs of his political community as a whole. That skill—the art, the prudence, the practical wisdom, the specific understanding possessed by the excellent statesman or politician—and not "a body of true propositions" concerning political matters, which is transmitted by teachers to pupils, is what was originally meant by "political science." A man who possesses "political science" is not merely able to deal properly with a large variety of situations in his own community; he can, in principle, manage well even the affairs of any other political community, be it "Greek" or "barbarian." While all political life is essentially the life of this or that political community, "political science," which essentially belongs to political life, is essentially "transferable" from one community to any other. A man like Themistocles was admired and listened to not only in Athens, but, after he had to flee from Athens, among the barbarians as well; such a man is admired because he is capable of giving sound political advice wherever he goes.[3]

"Political science" designated originally the skill by virtue of which a man could manage well the affairs of political communities by deed and by speech. The skill of speaking takes precedence over the skill of doing since all sensible action proceeds from deliberation, and the element of deliberation is speech. Accordingly, that part of political skill which first became the object of instruction was the skill of public speaking. "Political science" in a more precise sense, that is, as a skill that is essentially teachable, appeared first as rhetoric, or as a part of it. The teacher of rhetoric was not necessarily a politician or statesman; he was, however, a teacher of politicians or statesmen. Since his pupils belonged to the most different political communities, the content of his teaching could not possibly be bound up with the particular features of any individual political community. "Political science," on the level which it reached as a result of the exertions of the rhetoricians, is more "universal," is to an even higher degree "transferable," than is "political science" as the skill of the excellent statesman or politician: whereas strangers as statesmen or political advisers were an exception, strangers as teachers of rhetoric were the rule.[4]

Classical political philosophy rejected the identification of political science with rhetoric; it held that rhetoric, at its best, was only an instrument of political science. It did not, however, descend from the level of generality that had been reached by the rhetoricians. On the contrary, after that part

3. Xenophon, *Memorabilia* III 6, 2; Thucydides, I 138. See also Plato, *Lysis* 209d5–210b2, and *Republic* 494c7–d1. One of the purposes of the *Menexenus* is to illustrate the "transferable" character of political science: a sufficiently gifted foreign woman is as capable as Pericles, or more capable than he, to compose a most solemn speech to be delivered on behalf of the city of Athens.

4. Plato, *Protagoras* 319a1–2, and *Timaeus* 19e; also Aristotle, *Nicomachean Ethics* 1181a12 ff. as well as *Politics* 1264b33–34 and 1299a1–2; Isocrates, *Nicocles* 9; Cicero, *De oratore* III, 57.

of political skill which is the skill of speaking had been raised to the level of a distinct discipline, the classical philosophers could meet that challenge only by raising the whole of "political science," as far as possible or necessary, to the rank of a distinct discipline. By doing this they became the founders of political science in the precise and final sense of the term. And the way in which they did it was determined by the articulation natural to the political sphere.

"Political science" as the skill of the excellent politician or statesman consists in the right handling of individual situations; its immediate "products" are commands or decrees or advices effectively expressed, which are intended to cope with an individual case. Political life knows, however, a still higher kind of political understanding, which is concerned not with individual cases but, as regards each relevant subject, with all cases, and whose immediate "products"—laws and institutions—are meant to be permanent. The true legislators—"the fathers of the Constitution," as modern men would say—establish, as it were, the permanent framework within which the right handling of changing situations by excellent politicians or statesmen can take place. While it is true that the excellent statesman can act successfully within the most different frameworks of laws and institutions, the value of his achievement depends ultimately on the value of the cause in whose service he acts; and that cause is not his work but the work of him or those who made the laws and institutions of his community. The legislative skill is, therefore, the most "architectonic" political skill[5] that is known to political life.

5. Aristotle, *Nicomachean Ethics* 1141b24–29 (compare 1137b13); also Plato, *Gorgias* 464b7–8, and *Minos* 320c1–5; Cicero, *Offices* I, 75–76. The classical view was expressed as follows by Rousseau, who still shared it, or rather restored it: "s'il est vrai qu'un grand prince est un homme rare, que sera-ce d'un grand législateur? Le premier n'a qu'à suivre le modèle que l'autre doit proposer" ["if it is true that a great prince is a rare man, what about a great legislator? The first has only to follow the model that the other must propose."—Ed.] (*Contrat social*, II, 7).

Every legislator is primarily concerned with the individual community for which he legislates, but he has to raise certain questions which regard all legislation. These most fundamental and most universal political questions are naturally fit to be made the subject of the most "architectonic," the truly "architectonic" political knowledge: of that political science which is the goal of the political philosopher. This political science is the knowledge which would enable a man to teach legislators. The political philosopher who has reached his goal is the teacher of legislators.[6] The knowledge of the political philosopher is "transferable" in the highest degree. Plato demonstrated this *ad oculos** in his dialogue on legislation, by presenting in the guise of a stranger the philosopher who is a teacher of legislators.[7] He illustrated it less ambiguously by the comparison, which frequently occurs in his writings, of political science with medicine.

It is by being the teacher of legislators that the political philosopher is the umpire par excellence. All political conflicts that arise within the community are at least related to, if they do not proceed from, the most fundamental political controversy: the controversy as to what type of men should rule the community. And the right settlement of that controversy appears to be the basis of excellent legislation.

Classical political philosophy was related to political life directly, because its guiding subject was a subject of actual political controversy carried on in prephilosophic political life. Since all political controversies presuppose the exis-

6. Consider Plato, *Laws* 630b8–c4 and 631d–632d, and Aristotle, *Nicomachean Ethics* 1180a33 ff. and 1109b34 ff. as well as *Politics* 1297b37–38; cf. Isocrates, *To Nicocles* 6 and Montesquieu, *Esprit des Lois*, beginning of the 29th book. On the difference between political science proper and political skill see Thomas Aquinas' commentary on Aristotle's *Ethics* VI, lectio 7, and also Fārābī's *Enumeration of the Sciences*, Chapter 5.

7. Not to mention the fact that the authors of the *Politics* and the *Cyropaedia* were "strangers" when they wrote those books. Cf. *Politics* 1273b27–32.

* "before one's eyes"

tence of the political community, the classics are not primarily concerned with the question of whether and why there is, or should be, a political community; hence the question of the nature and purpose of the political community is not the guiding question for classical political philosophy. Similarly, to question the desirability or necessity of the survival and independence of one's political community normally means to commit the crime of treason; in other words, the ultimate aim of foreign policy is not essentially controversial. Hence classical political philosophy is not guided by questions concerning the external relations of the political community. It is concerned primarily with the inner structure of the political community, because that inner structure is essentially the subject of such political controversy as essentially involves the danger of civil war.[8]

The actual conflict of groups struggling for political power within the community naturally gives rise to the question what group should rule, or what compromise would be the best solution—that is to say, what political order would be the best order. Either the opposed groups are merely factions made up of the same type of men (such as parties of noblemen or adherents of opposed dynasties), or each of the opposed groups represents a specific type. Only in the latter case does the political struggle go to the roots of political life; then it becomes apparent to everyone, from everyday political life, that the question as to what type of men should have the decisive say is the subject of the most fundamental political controversy.

The immediate concern of that controversy is the best political order for the given political community, but every answer to that immediate question implies an answer to the universal question of the best political order as such. It does not require the exertions of philosophers to lay bare this implication, for the political controversy has a natural tendency to express itself in universal terms. A man who

---

8. Aristotle, *Politics* 1300b36–39; Rousseau, *Contrat social*, ii, 9.

rejects kingship for Israel cannot help using arguments against kingship as such; a man who defends democracy in Athens cannot help using arguments in favor of democracy as such. When they are confronted with the fact that monarchy is the best political order, say, for Babylon, the natural reaction of such men will be that this fact shows the inferiority of Babylon and not that the question of the best political order does not make sense.

The groups, or types, whose claims to rule were considered by the classical philosophers were "the good" (men of merit), the rich, the noble, and the multitude, or the poor citizens; in the foreground of the political scene in the Greek cities, as well as in other places, was the struggle between the rich and the poor. The claim to rule which is based on merit, on human excellence, on "virtue," appeared to be least controversial: courageous and skillful generals, incorruptible and equitable judges, wise and unselfish magistrates, are generally preferred. Thus "aristocracy" (rule of the best) presented itself as the natural answer of all good men to the natural question of the best political order. As Thomas Jefferson put it, "That form of government is the best, which provides the most effectually for a pure selection of [the] natural *aristoi* into offices of the government."[9]

What is to be understood by "good men" was known also from political life: good men are those who are willing, and able, to prefer the common interest to their private interest and to the objects of their passions, or those who, being able to discern in each situation what is the noble or right thing to do, do it because it is noble and right and for no ulterior reason. It was also generally recognized that this answer gives rise to further questions of almost overwhelming political significance: that results which are generally considered desirable can be achieved by men of dubious character or by the use of unfair means; that "just" and

9. Letter to John Adams, October 28, 1813.

"useful" are not simply identical; that virtue may lead to ruin.[10]

Thus the question guiding classical political philosophy, the typical answer that it gave, and the insight into the bearing of the formidable objections to it, belong to prephilosophic political life, or precede political philosophy. Political philosophy goes beyond prephilosophic political knowledge by trying to understand fully the implications of these prephilosophic insights, and especially by defending the second of them against the more or less "sophisticated" attacks made by bad or perplexed men.

When the prephilosophic answer is accepted, the most urgent question concerns the "materials" and institutions which would be most favorable to "the rule of the best." It is primarily by answering this question, by thus elaborating a "blueprint" of the best polity, that the political philosopher becomes the teacher of legislators. The legislator is strictly limited in his choice of institutions and laws by the character of the people for whom he legislates, by their traditions, by the nature of their territory, by their economic conditions, and so on. His choosing this or that law is normally a compromise between what he would wish and what circumstances permit. To effect that compromise intelligently, he must first know what he wishes, or, rather, what would be most desirable in itself. The political philosopher can answer that question because he is not limited in his reflections by any particular set of circumstances, but is free to choose the most favorable conditions that are possible—ethnic, climatic, economic, and other—and thus to determine what laws and institutions would be preferable under those conditions.[11] After that, he tries to bridge the gulf between what is most desirable in itself and what is possible in given circumstances, by discussing what polity,

10. See Aristotle, *Nicomachean Ethics* 1094b18 ff.; Xenophon, *Memorabilia* IV 2, 32 ff.

11. See Aristotle, *Politics* 1265a17 ff. and 1325b33–40; Plato, *Laws* 857e8–858c3; Cicero, *Republic* I, 33.

and what laws, would be best under various types of more or less unfavorable conditions, and even what kinds of laws and measures are appropriate for preserving any kind of polity, however defective. By thus erecting on the "normative" foundation of political science a "realistic" structure, or, to speak somewhat more adequately, by thus supplementing political physiology with political pathology and therapeutics, he does not retract or even qualify, he rather confirms, his view that the question of the best polity is necessarily the guiding question.[12]

By the best political order the classical philosopher understood that political order which is best always and everywhere.[13] This does not mean that he conceived of that order as necessarily good for every community, as "a perfect solution for all times and for every place": a given community may be so rude or so depraved that only a very inferior type of order can "keep it going." But it does mean that the goodness of the political order realized anywhere and at any time can be judged only in terms of that political order which is best absolutely. "The best political order" is, then, not intrinsically Greek: it is no more intrinsically Greek than health, as is shown by the parallelism of political science and medicine. But just as it may happen that the members of one nation are more likely to be healthy and strong than those of others, it may also happen that one nation has a greater natural fitness for political excellence than others.

When Aristotle asserted that the Greeks had a greater natural fitness for political excellence than the nations of the north and those of Asia, he did not assert, of course, that political excellence was identical with the quality of being Greek or derivative from it; otherwise he could not have praised the institutions of Carthage as highly as the institutions of the most renowned Greek cities. When Soc-

12. See Plato, *Laws* 739b8 ff., and the beginning of the fourth book of Aristotle's *Politics*.
13. Aristotle, *Nicomachean Ethics* 1135a4–5.

rates asked Glaucon in the *Republic* whether the city that Glaucon was founding would be a Greek city, and Glaucon answered emphatically in the affirmative, neither of them said any more than that a city founded by Greeks would necessarily be a Greek city. The purpose of this truism, or rather of Socrates' question, was to induce the warlike Glaucon to submit to a certain moderation of warfare: since a general prohibition of wars was not feasible, at least warfare among Greeks should keep within certain limits. The fact that a perfect city founded by Glaucon would be a Greek city does not imply that any perfect city was necessarily Greek: Socrates considered it possible that the perfect city, which certainly did not exist at that time anywhere in Greece, existed at that time "in some barbarian place."[14] Xenophon went so far as to describe the Persian Cyrus as *the* perfect ruler, and to imply that the education Cyrus received in Persia was superior even to Spartan education; and he did not consider it impossible that a man of the rank of Socrates would emerge among the Armenians.[15]

Because of its direct relation to political life, classical political philosophy was essentially "practical"; on the other hand, it is no accident that modern political philosophy frequently calls itself political "theory."[16] The primary concern of the former was not the description, or understanding, of political life, but its right guidance. Hegel's demand that political philosophy refrain from construing a state as it ought to be, or from teaching the state how it should be,

14. Plato, *Republic* 427c2–3, 470e4 ff. and 499c7–9; see also *Laws* 739c3 (compare *Republic* 373e, with *Phaedo* 66c5–7); also *Theaetetus* 175a1–5, *Politicus* 262c8–263a1, *Cratylus* 390a, *Phaedo* 78a3–5, and *Laws* 656d–657b and 799a ff.; also *Minos* 316d.

15. *Cyropaedia* I 1 and 2, III 1, 38–40; compare II 2, 26.

16. Hegel, *Vorlesungen ueber die Geschichte der Philosophie*, ed. Michelet-Glockner, I, 291: "Wir werden ueberhaupt die praktische Philosophie nicht spekulativ werden sehen, bis auf die neuesten Zeiten." ["We will at no time see practical philosophy becoming speculative until the most recent times."—Ed.] Cf. Schelling, *Studium Generale*, ed. Glockner, 94–95.

and that it try to understand the present and actual state as something essentially rational, amounts to a rejection of the *raison d'être* of classical political philosophy. In contrast with present-day political science, or with well-known interpretations of present-day political science, classical political philosophy pursued practical aims and was guided by, and culminated in, "value judgments." The attempt to replace the quest for the best political order by a purely descriptive or analytical political science which refrains from "value judgments" is, from the point of view of the classics, as absurd as the attempt to replace the art of making shoes, that is, good and well-fitting shoes, by a museum of shoes made by apprentices, or as the idea of a medicine which refuses to distinguish between health and sickness.

Since political controversies are concerned with "good things" and "just things," classical political philosophy was naturally guided by considerations of "goodness" and "justice." It started from the moral distinctions as they are made in everyday life, although it knew better than the dogmatic skeptic of our time the formidable theoretical objections to which they are exposed. Such distinctions as those between courage and cowardice, justice and injustice, human kindness and selfishness, gentleness and cruelty, urbanity and rudeness, are intelligible and clear for all practical purposes, that is, in most cases, and they are of decisive importance in guiding our lives: this is a sufficient reason for considering the fundamental political questions in their light.

In the sense in which these distinctions are politically relevant, they cannot be "demonstrated," they are far from being perfectly lucid, and they are exposed to grave theoretical doubts. Accordingly, classical political philosophy limited itself to addressing men who, because of their natural inclinations as well as their upbringing, took those distinctions for granted. It knew that one can perhaps silence but not truly convince such people as have no "taste" for the moral distinctions and their significance: not even Socrates himself could convert, though he could silence, such men as Meletus and Callicles, and he admitted the limits set to demonstrations in this sphere by taking recourse to "myths."

The political teaching of the classical philosophers, as distinguished from their theoretical teaching, was primarily addressed not to all intelligent men, but to all decent men.[17] A political teaching which addressed itself equally to decent and indecent men would have appeared to them from the outset as unpolitical, that is, as politically, or socially, irresponsible; for if it is true that the well-being of the political community requires that its members be guided by considerations of decency or morality, the political community cannot tolerate a political science which is morally "neutral" and which therefore tends to loosen the hold of moral principles on the minds of those who are exposed to it. To express the same view somewhat differently, even if it were true that when men are talking of right they are thinking only of their interests, it would be equally true that that reserve is of the essence of political man, and that by emancipating oneself from it one would cease to be a political man or to speak his language.

Thus the attitude of classical political philosophy toward political things was always akin to that of the enlightened statesman; it was not the attitude of the detached observer who looks at political things in the way in which a zoologist looks at the big fishes swallowing the small ones, or that of the social "engineer" who thinks in terms of manipulating or conditioning rather than in terms of education or liberation, or that of the prophet who believes that he knows the future.

In brief, the root of classical political philosophy was the fact that political life is characterized by controversies between groups struggling for power within the political community. Its purpose was to settle those political controversies

17. See Aristotle, *Nicomachean Ethics* 1095b4–6 and 1140b13–18; Cicero, *Laws* I, 37–39.

which are of a fundamental and typical character in the spirit not of the partisan but of the good citizen, and with a view to such an order as would be most in accordance with the requirements of human excellence. Its guiding subject was the most fundamental politically controversial subject, understood in the way, and in the terms, in which it was understood in prephilosophic political life.

In order to perform his function, the philosopher had to raise an ulterior question which is never raised in the political arena. That question is so simple, elementary, and unobtrusive that it is, at first, not even intelligible, as is shown by a number of occurrences described in the Platonic dialogues. This distinctly philosophic question is "What is virtue?" What is that virtue whose possession—as everyone admits spontaneously or is reduced to silence by unanswerable arguments—gives a man the highest right to rule? In the light of this question the common opinions about virtue appear at the outset as unconscious attempts to answer an unconscious question. On closer examination their radical insufficiency is more specifically revealed by the fact that some of them are contradicted by other opinions which are equally common. To reach consistency, the philosopher is compelled to maintain one part of common opinion and to give up the other part which contradicts it; he is thus driven to adopt a view that is no longer generally held, a truly paradoxical view, one that is generally considered "absurd" or "ridiculous."

Nor is that all. He is ultimately compelled to transcend not merely the dimension of common opinion, of political opinion, but the dimension of political life as such; for he is led to realize that the ultimate aim of political life cannot be reached by political life, but only by a life devoted to contemplation, to philosophy. This finding is of crucial importance for political philosophy, since it determines the limits set to political life, to all political action and all political planning. Moreover, it implies that the highest subject of political philosophy is the philosophic life: philosophy—not as a teaching or as a body of knowledge, but as a way of life—offers, as it were, the solution to the problem that keeps political life in motion. Ultimately, political philosophy transforms itself into a discipline that is no longer concerned with political things in the ordinary sense of the term: Socrates called his inquiries a quest for "the *true* political skill," and Aristotle called his discussion of virtue and related subjects "a *kind* of political science."[18]

No difference between classical political philosophy and modern political philosophy is more telling than this: the philosophic life, or the life of "the wise," which was the highest subject of classical political philosophy, has in modern times almost completely ceased to be a subject of political philosophy. Yet even this ultimate step of classical political philosophy, however absurd it seemed to the common opinion, was nevertheless "divined" by prephilosophic political life: men wholly devoted to the political life were sometimes popularly considered "busybodies," and their unresting habits were contrasted with the greater freedom and the higher dignity of the more retired life of men who were "minding their own business."[19]

The direct relation of classical political philosophy to prephilosophic political life was due not to the undeveloped character of classical philosophy or science, but to mature reflection. This reflection is summed up in Aristotle's description of political philosophy as "the philosophy concerning the human things." This description reminds us of the almost overwhelming difficulty which had to be overcome before philosophers could devote any serious attention to political things, to human things. The "human things" were distinguished from the "divine things" or the

---

18. Plato, *Gorgias* 521d7; Aristotle, *Nicomachean Ethics* 1094b11 and 1130b26–29 (*Rhetoric* 1356a25 f.).

19. Aristotle, *Nicomachean Ethics* 1142a1–2 (compare 1177a25 ff.), and *Metaphysics* 982b25–28; Plato, *Republic* 620c4–7 and 549c2 ff., and *Theaetetus* 172c8 ff. and 173c8 ff. See also Xenophon, *Memorabilia* I 2, 47 ff. and II 9, 1.

"natural things," and the latter were considered absolutely superior in dignity to the former.[20] Philosophy, therefore, was at first exclusively concerned with the natural things. Thus, in the beginning, philosophic effort was concerned only negatively, only accidentally, with political things. Socrates himself, the founder of political philosophy, was famous as a philosopher before he ever turned to political philosophy. Left to themselves, the philosophers would not descend again to the "cave" of political life, but would remain outside in what they considered "the island of the blessed"—contemplation of the truth.[21]

But philosophy, being an attempt to rise from opinion to sceince, is necessarily related to the sphere of opinion as its essential starting point, and hence to the political sphere. Therefore the political sphere is bound to advance into the focus of philosophic interest as soon as philosophy starts to reflect on its own doings. To understand fully its own purpose and nature, philosophy has to understand its essential starting point, and hence the nature of political things.

The philosophers, as well as other men who have become aware of the possibility of philosophy, are sooner or later driven to wonder "Why philosophy?" Why does human life need philosophy, why is it good, why is it right, that opinions about the nature of the whole should be replaced by genuine knowledge of the nature of the whole? Since human life is living together or, more exactly, is political life, the question "Why philosophy?" means "Why does political life need philosophy?" This question calls philosophy before the tribunal of the political community: it makes philosophy politically responsible. Like Plato's perfect city itself, which, once established, does not permit the philosophers to

20. Aristotle, *Nicomachean Ethics* 1181b15, 1141a20–b9, 1155b2 ff., and 1177b30 ff. Compare the typical disagreement between the philosopher and the legislator in Plato's *Laws* 804b5–c1, with his *Meno* 94e3–4, and *Apologia Socratis* 23a6–7 (also *Republic* 517d4–5, *Theaetetus* 175c5, and *Politicus* 267e9 ff.). Compare also Xenophon, *Memorabilia* I 1, 11–16, and Seneca, *Naturales Quaestiones* I, beginning.

21. Plato, *Republic* 519b7–d7; compare *ibid.*, 521b7–10.

devote themselves any longer exclusively to contemplation, this question, once raised, forbids the philosophers any longer to disregard political life altogether. Plato's *Republic* as a whole, as well as other political works of the classical philosophers, can best be described as an attempt to supply a political justification for philosophy by showing that the well-being of the political community depends decisively on the study of philosophy. Such a justification was all the more urgent since the meaning of philosophy was by no means generally understood, and hence philosophy was distrusted and hated by many well-meaning citizens.[22] Socrates himself fell victim to the popular prejudice against philosophy.

To justify philosophy before the tribunal of the political community means to justify philosophy in terms of the political community, that is to say, by means of a kind of argument which appeals not to philosophers as such, but to citizens as such. To prove to citizens that philosophy is permissible, desirable, or even necessary, the philosopher has to follow the example of Odysseus and start from premises that are generally agreed upon, or from generally accepted opinions:[23] he has to argue *ad hominem* or "dialectically." From this point of view, the adjective "political" in the expression "political philosophy" designates not so much a subject matter as a manner of treatment;[24] from this point of view, I say, "political philosophy" means primarily not the philosophic treatment of politics, but the political, or popular, treatment of philosophy, or the political introduc-

22. Plato, *Republic* 520b2–3 and 494a4–10, *Phaedo* 64b, and *Apologia Socratis* 23d1–7. Compare Cicero, *Tusculanae disputationes* II 1, 4, and *De officiis* II 1, 2, and Plutarch, *Nicias* 23.

23. Xenophon, *Memorabilia* IV 6, 15.

24. Aristotle, *Politics* 1275b25 (compare J. F. Gronovius' note to Grotius, *De jure belli*, Prolegomena, § 44) and *Nicomachean Ethics* 1171a15–20; Polybius, v 33.5; see also Locke, *Essay Concerning Human Understanding*, III, 9, §§ 3 and 22. Note especially the derogatory meaning of "political" in the term "political virtue": Plato, *Phaedo* 82a10 ff., and *Republic* 430c3–5, and Aristotle, *Nicomachean Ethics* 1116a17 ff.

tion to philosophy—the attempt to lead the qualified citizens, or rather their qualified sons, from the political life to the philosophic life. This deeper meaning of "political philosophy" tallies well with its ordinary meaning, for in both cases "political philosophy" culminates in praise of the philosophic life. At any rate, it is ultimately because he means to justify philosophy before the tribunal of the political community, and hence on the level of political discussion, that the philosopher has to understand the political things exactly as they are understood in political life.

In his political philosophy the philosopher starts, then, from that understanding of political things which is natural to prephilosophic political life. At the beginning, the fact that a certain habitual attitude or a certain way of acting is generally praised is a sufficient reason for considering that attitude, or that way of acting, a virtue. But the philosopher is soon compelled, or able, to transcend the dimension of prephilosophic understanding by raising the crucial question "What is virtue?" The attempt to answer this question leads to a critical distinction between the generally praised attitudes which are rightly praised, and those which are not; and it leads to the recognition of a certain hierarchy, unknown in prephilosophic life, of the different virtues. Such a philosophic critique of the generally accepted views is at the bottom of the fact that Aristotle, for example, omitted piety and sense of shame from his list of virtues,[25] and that his list starts with courage and moderation (the least intellectual virtues) and, proceeding via liberality, magnanimity, and the virtues of private relations, to justice, culminates in the dianoetic virtues.[26] Moreover, insight into the limits of the moral-political sphere as a whole can be expounded fully only by answering the ques-

25. *Eudemian Ethics* 1221a1.
26. *Nicomachean Ethics* 1117b23 ff., and *Rhetoric* I 5, 6. See also Plato, *Laws* 630c ff. and 963e, and *Phaedrus* 247d5–7; Xenophon, *Memorabilia* IV 8, 11 (compare his *Apologia Socratis* 14–16); Thomas Aquinas, *Summa theologica* 2, 2, qu. 129 art. 2 and qu. 58 art. 12.

tion of the nature of political things. This question marks the limit of political philosophy as a practical discipline: while essentially practical in itself, the question functions as an entering wedge for others whose purpose is no longer to guide action but simply to understand things as they are.[27]

27. See, for example, Aristotle, *Politics* 1258b8 ff.. 1279b11 ff., and 1299a28 ff.

The Three Waves
of Modernity

Toward the end of World War I, there appeared a book
with the ominous title *The Decline, or Setting, of the West.*
Spengler understood by the West not what we are in the
habit of calling Western Civilization, the civilization that
originated in Greece, but a culture which emerged around
the year 1000 in Northern Europe; it includes, above all,
modern western culture. He predicted then the decline, or
setting, of modernity. His book was a powerful document
to the crisis of modernity. That such a crisis exists is now
obvious to the meanest capacities. To understand the crisis
of modernity, we must first understand the character of
modernity.

The crisis of modernity reveals itself in the fact, or consists in the fact, that modern western man no longer knows
what he wants—that he no longer believes that he can
know what is good and bad, what is right and wrong. Until
a few generations ago, it was generally taken for granted
that man can know what is right and wrong, what is the
just or the good or the best order of society—in a word
that political philosophy is possible and necessary. In our
time this faith has lost its power. According to the predominant view, political philosophy is impossible: it was a
dream, perhaps a noble dream, but at any rate a dream.
While there is broad agreement on this point, opinions

differ as to why political philosophy was based on a fundamental error. According to a very widespread view, all knowledge which deserves the name is scientific knowledge; but scientific knowledge cannot validate value judgments; it is limited to factual judgments; yet political philosophy presupposes that value judgments can be rationally validated. According to a less widespread but more sophisticated view, the predominant separation of facts from values is not tenable: the categories of theoretical understanding imply, somehow, principles of evaluation; but those principles of evaluation together with the categories of understanding are historically variable; they change from epoch to epoch; hence it is impossible to answer the question of right and wrong or of the best social order in a universally valid manner, in a manner valid for all historical epochs, as political philosophy requires.

The crisis of modernity is then primarily the crisis of modern political philosophy. This may seem strange: why should the crisis of a culture primarily be the crisis of one academic pursuit among many? But political philosophy is not essentially an academic pursuit: the majority of the great political philosophers were not university professors. Above all, as is generally admitted, modern culture is emphatically rationalistic, believing in the power of reason; surely if such a culture loses its faith in reason's ability to validate its highest aims, it is in a crisis.

What then is the peculiarity of modernity? According to a very common notion, modernity is secularized biblical faith; the other-worldly biblical faith has become radically this-worldly. Most simply: not to hope for life in heaven but to establish heaven on earth by purely human means. But this is exactly what Plato claims to do in his *Republic*: to bring about the cessation of all evil on earth by purely human means. And surely Plato cannot be said to have secularized biblical faith. If one wishes to speak of the secularization of biblical faith, one must then be somewhat more specific. E.g., it is asserted that the spirit of modern capitalism is of puritan origin. Or, to give another example, Hobbes conceives of man in terms of a fundamental polarity of evil pride and salutary fear of violent death; everyone can see that this is a secularized version of the biblical polarity of sinful pride and salutary fear of the Lord. Secularization means, then, the preservation of thoughts, feelings, or habits of biblical origin after the loss or atrophy of biblical faith. But this definition does not tell us anything as to what kind of ingredients are preserved in secularizations. Above all it does not tell us what secularization is, except negatively: loss or atrophy of biblical faith. Yet modern man was originally guided by a positive project. Perhaps that positive project could not have been conceived without the help of surviving ingredients of biblical faith; but whether this is in fact the case cannot be decided before one has understood that project itself.

But can one speak of a single project? Nothing is more characteristic of modernity than the immense variety and the frequency of radical change within it. The variety is so great that one may doubt whether one can speak of modernity as something which is one. Mere chronology does not establish meaningful unity: there may be thinkers in modern times who do not think in a modern manner. How then can one escape arbitrariness or subjectivism? By modernity we understand a radical modification of premodern political philosophy—a modification which comes to sight first as a rejection of premodern political philosophy. If premodern political philosophy possesses a fundamental unity, a physiognomy of its own, modern political philosophy, its opponent, will have the same distinction at least by reflection. We are led to see that this is in fact the case after having fixed the beginning of modernity by means of a nonarbitrary criterion. If modernity emerged through a break with premodern thought, the great minds who achieved that break must have been aware of what they were doing. Who, then, is the first political philosopher who explicitly rejected all earlier political philosophy as fundamentally insufficient and even unsound? There is no difficulty regarding the answer: the man in question was Hobbes. Yet closer study shows that Hobbes's radical break with the tradition of political philosophy only continues, if in a very original manner, what had been done in the first place by Machiavelli. Machiavelli questioned, in fact, no less radically than Hobbes the value of traditional political philosophy; he claimed, in fact, no less clearly than Hobbes that the true political philosophy begins with him, although he stated his claim in a somewhat more subdued language than Hobbes was going to do.

There are two utterances of Machiavelli which indicate his broad intention with the greatest clarity. The first is to this effect: Machiavelli is in profound disagreement with the view of others regarding how a prince should conduct himself toward his subjects or friends; the reason for this disagreement is that he is concerned with the factual, practical truth and not with fancies; many have imagined commonwealths and principalities which never were, because they looked at how men ought to live instead of how men do in fact live. Machiavelli opposes to the idealism of traditional political philosophy a realistic approach to political things. But this is only half of the truth (or in other words his realism is of a peculiar kind). The other half is stated by Machiavelli in these terms: fortuna is a woman who can be controlled by the use of force. To understand the bearing of these two utterances, one must remind oneself of the fact that classical political philosophy was a quest for the best political order, or the best regime as a regime most conducive to the practice of virtue or of how men should live, and that according to classical political philosophy the establishment of the best regime depends necessarily on uncontrollable, elusive fortuna or chance. According to Plato's *Republic*, e.g., the coming into being of the best regime depends on the coincidence, the unlikely coming together, of philosophy and political power. The so-called realist Aristotle agrees with Plato in these two most important respects: the best regime is the order most conducive to the practice of virtue, and the actualization of the best regime depends on chance. For according to Aristotle the best regime cannot be established if the proper matter is not available, i.e., if the nature of the available territory and of the available people is not fit for the best regime; whether or not that matter is available depends in no way on the art of the founder, but on chance. Machiavelli seems to agree with Aristotle by saying that one cannot establish the desirable political order if the matter is corrupt, i.e., if the people is corrupt; but what for Aristotle is an impossibility is for Machiavelli only a very great difficulty: the difficulty can be overcome by an outstanding man who uses extraordinary means in order to transform a corrupt matter into a good matter; that obstacle to the establishment of the best regime which is man as matter, the human material, can be overcome because that matter can be transformed.

What Machiavelli calls the imagined commonwealths of the earlier writers is based on a specific understanding of nature which he rejects, at least implicitly. According to that understanding, all natural beings, at least all living beings, are directed towards an end, a perfection for which they long; there is a specific perfection which belongs to each specific nature; there is especially perfection of man which is determined by the nature of man as the rational and social animal. Nature supplies the standard, a standard wholly independent of man's will; this implies that nature is good. Man has a definite place within the whole, a very exalted place; one can say that man is the measure of all things or that man is the microcosm, but he occupies that place by nature; man has his place in an order which he did not originate. "Man is the measure of all things" is the very opposite of "man is the master of all things." Man has a place within the whole: man's power is limited; man cannot overcome the limitations of his nature. Our nature is enslaved in many ways (Aristotle) or we are the playthings of the gods (Plato). This limitation shows itself in particular in the ineluctable power of chance. The good life is the life according to nature, which means to stay within certain limits; virtue is essentially moderation. There is no difference in this respect between classical political philosophy and classical hedonism which is unpolitical: not the maximum of pleasures but the purest pleasures are desirable; happiness depends decisively on the limitation of our desires.

In order to judge properly of Machiavelli's doctrine, we must consider that in the crucial respect there is agreement between classical philosophy and the Bible, between Athens and Jerusalem, despite the profound difference and even antagonism between Athens and Jerusalem. According to the Bible man is created in the image of God; he is given the rule over all terrestrial creatures: he is not given the rule over the whole; he has been put into a garden to work it and to guard it; he has been assigned a place; righteousness is obedience to the divinely established order, just as in classical thought justice is compliance with the natural order; to the recognition of elusive chance corresponds the recognition of inscrutable providence.

Machiavelli rejects the whole philosophic and theological tradition. We can state his reasoning as follows. The traditional views either lead to the consequence that the political things are not taken seriously (Epicureanism) or else that they are understood in the light of an imaginary perfection—of imagined commonwealths and principalities, the most famous of them being the kindom of God. One must start from how men do live; one must lower one's sights. The immediate corollary is the reinterpretation of virtue: virtue must not be understood as that for the sake of which the commonwealth exists, but virtue exists exclusively for the sake of the commonwealth; political life proper is not subject to morality; morality is not possible outside of political society; it presupposes political society; political society cannot be established and preserved by staying within the limits of morality, for the simple reason that the effect or the conditioned cannot precede the cause or condition. Furthermore, the establishment of political society and even of the most desirable political society does not depend on chance, for chance can be conquered or corrupt matter can be transformed into incorrupt matter. There is a guarantee for the solution of the political problem because a) the goal is lower, i.e., in harmony with what most men actually desire and b) chance can be conquered. The political problem becomes a technical problem. As Hobbes puts it, "when commonwealths come to be dissolved by intestine discord, the fault is not in men as they are the matter but as they are the makers of them." The matter is not corrupt or vicious; there is no evil in men which cannot be controlled; what is required is not divine grace, morality, nor formation of character, but institutions with teeth in them. Or, to quote Kant, the establishment of the right social order does not require, as people are in the habit of saying, a nation of angels: "hard as it may sound, the problem of establishing the state [i.e., the just state] is soluble even for a nation of devils, provided they have sense," i.e., provided their selfishness is enlightened; the fundamental political problem is simply one of "a good organization of the state of which man is indeed capable."

In order to do justice to the change effected by Machiavelli, one must consider two great changes which occurred after his time but which were in harmony with his spirit. The first is the revolution in natural science, i.e., the emergence of modern natural science. The rejection of final causes (and therewith also of the concept of chance) destroyed the theoretical basis of classical political philosophy. The new natural science differs from the various forms of the older one not only because of its new understanding of nature but also and especially because of its new understanding of science: knowledge is no longer understood as fundamentally receptive; the initiative in understanding is with man, not with the cosmic order; in seeking knowledge man calls nature before the tribunal of his reason; he "puts nature to the question" (Bacon); knowing is a kind of making; human understanding prescribes nature its laws; man's power is infinitely greater than was hitherto believed; not only can man transform corrupt human matter into incorrupt human matter, or conquer chance—all truth and meaning originate in man; they are not inherent in a cosmic order which exists independently of man's activity. Correspondingly, poetry is no longer understood as inspired imitation or reproduction but as creativity. The purpose of science is reinterpreted: *propter potentiam,* for the relief of man's estate, for the conquest of nature, for the maximum control, the systematic control of the natural conditions of human life. Conquest of nature implies that nature is the enemy, a chaos to be reduced to order; everything good is due to man's labor rather than to nature's gift: nature supplies only the almost worthless materials. Accordingly the political society is in no way natural: the state is simply an artifact, due to convenants; man's perfection is not the natural end of man but an ideal freely formed by man.

The second post-Machiavellian change which is in harmony with his spirit concerns political or moral philosophy alone. Machiavelli had completely severed the connection between politics and natural law or natural right, i.e., with justice understood as something independent of human arbitrariness. The Machiavellian revolution acquired its full force only when that connection was restored: when justice, or natural right, were reinterpreted in Machiavelli's spirit. This was the work primarily of Hobbes. One can describe the change effected by Hobbes as follows: whereas prior to him natural law was understood in the light of a hierarchy of man's ends in which self-preservation occupied the lowest place, Hobbes understood natural law in terms of self-preservation alone; in connection with this, natural law came to be understood primarily in terms of the right of self-preservation as distinguished from any obligation or duty—a development which culminates in the substitution of the rights of man for natural law (nature replaced by man, law replaced by rights). Already in Hobbes himself the natural right to self-preservation includes the right to "corporeal liberty" and to a condition in which man is not weary of life: it approaches the right to comfortable self-preservation which is the pivot of Locke's teaching. I can here only assert that the increased emphasis on economics is a consequence of this. Eventually we arrive at the view that universal affluence and peace is the necessary and sufficient condition of perfect justice.

The second wave of modernity begins with Rousseau. He changed the moral climate of the west as profoundly as Machiavelli. Just as I did in the case of Machiavelli, I shall describe the character of Rousseau's thought by commenting on two or three sentences of his. The characteristics of the first wave of modernity were the reduction of the moral and political problem to a technical problem, and the concept of nature as in need of being overlaid by civilization as a mere artifact. Both characteristics became the targets of Rousseau's critique. As for the first, "the ancient politicians spoke unceasingly of manners and virtue; ours speak of nothing but trade and money." Rousseau protested in the name of virtue, of the genuine, nonutilitarian virtue of the classical republics against the degrading and enervating doctrines of his predecessors; he opposed both the stifling spirit of the absolute monarchy and the more or less cynical commercialism of the modern republics. Yet he could not restore the classical concept of virtue as the natural end of man, as the perfection of man's nature; he was forced to reinterpret virtue because he took over the modern concept of the state of nature as the state in which man finds himself at the beginning. He did not merely take over this concept from Hobbes and Hobbes's successors; he thought it through to its conclusion: "the philosophers who have examined the foundations of society have all of them felt the necessity to go back to the state of nature, but not one of them has arrived there." Rousseau did arrive there because he saw that man in the state of nature is a man stripped of everything which he has acquired by his own efforts. Man in the state of nature is subhuman or prehuman; his humanity or rationality have been acquired in a long process. In post-Rousseauan language, man's humanity is due not to nature but to history, to the historical process, a singular or unique process which is not teleological: the end of the process or its peak was not foreseen or foreseeable but it came to sight only with the approach of the possibility of fully actualizing man's rationality or humanity. The concept of history, i.e., of the historical process as a single process in which man becomes human without intending it, is a consequence of Rousseau's radicalization of the Hobbesean concept of the state of nature.

Yet how can we know that a certain state in man's development is the peak? Or, more generally, how can we distinguish good from bad if man is by nature subhuman, if the state of nature is subhuman? Let us repeat: Rousseau's natural man lacks not merely, as Hobbes's natural man does, sociality, but rationality as well; he is not the rational animal but the animal which is a free agent or, more precisely, which possesses an almost unlimited perfectibility or malleability. But how ought he to be molded or to mold himself? Man's nature seems to be wholly insufficient to give him guidance. The guidance which it gives him is limited to this: under certain conditions, i.e., in a certain stage of his development, man is unable to preserve himself except by establishing civil society; yet he would endanger his self-preservation if he did not make sure that civil society has a definite structure, a structure conducive to his self-preservation: man must get within society the full equivalent of the freedom which he possessed in the state of nature; all members of society must be equally subject and wholly subject to the laws to the making of which everyone must have been able to contribute; there must not be any possibility of appealing from the laws, the positive laws, to a higher law, a natural law, for such an appeal would endanger the rule of laws. The source of the positive law, and of nothing but the positive law, is the general will; a will inherent or immanent in properly constituted society takes the place of the transcendent natural law. Modernity started from the dissatisfaction with the gulf between the is and the ought, the actual and the ideal; the solution suggested in the first wave was: to bring the ought nearer to the is by lowering the ought, by conceiving of the ought as not making too high demands on men, or as being in agreement with man's most powerful and most common passion; in spite of this lowering, the fundamental difference between the is and the ought remained; even Hobbes could not simply deny the legitimacy of the appeal from the is, the established order, to the ought, the natural or moral law. Rousseau's concept of the general will which as such cannot err—which by merely being is what it ought to be—showed how the gulf between the is and the ought can be overcome. Strictly speaking, Rousseau showed this only under the condition that his doctrine of the general will, his political doctrine proper, is linked with his doctrine of the historical process, and this linking was the work of Rousseau's great successors, Kant and Hegel, rather than of Rousseau himself. According to this view, the rational or just society, the society characterized by the existence of a general will known to be the general will, i.e., the ideal, is necessarily actualized by the historical process without men's intending to actualize it.

Why can the general will not err? Why is the general will necessarily good? The answer is: it is good because it is rational, and it is rational because it is general; it emerges through the generalization of the particular will, of the will which as such is not good. What Rousseau has in mind is the necessity in a republican society for everyone to transform his wishes, his demands on his fellows, into the form of laws; he cannot leave it at saying: "I do not wish to pay taxes"; he must propose a law abolishing taxes; in transforming his wish into a possible law, he realizes the folly of his primary or particular will. It is then the mere generality of a will which vouches for its goodness; it is not necessary to have recourse to any substantive consideration, to any consideration of what man's nature, his natural perfection, requires. This epoch-making thought reached full clarity in Kant's moral doctrine: the sufficient test for the goodness of maxims is their susceptibility of becoming principles of universal legislation; the mere form of rationality, i.e. universality, vouches for the goodness of the content. Therefore, the moral laws, as laws of freedom, are no longer understood as natural laws. Moral and political ideals are established without reference to man's nature: man is radically liberated from the tutelage of nature. Arguments against the ideal which are taken from man's nature, as known by the uncontestable experience of the ages, are no longer of importance: what is called man's nature is merely the result of man's development hitherto; it is merely man's past, which cannot give any guidance for man's possible future; the only guidance regarding the future, regarding what men ought to do or aspire to, is supplied by reason. Reason replaces nature. This is the meaning of the assertion that the ought has no basis whatever in the is.

This much about Rousseau's thought which inspired Kant and German idealistic philosophy, the philosophy of freedom. But there is another fundamental thought of Rousseau, no less important than the one indicated which was indeed abandoned by Kant and his successors but which bore fruit in another part of the modern globe. German idealism accepted and radicalized the notion of the general will and the implications of that concept. It abandoned Rousseau's own qualification of this line of reasoning. "Man was born free, and everywhere he is in chains. How has this change taken place? I do not know. What can make that change legitimate? I believe I can answer that question." I.e.: the free society, the society characterized by the existence within it of a general will, is distinguished from a despotically ruled society as legitimate bondage from illegitimate bondage; it is itself bondage. Man cannot find his freedom in any society; he can find his freedom only by returning from society, however good and legitimate, to nature. In other words, self-preservation, the content of the fundamental natural right from which the social contract is derived, is not the fundamental fact; self-preservation would not be good if mere life, mere existence, were not good. The goodness of mere existence is experienced in the sentiment of existence. It is this sentiment which gives rise to the concern with preservation of existence, to all human activity; but that concern prevents the fundamental enjoyment and makes man miserable. Only by returning to the fundamental experience can man become happy; only few men are able to achieve this while almost all men are capable of acting in conformity with the derivative right of self-preservation, i.e. of living as citizens. Of the citizen it is required that he does his duty; the citizen must be virtuous. But virtue is not goodness. Goodness (sensibility, compassion) without a sense of duty or obligation, without effort—no virtue without effort—is the preserve of the natural man, of the man who lives on the fringes of society without being a part of it. There is an unbridgeable gulf between the world of virtue, reason, moral freedom, history on the one hand and nature, natural freedom, and goodness on the other.

At this point a general remark on the notion of modernity seems to be appropriate. Modernity was understood from the beginning in contradistinction to antiquity; modernity could therefore include the medieval world. The difference between the modern and the medieval on the one hand, and antiquity on the other, was reinterpreted around 1800 as the difference between the romantic and the classic. In the narrower sense, romanticism meant the movement of thought and feeling which was initiated by Rousseau. Surely romanticism is more clearly modern than classicism in any of its forms. Perhaps the greatest document of the fertile conflict between modernity and antiquity understood as the conflict between the romantic and the classic is Goethe's *Faust*. Faust is called by the Lord himself "a good man." That good man commits atrocious crimes, both private and public ones. I shall not speak here of the fact that he is redeemed by performing salutary public action, an action which enables him to stand on free soil with a free people, and that this salutary political action is not criminal or revolutionary but strictly legitimate: it is rendered possible by his receiving a fief from the German emperor. I limit myself to stressing the fact that Faust's goodness is decidedly not virtue—i.e., that the moral horizon of Goethe's most famous work has been opened by Rousseau. It is true that Faust's goodness is not identical with goodness in Rousseau's sense. While Rousseau's goodness goes together with abstention from action, with a kind of rest, Faust's goodness is unrest, infinite striving, dissatisfaction with everything finite, finished, complete, "classic." The significance of Faust for modernity, for the way in which modern man understands himself as modern man, was properly appreciated by Spengler, who called modern man Faustic man. We may say that Spengler replaced "romantic" by "Faustic" in describing the character of modernity.

Just as the second wave of modernity is related to Rousseau, the third wave is related to Nietzsche. Rousseau confronts us with the antinomy of nature on the one hand, and of civil society, reason, morality, history on the other, in such a way that the fundamental phenomenon is the beatific sentiment of existence—of union and communion with nature—which belongs altogether on the side of nature as distinguished from reason and society. The third wave may be described as being constituted by a new understanding of the sentiment of existence: that sentiment is the experience of terror and anguish rather than of harmony and peace, and it is the sentiment of historic existence as necessarily tragic; the human problem is indeed insoluble as a social problem, as Rousseau had said, but there is no escape from the human to nature; there is no possibility of genuine happiness, or the highest of which man is capable has nothing to do with happiness.

I quote Nietzsche: "All philosophers have the common defect that they start from present-day man and believe that they can reach their goal by an analysis of present-day man. Lack of historical sense is the inherited defect of all philosophers." Nietzsche's critique of all earlier philosophers is a restatement of Rousseau's critique of all earlier philosophers. But what makes much sense in Rousseau is very strange in Nietzsche; for between Rousseau and Nietzsche there has taken place the discovery of history; the century between Rousseau and Nietzsche is the age of historical sense. Nietzsche implies: the essence of history has hitherto been misunderstood. The most powerful philosopher of history was Hegel. For Hegel the historical process was a rational and reasonable process, a progress, culminating in the rational state, the postrevolutionary state. Christianity is the true or absolute religion; but Christianity consists in its reconciliation with the world, the *saeculum,* in its complete secularization, a process begun with the Reformation, continued by the Enlightenment, and completed in the postrevolutionary state, which is the first state consciously based upon the recognition of the rights of man. In the case of Hegel, we are indeed compelled to say that the essence of modernity is secularized Christianity, for secularization is Hegel's conscious and explicit intention. According to Hegel there is then a peak and end of history; this makes it possible for him to reconcile the idea of philosophic truth with the fact that every philosopher is a son of his time: the true and final philosophy belongs to the absolute moment in history, to the peak of history. Post-Hegelian thought rejected the notion that there can be an end or peak of history, i.e., it understood the historical process as unfinished and unfinishable, and yet it maintained the now baseless belief in the rationality or progressive character of the historical process. Nietzsche was the first to face this situation. The insight that all principles of thought and action are historical cannot be attenuated by the baseless hope that the historical sequence of these principles is progressive or that the historical process has an intrinsic meaning, an intrinsic directedness. All ideals are the outcome of human creative acts, of free human projects that form that horizon within which specific cultures were possible; they do not order themselves into a system; and there is no possibility of a genuine synthesis of them. Yet all known ideals claimed to have an objective support: in nature or in god or in reason. The historical insight destroys that claim and therewith all known ideals. But precisely the realization of the true origin of all ideals—in human creations or projects—makes possible a radically new kind of project, the transvaluation of all values, a project that is in agreement with the new insight yet not deducible from it (for otherwise it would not be due to a creative act).

But does all this not imply that the truth has finally been discovered—the truth about all possible principles of thought and action? Nietzsche seems to hesitate between admitting this and presenting his understanding of the truth as his project or his interpretation. Yet in fact he did the former; he believed he had discovered the fundamental unity between man's creativity and all beings: "wherever I found life, I found will to power." The transvaluation of all values which Nietzsche tries to achieve is ultimately justified by the fact that its root is the highest will to power —a higher will to power than the one which gave rise to all earlier values. Not man as he hitherto was, even at his highest, but only the Over-man will be able to live in accordance with the transvalution of all values. The final insight into being leads to the final ideal. Nietzsche does not, like Hegel, claim that the final insight succeeds the actualization of the final ideal but rather that the final insight opens the way for the actualization of the final ideal. In this respect Nietzsche's view resembles Marx's. But there is this fundamental difference between Nietzsche and Marx:

for Marx the coming of the classless society is necessary, whereas for Nietzsche the coming of the Over-man depends on man's free choice. Only one thing is certain for Nietzsche regarding the future: the end has come for man as he was hitherto; what will come is either the Over-man or the Last-man. The last man, the lowest and most decayed man, the herd man without any ideals and aspirations, but well fed, well clothed, well housed, well medicated by ordinary physicians and by psychiatrists is Marx's man of the future seen from an anti-Marxist point of view. Yet in spite of the radical opposition between Marx and Nietzsche, the final state of the peak is characterized in the eyes of both Marx and Nietzsche by the fact that it marks the end of the rule of chance: man will be for the first time the master of his fate.

There is one difficulty peculiar to Nietzsche. For Nietzsche all genuinely human life, every high culture has necessarily a hierarchic or aristocratic character; the highest culture of the future must be in accordance with the natural order of rank among men which Nietzsche, in principle, understands along Platonic lines. Yet how can there be a natural order of rank, given the, so to speak, infinite power of the Over-man? For Nietzsche, too, the fact that almost all men are defective or fragmentary cannot be due to an authoritative nature but can be no more than an inheritance of the past, or of history as it has developed hitherto. To avoid this difficulty, i.e. to avoid the longing for the equality of all men when man is at the peak of his power, Nietzsche needs nature or the past as authoritative or at least inescapable. Yet since it is no longer for him an undeniable fact, he must will it, or postulate it. This is the meaning of his doctrine of eternal return. The return of the past, of the whole past, must be willed, if the Over-man is to be possible.

Surely the nature of man is will to power and this means on the primary level the will to overpower others: man does not by nature will equality. Man derives enjoyment from overpowering others as well as himself. Whereas Rousseau's natural man is compassionate, Nietzsche's natural man is cruel.

What Nietzsche says in regard to political action is much more indefinite and vague than what Marx says. In a sense, all political use of Nietzsche is a perversion of his teaching. Nevertheless, what he said was read by political men and inspired them. He is as little responsible for fascism as Rousseau is responsible for Jacobinism. This means, however, that he is as much responsible for fascism as Rousseau was for Jacobinism.

I draw a political conclusion from the foregoing remarks. The theory of liberal democracy, as well as of communism, originated in the first and second waves of modernity; the political implication of the third wave proved to be fascism. Yet this undeniable fact does not permit us to return to the earlier forms of modern thought: the critique of modern rationalism or of the modern belief in reason by Nietzsche cannot be dismissed or forgotten. This is the deepest reason for the crisis of liberal democracy. The theoretical crisis does not necessarily lead to a practical crisis, for the superiority of liberal democracy to communism, Stalinist or post-Stalinist, is obvious enough. And above all, liberal democracy, in contradistinction to communism and fascism, derives powerful support from a way of thinking which cannot be called modern at all: the premodern thought of our western tradition.

Natural Right and
the Historical Approach

The attack on natural right in the name of history takes, in most cases, the following form: natural right claims to be a right that is discernible by human reason and is universally acknowledged; but history (including anthropology) teaches us that no such right exists; instead of the supposed uniformity, we find an indefinite variety of notions of right or justice. Or, in other words, there cannot be natural right if there are no immutable principles of justice, but history shows us that all principles of justice are mutable. One cannot understand the meaning of the attack on natural right in the name of history before one has realized the utter irrelevance of this argument. In the first place, "consent of all mankind" is by no means a necessary condition of the existence of natural right. Some of the greatest natural right teachers have argued that, precisely if natural right is rational, its discovery presupposes the cultivation of reason, and therefore natural right will not be known universally: one ought not even to expect any real knowledge of natural right among savages.[1] In other words, by

1. Consider Plato, *Republic* 456b12–c2, 452a7–8 and c6–d1; *Laches* 184d1–185a3; Hobbes. *De cive*, II, 1; Locke, *Two Treatises of Civil Government*, Book II, sec. 12, in conjunction with *An Essay on the Human Understanding*, Book I, chap. iii. Compare Rousseau, *Discours sur l'origine de l'inégalité*, Preface; Montesquieu, *De l'esprit des lois*, I, 1–2; also Marsilius, *Defensor pacis* ii. 12. 8.

proving that there is no principle of justice that has not been denied somewhere or at some time, one has not yet proved that any given denial was justified or reasonable. Furthermore, it has always been known that different notions of justice obtain at different times and in different nations. It is absurd to claim that the discovery of a still greater number of such notions by modern students has in any way affected the fundamental issue. Above all, knowledge of the indefinitely large variety of notions of right and wrong is so far from being incompatible with the idea of natural right that it is the essential condition for the emergence of that idea: realization of the variety of notions of right is *the* incentive for the quest for natural right. If the rejection of natural right in the name of history is to have any significance, it must have a basis other than historical evidence. Its basis must be a philosophic critique of the possibility, or of the knowability, of natural right—a critique somehow connected with "history."

The conclusion from the variety of notions of right to the nonexistence of natural right is as old as political philosophy itself. Political philosophy seems to begin with the contention that the variety of notions of right proves the nonexistence of natural right or the conventional character of all right.[2] We shall call this view "conventionalism." To clarify the meaning of the present-day rejection of natural right in the name of history, we must first grasp the specific difference between conventionalism, on the one hand, and "the historical sense" or "the historical consciousness" characteristic of nineteenth- and twentieth-century thought, on the other.[3]

2. Aristotle, *Nicomachean Ethics* 1134b24–27.
3. The legal positivism of the nineteenth and twentieth centuries cannot be simply identified with either conventionalism or historicism. It seems, however, that it derives its strength ultimately from the generally accepted historicist premise (see particularly Karl Bergbohm, *Jurisprudenz und Rechtsphilosophie,* I [Leipzig, 1892], 409 ff.). Bergbohm's strict argument against the possibility of natural right (as distinguished from the argument that is meant merely to show the dis-

Conventionalism presupposed that the distinction between nature and convention is the most fundamental of all distinctions. It implied that nature is of incomparably higher dignity than convention or the fiat of society, or that nature is the norm. The thesis that right and justice are conventional meant that right and justice have no basis in nature, that they are ultimately against nature, and that they have their ground in arbitrary decisions, explicit or implicit, of communities: they have no basis but some kind of agreement, and agreement may produce peace but it cannot produce truth. The adherents of the modern historical view, on the other hand, reject as mythical the premise that nature is the norm; they reject the premise that nature is of higher dignity than any works of man. On the contrary, either they conceive of man and his works, his varying notions of justice included, as equally natural as all other real things, or else they assert a basic dualism between the realm of nature and the realm of freedom or history. In the latter case, they imply that the world of man, of human creativity, is exalted far above nature. Accordingly, they do not conceive of the notions of right and wrong as fundamentally arbitrary. They try to discover their causes; they try to make intelligible their variety and sequence; in tracing them to acts of freedom, they insist on the fundamental difference between freedom and arbitrariness.

What is the significance of the difference between the old and the modern view? Conventionalism is a particular form of classical philosophy. There are obviously profound differences between conventionalism and the position taken by Plato, for example. But the classical opponents agree in regard to the most fundamental point: both admit that the

---

astrous consequences of natural right for the positive legal order) is based on "the undeniable truth that nothing eternal and absolute exists except the One Whom man cannot comprehend, but only divine in a spirit of faith" (p. 416 n.), that is, on the assumption that "the standards with reference to which we pass judgment on the historical, positive law . . . are themselves absolutely the progeny of their time and are always historical and relative" (p. 450 n.).

distinction between nature and convention is fundamental. For this distinction is implied in the idea of philosophy. Philosophizing means to ascend from the cave to the light of the sun, that is, to the truth. The cave is the world of opinion as opposed to knowledge. Opinion is essentially variable. Men cannot live, that is, they cannot live together, if opinions are not stabilized by social fiat. Opinion thus becomes authoritative opinion or public dogma or Weltanschauung. Philosophizing means, then, to ascend from public dogma to essentially private knowledge. The public dogma is originally an inadequate attempt to answer the question of the all-comprehensive truth or of the eternal order.[4] Any inadequate view of the eternal order is, from the point of view of the eternal order, accidental or arbitrary; it owes its validity not to its intrinsic truth but to social fiat or convention. The fundamental premise of conventionalism is, then, nothing other than the idea of philosophy as the attempt to grasp the eternal. The modern opponents of natural right reject precisely this idea. According to them, all human thought is historical and hence unable ever to grasp anything eternal. Whereas, according to the ancients, philosophizing means to leave the cave, according to our contemporaries all philosophizing essentially belongs to a "historical world," "culture," "civilization," "Weltanschauung," that is, to what Plato had called the cave. We shall call this view "historicism."

We have noted before that the contemporary rejection of natural right in the name of history is based, not on historical evidence, but on a philosophic critique of the possibility or knowability of natural right. We note now that the philosophic critique in question is not particularly a critique of natural right or of moral principles in general. It is a critique of human thought as such. Nevertheless, the critique of natural right played an important role in the formation of historicism.

4. Plato, *Minos* 314b10–315b2.

Historicism emerged in the nineteenth century under the protection of the belief that knowledge, or at least divination, of the eternal is possible. But it gradually undermined the belief which had sheltered it in its infancy. It suddenly appeared within our lifetime in its mature form. The genesis of historicism is inadequately understood. In the present state of our knowledge, it is difficult to say at what point in the modern development the decisive break occurred with the "unhistorical" approach that prevailed in all earlier philosophy. For the purpose of a summary orientation, it is convenient to start with the moment when the previously subterranean movement came to the surface and began to dominate the social sciences in broad daylight. That moment was the emergence of the historical school.

The thoughts that guided the historical school were very far from being of a purely theoretical character. The historical school emerged in reaction to the French Revolution and to the natural right doctrines that had prepared that cataclysm. In opposing the violent break with the past, the historical school insisted on the wisdom and on the need of preserving or continuing the traditional order. This could have been done without a critique of natural right as such. Certainly, premodern natural right did not sanction reckless appeal from the established order, or from what was actual here and now, to the natural or rational order. Yet the founders of the historical school seemed to have realized somehow that the acceptance of any universal or abstract principles has necessarily a revolutionary, disturbing, unsettling effect as far as thought is concerned, and that this effect is wholly independent of whether the principles in question sanction, generally speaking, a conservative or a revolutionary course of action. For the recognition of universal principles forces man to judge the established order, or what is actual here and now, in the light of the natural or rational order; and what is actual here and now is more likely than not to fall short of the universal and unchangeable norm.[5] The recognition of universal principles thus tends to prevent men from wholeheartedly identifying themselves with, or accepting, the social order that fate has allotted to them. It tends to alienate them from their place on the earth. It tends to make them strangers, and even strangers on the earth.

By denying the significance, if not the existence, of universal norms, the eminent conservatives who founded the historical school were, in fact, continuing and even sharpening the revolutionary effort of their adversaries. That effort was inspired by a specific notion of the natural. It was directed against both the unnatural or conventional and the supernatural or otherworldly. The revolutionists assumed, we may say, that the natural is always individual and that therefore the uniform is unnatural or conventional. The human individual was to be liberated or to liberate himself so that he could pursue not just his happiness but his own version of happiness. This meant, however, that one universal and uniform goal was set up for all men: the natural right of each individual was a right uniformly belonging to every man as man. But uniformity was said to be unnatural and hence bad. It was evidently impossible to individualize rights in full accordance with the natural diversity of individuals. The only kinds of rights that were neither incompatible with social life nor uniform were "historical" rights: rights of Englishmen, for example, in contradistinction to the rights of man. Local and temporal variety seemed to supply a safe and solid middle ground between antisocial individualism and unnatural universality. The historical school did not discover the local and temporal variety of notions of justice: the obvious does not have to be discovered. The utmost one

---

5. ". . . [les] imperfections [des États], s'ils en ont, comme la seule diversité, qui est entre eux suffit pour assurer que plusieurs en ont . . ." [". . . [the] imperfections [of States], if they have any, as the mere diversity, which exists between them suffices to insure that several have them . . ."—Ed.] (Descartes, *Discours de la méthode*, Part II).

could say is that it discovered the value, the charm, the inwardness of the local and temporal, or that it discovered the superiority of the local and temporal to the universal. It would be more cautious to say that, radicalizing the tendency of men like Rousseau, the historical school asserted that the local and the temporal have a higher value than the universal. As a consequence, what claimed to be universal appeared eventually as derivative from something locally and temporally confined, as the local and temporal *in statu evanescendi.** The natural law teaching of the Stoics, for example, was likely to appear as a mere reflex of a particular temporal state of a particular local society—of the dissolution of the Greek city.

The effort of the revolutionists was directed against all otherworldliness[6] or transcendence. Transcendence is not a preserve of revealed religion. In a very important sense it was implied in the original meaning of political philosophy as the quest for the natural or best political order. The best regime, as Plato and Aristotle understood it, is, and is meant to be, for the most part, different from what is actual here and now or beyond all actual orders. This view of the transcendence of the best political order was profoundly modified by the way in which "progress" was understood in the eighteenth century, but it was still preserved in that eighteenth-century notion. Otherwise, the theorists of the French Revolution could not have condemned all or almost all social orders which had ever been in existence. By denying the significance, if not the existence, of universal norms, the historical school destroyed the only solid basis

6. As regards the tension between the concern with the history of the human race and the concern with life after death, see Kant's "Idea for a universal history with cosmopolitan intent," proposition 9 (*The Philosophy of Kant,* ed. C. J. Friedrich ["Modern Library"], p. 130). Consider also the thesis of Herder, whose influence on the historical thought of the nineteenth century is well known, that "the five acts are in this life" (see M. Mendelssohn, *Gesammelte Schriften, Jubiläums-Ausgabe,* III, 1, pp. xxx–xxxii).

* "in the state of fading away"

of all efforts to transcend the actual. Historicism can therefore be described as a much more extreme form of modern
this-worldliness than the French radicalism of the eighteenth century had been. It certainly acted as if it intended
to make men absolutely at home in "this world." Since
any universal principles make at least most men potentially
homeless, it depreciated universal principles in favor of historical principles. It believed that, by understanding their
past, their heritage, their historical situation, men could
arrive at principles that would be as objective as those of
the older, prehistoricist political philosophy had claimed to
be and, in addition, would not be abstract or universal and
hence harmful to wise action or to a truly human life, but
concrete or particular—principles fitting the particular age
or particular nation, principles relative to the particular
age or particular nation.

   In trying to discover standards which, while being objective, were relative to particular historical situations, the historical school assigned to historical studies a much greater
importance than they had ever possessed. Its notion of what
one could expect from historical studies was, however, not
the outcome of historical studies but of assumptions that
stemmed directly or indirectly from the natural right doctrine of the eighteenth century. The historical school assumed the existence of folk minds, that is, it assumed that
nations or ethnic groups are natural units, or it assumed
the existence of general laws of historical evolution, or it
combined both assumptions. It soon appeared that there
was a conflict between the assumptions that had given the
decisive impetus to historical studies and the results, as well
as the requirements, of genuine historical understanding.
In the moment these assumptions were abandoned, the infancy of historicism came to its end.

   Historicism now appeared as a particular form of positivism, that is, of the school which held that theology and
metaphysics had been superseded once and for all by positive science or which identified genuine knowledge of re-

ality with the knowledge supplied by the empirical sciences. Positivism proper had defined "empirical" in terms of the procedures of the natural sciences. But there was a glaring contrast between the manner in which historical subjects were treated by positivism proper and the manner in which they were treated by the historians who really proceeded empirically. Precisely in the interests of empirical knowledge it became necessary to insist that the methods of natural science be not considered authoritative for historical studies. In addition, what "scientific" psychology and sociology had to say about man proved to be trivial and poor if compared with what could be learned from the great historians. Thus history was thought to supply the only empirical, and hence the only solid, knowledge of what is truly human, of man as man: of his greatness and misery. Since all human pursuits start from and return to man, the empirical study of humanity could seem to be justified in claiming a higher dignity than all other studies of reality. History—history divorced from all dubious or metaphysical assumptions—became the highest authority.

But history proved utterly unable to keep the promise that had been held out by the historical school. The historical school had succeeded in discrediting universal or abstract principles; it had thought that historical studies would reveal particular or concrete standards. Yet the unbiased historian had to confess his inability to derive any norms from history: no objective norms remained. The historical school had obscured the fact that particular or historical standards can become authoritative only on the basis of a universal principle which imposes an obligation on the individual to accept, or to bow to, the standards suggested by the tradition or the situation which has molded him. Yet no universal principle will ever sanction the acceptance of every historical standard or of every victorious cause: to conform with tradition or to jump on "the wave of the future" is not obviously better, and it is certainly not always better than to burn what one has worshiped or to resist the "trend of history." Thus all standards suggested by history as such proved to be fundamentally ambiguous and therefore unfit to be considered standards. To the unbiased historian, "the historical process" revealed itself as the meaningless web spun by what men did, produced, and thought, no more than by unmitigated chance —a tale told by an idiot. The historical standards, the standards thrown up by this meaningless process, could no longer claim to be hallowed by sacred powers behind that process. The only standards that remained were of a purely subjective character, standards that had no other support than the free choice of the individual. No objective criterion henceforth allowed the distinction between good and bad choices. Historicism culminated in nihilism. The attempt to make man absolutely at home in this world ended in man's becoming absolutely homeless.

The view that "the historical process" is a meaningless web or that there is no such thing as the "historical process" was not novel. It was fundamentally the classical view. In spite of considerable opposition from different quarters, it was still powerful in the eighteenth century. The nihilistic consequence of historicism could have suggested a return to the older, prehistoricist view. But the manifest failure of the practical claim of historicism, that it could supply life with a better, a more solid, guidance than the prehistoricist thought of the past had done, did not destroy the prestige of the alleged theoretical insight due to historicism. The mood created by historicism and its practical failure was interpreted as the unheard-of experience of the true situation of man as man—of a situation which earlier man had concealed from himself by believing in universal and unchangeable principles. In opposition to the earlier view, the historicists continued to ascribe decisive importance to that view of man that arises out of historical studies, which as such are particularly and primarily concerned not with the permanent and universal but with the variable and unique. History as history seems to present to us the depressing spectacle of a disgraceful variety of thoughts and beliefs and, above all, of the passing-away of every thought and belief ever held by men. It seems to show that all human thought is dependent on unique historical contexts that are preceded by more or less different contexts and that emerge out of their antecedents in a fundamentally unpredictable way: the foundations of human thought are laid by unpredictable experiences or decisions. Since all human thought belongs to specific historical situations, all human thought is bound to perish with the situation to which it belongs and to be superseded by new, unpredictable thoughts.

The historicist contention presents itself today as amply supported by historical evidence, or even as expressing an obvious fact. But if the fact is so obvious, it is hard to see how it could have escaped the notice of the most thoughtful men of the past. As regards the historical evidence, it is clearly insufficient to support the historicist contention. History teaches us that a given view has been abandoned in favor of another view by all men, or by all competent men, or perhaps only by the most vocal men; it does not teach us whether the change was sound or whether the rejected view deserved to be rejected. Only an impartial analysis of the view in question—an analysis that is not dazzled by the victory or stunned by the defeat of the adherents of the view concerned—could teach us anything regarding the worth of the view and hence regarding the meaning of the historical change. If the historicist contention is to have any solidity, it must be based not on history but on philosophy: on a philosophic analysis proving that all human thought depends ultimately on fickle and dark fate and not on evident principles accessible to man as man. The basic stratum of that philosophic analysis is a "critique of reason" that allegedly proves the impossibility of theoretical metaphysics and of philosophic ethics or natural right. Once all metaphysical and ethical views can be assumed to be, strictly speaking, untenable, that is, untenable as regards their claim to be simply true, their historical fate necessarily appears to be deserved. It then becomes a plausible, although not very important, task to trace the prevalence, at different times, of different metaphysical and ethical views, to the times at which they prevailed. But this leaves still intact the authority of the positive sciences. The second stratum of the philosophical analysis underlying historicism is the proof that the positive sciences rest on metaphysical foundations.

Taken by itself, this philosophic critique of philosophic and scientific thought—a continuation of the efforts of Hume and of Kant—would lead to skepticism. But skepticism and historicism are two entirely different things. Skepticism regards itself as, in principle, coeval with human thought; historicism regards itself as belonging to a specific historical situation. For the skeptic, all assertions are uncertain and therefore essentially arbitrary; for the historicist, the assertions that prevail at different times and in different civilizations are very far from being arbitrary. Historicism stems from a nonskeptical tradition—from that modern tradition which tried to define the limits of human knowledge and which therefore admitted that, within certain limits, genuine knowledge is possible. In contradistinction to all skepticism, historicism rests at least partly on such a critique of human thought as claims to articulate what is called "the experience of history."

No competent man of our age would regard as simply true the complete teaching of any thinker of the past. In every case, experience has shown that the originator of the teaching took things for granted which must not be taken for granted or that he did not know certain facts or possibilities which were discovered in a later age. Up to now, all thought has proved to be in need of radical revisions or to be incomplete or limited in decisive respects. Furthermore, looking back at the past, we seem to observe that every progress of thought in one direction was bought at the price of a retrogression of thought in another respect:

when a given limitation was overcome by a progress of thought, earlier important insights were invariably forgotten as a consequence of that progress. On the whole, there was then no progress, but merely a change from one type of limitation to another type. Finally, we seem to observe that the most important limitations of earlier thought were of such a nature that they could not possibly have been overcome by any effort of the earlier thinkers; to say nothing of other considerations, any effort of thought which led to the overcoming of specific limitations led to blindness in other respects. It is reasonable to assume that what has invariably happened up to now will happen again and again in the future. Human thought is essentially limited in such a way that its limitations differ from historical situation to historical situation and that the limitation characteristic of the thought of a given epoch cannot be overcome by any human effort. There always have been and there always will be surprising, wholly unexpected changes of outlook which radically modify the meaning of all previously acquired knowledge. No view of the whole, and in particular no view of the whole of human life, can claim to be final or universally valid. Every doctrine, however seemingly final, will be superseded sooner or later by another doctrine. There is no reason to doubt that earlier thinkers had insights which are wholly inaccessible to us and which cannot become accessible to us, however carefully we might study their works, because our limitations prevent us from even suspecting the possibility of the insights in question. Since the limitations of human thought are essentially unknowable, it makes no sense to conceive of them in terms of social, economic, and other conditions, that is, in terms of knowable or analyzable phenomena: the limitations of human thought are set by fate.

The historicist argument has a certain plausibility which can easily be accounted for by the preponderance of dogmatism in the past. We are not permitted to forget Voltaire's complaint: "nous avons des bacheliers qui savent tout ce que ces grands hommes ignoraient."[7] Apart from this, many thinkers of the first rank have propounded all-comprehensive doctrines which they regarded as final in all important respects—doctrines which invariably have proved to be in need of radical revision. We ought therefore to welcome historicism as an ally in our fight against dogmatism. But dogmatism—or the inclination "to identify the goal of our thinking with the point at which we have become tired of thinking"[8]—is so natural to man that it is not likely to be a preserve of the past. We are forced to suspect that historicism is the guise in which dogmatism likes to appear in our age. It seems to us that what is called the "experience of history" is a bird's-eye view of the history of thought, as that history came to be seen under the combined influence of the belief in necessary progress (or in the impossibility of returning to the thought of the past) and of the belief in the supreme value of diversity or uniqueness (or of the equal right of all epochs or civilizations). Radical historicism does not seem to be in need of those beliefs any more. But it has never examined whether the "experience" to which it refers is not an outcome of those questionable beliefs.

When speaking of the "experience" of history, people imply that this "experience" is a comprehensive insight which arises out of historical knowledge but which cannot be reduced to historical knowledge. For historical knowledge is always extremely fragmentary and frequently very uncertain, whereas the alleged experience is supposedly global and certain. Yet it can hardly be doubted that the alleged experience ultimately rests on a number of historical observations. The question, then, is whether these observations entitle one to assert that the acquisition of new

7. ["... we have bachelors of arts who know everything which those great men were ignorant of"—Ed.] "Âme," *Dictionnaire philosophique,* ed. J. Benda, I, 19.
8. See Lessing's letter to Mendelssohn of January 9, 1771.

important insights necessarily leads to the forgetting of earlier important insights and that the earlier thinkers could not possibly have thought of fundamental possibilities which came to the center of attention in later ages. It is obviously untrue to say, for instance, that Aristotle could not have conceived of the injustice of slavery, for he did conceive of it. One may say, however, that he could not have conceived of a world state. But why? The world state presupposes such a development of technology as Aristotle could never have dreamed of. That technological development, in its turn, required that science be regarded as essentially in the service of the "conquest of nature" and that technology be emancipated from any moral and political supervision. Aristotle did not conceive of a world state because he was absolutely certain that science is essentially theoretical and that the liberation of technology from moral and political control would lead to disastrous consequences: the fusion of science and the arts together with the unlimited or uncontrolled progress of technology has made universal and perpetual tyranny a serious possibility. Only a rash man would say that Aristotle's view—that is, his answers to the questions of whether or not science is essentially theoretical and whether or not technological progress is in need of strict moral or political control—has been refuted. But whatever one might think of his answers, certainly the fundamental questions to which they are the answers are identical with the fundamental questions that are of immediate concern to us today. Realizing this, we realize at the same time that the epoch which regarded Aristotle's fundamental questions as obsolete completely lacked clarity about what the fundamental issues are.

Far from legitimizing the historicist inference, history seems rather to prove that all human thought, and certainly all philosophic thought, is concerned with the same fundamental themes or the same fundamental problems, and therefore that there exists an unchanging framework which persists in all changes of human knowledge of both facts and principles. This inference is obviously compatible with the fact that clarity about these problems, the approach to them, and the suggested solutions to them differ more or less from thinker to thinker or from age to age. If the fundamental problems persist in all historical change, human thought is capable of transcending its historical limitation or of grasping something trans-historical. This would be the case even if it were true that all attempts to solve these problems are doomed to fail and that they are doomed to fail on account of the "historicity" of "all" human thought.

To leave it at this would amount to regarding the cause of natural right as hopeless. There cannot be natural right if all that man could know about right were the problem of right, or if the question of the principles of justice would admit of a variety of mutually exclusive answers, none of which could be proved to be superior to the others. There cannot be natural right if human thought, in spite of its essential incompleteness, is not capable of solving the problem of the principles of justice in a genuine and hence universally valid manner. More generally expressed, there cannot be natural right if human thought is not capable of acquiring genuine, universally valid, final knowledge within a limited sphere or genuine knowledge of specific subjects. Historicism cannot deny this possibility. For its own contention implies the admission of this possibility. By asserting that all human thought, or at least all relevant human thought, is historical, historicism admits that human thought is capable of acquiring a most important insight that is universally valid and that will in no way be affected by any future surprises. The historicist thesis is not an isolated assertion: it is inseparable from a view of the essential structure of human life. This view has the same transhistorical character or pretension as any natural right doctrine.

The historicist thesis is then exposed to a very obvious difficulty which cannot be solved but only evaded or obscured by considerations of a more subtle character. Historicism asserts that all human thoughts or beliefs are historical, and hence deservedly destined to perish; but historicism itself is a human thought; hence historicism can be of only temporary validity, or it cannot be simply true. To assert the historicist thesis means to doubt it and thus to transcend it. As a matter of fact, historicism claims to have brought to light a truth which has come to stay, a truth valid for all thought, for all time: however much thought has changed and will change, it will always remain historical. As regards the decisive insight into the essential character of all human thought and therewith into the essential character or limitation of humanity, history has reached its end. The historicist is not impressed by the prospect that historicism may be superseded in due time by the denial of historicism. He is certain that such a change would amount to a relapse of human thought into its most powerful delusion. Historicism thrives on the fact that it inconsistently exempts itself from its own verdict about all human thought. The historicist thesis is self-contradictory or absurd. We cannot see the historical character of "all" thought—that is, of all thought with the exception of the historicist insight and its implications—without transcending history, without grasping something trans-historical.

If we call all thought that is radically historical a "comprehensive world view" or a part of such a view, we must say: historicism is not itself a comprehensive world view but an analysis of all comprehensive world views, an exposition of the essential character of all such views. Thought that recognizes the relativity of all comprehensive views has a different character from thought which is under the spell of, or which adopts, a comprehensive view. The former is absolute and neutral; the latter is relative and committed. The former is a theoretical insight that transcends history; the latter is the outcome of a fateful dispensation.

The radical historicist refuses to admit the trans-historical character of the historicist thesis. At the same time he recognizes the absurdity of unqualified historicism as a theoretical thesis. He denies, therefore, the possibility of a theoretical or objective analysis, which as such would be trans-historical, of the various comprehensive views or "historical worlds" or "cultures." This denial was decisively prepared by Nietzsche's attack on nineteenth-century historicism, which claimed to be a theoretical view. According to Nietzsche, the theoretical analysis of human life that realizes the relativity of all comprehensive views, and thus depreciates them, would make human life itself impossible, for it would destroy the protecting atmosphere within which life or culture or action is alone possible. Moreover, since the theoretical analysis has its basis outside of life, it will never be able to understand life. The theoretical analysis of life is noncommittal and fatal to commitment, but life means commitment. To avert the danger to life, Nietzsche could choose one of two ways: he could insist on the strictly esoteric character of the theoretical analysis of life —that is, restore the Platonic notion of the noble delusion —or else he could deny the possibility of theory proper and so conceive of thought as essentially subservient to, or dependent on, life or fate. If not Nietzsche himself, at any rate his successors adopted the second alternative.[9]

The thesis of radical historicism can be stated as follows. All understanding, all knowledge, however limited and "scientific," presupposes a frame of reference; it presupposes a horizon, a comprehensive view within which understanding and knowing take place. Only such a comprehensive vision makes possible any seeing, any observation, any orientation.

9. For the understanding of this choice, one has to consider its connection with Nietzsche's sympathy with "Callicles," on the one hand, and his preferring the "tragic life" to the theoretical life, on the other (see Plato, *Gorgias* 481d and 502b ff., and *Laws* 658d2–5; compare Nietzsche's *Vom Nutzen und Nachteil der Historie für das Leben* [Insel-Bücherei, ed.], p. 73). This passage reveals clearly the fact that Nietzsche adopted what one may consider the fundamental premise of the historical school.

The comprehensive view of the whole cannot be validated by reasoning, since it is the basis of all reasoning. Accordingly, there is a variety of such comprehensive views, each as legitimate as any other: we have to choose such a view without any rational guidance. It is absolutely necessary to choose one; neutrality or suspension of judgment is impossible. Our choice has no support but itself; it is not supported by any objective or theoretical certainty; it is separated from nothingness, the complete absence of meaning, by nothing but our choice of it. Strictly speaking, we cannot choose among different views. A single comprehensive view is imposed on us by fate: the horizon within which all our understanding and orientation take place is produced by the fate of the individual or of his society. All human thought depends on fate, on something that thought cannot master and whose workings it cannot anticipate. Yet the support of the horizon produced by fate is ultimately the choice of the individual, since that fate has to be accepted by the individual. We are free in the sense that we are free either to choose in anguish the world view and the standards imposed on us by fate or else to lose ourselves in illusory security or in despair.

The radical historicist asserts, then, that only to thought that is itself committed or "historical" does other committed or "historical" thought disclose itself, and, above all, that only to thought that is itself committed or "historical" does the true meaning of the "historicity" of all genuine thought disclose itself. The historicist thesis expresses a fundamental experience which, by its nature, is incapable of adequate expression on the level of noncommitted or detached thought. The evidence of that experience may indeed be blurred, but it cannot be destroyed by the inevitable logical difficulties from which all expressions of such experiences suffer. With a view to his fundamental experience, the radical historicist denies that the final and, in this sense, trans-historical character of the historicist thesis makes doubtful the content of that thesis. The final and irrevocable insight into the historical character of all thought would transcend history only if that insight were accessible to man as man and hence, in principle, at all times; but it does not transcend history if it essentially belongs to a specific historic situation. It belongs to a specific historic situation: that situation is not merely the condition of the historicist insight but its source.[10]

All natural right doctrines claim that the fundamentals of justice are, in principle, accessible to man as man. They presuppose, therefore, that a most important truth can, in principle, be accessible to man as man. Denying this presupposition, radical historicism asserts that the basic insight into the essential limitation of all human thought is not accessible to man as man, or that it is not the result of the progress or the labor of human thought, but that it is an unforeseeable gift of unfathomable fate. It is due to fate that the essential dependence of thought on fate is realized now, and was not realized in earlier times. Historicism has this in common with all other thought, that it depends on fate. It differs from all other thought in this, that, thanks to fate, it has been given to realize the radical dependence of thought on fate. We are absolutely ignorant of the surprises which fate may have in store for later generations, and fate may in the future again conceal what it has revealed to us; but this does not impair the truth of that revelation. One does not have to transcend history in order to see the historical character of all thought: there is a privileged moment, an absolute moment in the historical process, a moment in which the essential character of all thought becomes transparent. In exempting itself from its own verdict, historicism claims merely to mirror the character of historical reality or to be true to the facts; the self-contradictory character of the historicist thesis should be charged not to historicism but to reality.

10. The distinction between "condition" and "source" corresponds to the difference between Aristotle's "history" of philosophy in the first book of the *Metaphysics* and historicist history.

The assumption of an absolute moment in history is essential to historicism. In this, historicism surreptitiously follows the precedent set in a classic manner by Hegel. Hegel had taught that every philosophy is the conceptual expression of the spirit of its time, and yet he maintained the absolute truth of his own system of philosophy by ascribing absolute character to his own time; he assumed that his own time was the end of history and hence the absolute moment. Historicism explicitly denies that the end of history has come, but it implicitly asserts the opposite: no possible future change of orientation can legitimately make doubtful the decisive insight into the inescapable dependence of thought on fate, and therewith into the essential character of human life; in the decisive respect the end of history, that is, of the history of thought, has come. But one cannot simply assume that one lives or thinks in the absolute moment; one must show, somehow, how the absolute moment can be recognized as such. According to Hegel, the absolute moment is the one in which philosophy, or quest for wisdom, has been transformed into wisdom, that is, the moment in which the fundamental riddles have been fully solved. Historicism, however, stands or falls by the denial of the possibility of theoretical metaphysics and of philosophic ethics or natural right; it stands or falls by the denial of the solubility of the fundamental riddles. According to historicism, therefore, the absolute moment must be the moment in which the insoluble character of the fundamental riddles has become fully manifest or in which the fundamental delusion of the human mind has been dispelled.

But one might realize the insoluble character of the fundamental riddles and still continue to see in the understanding of these riddles the task of philosophy; one would thus merely replace a nonhistoricist and dogmatic philosophy by a nonhistoricist and skeptical philosophy. Historicism goes beyond skepticism. It assumes that philosophy, in the full and original sense of the term, namely, the attempt to replace opinions about the whole by knowledge of the whole, is not only incapable of reaching its goal but absurd, because the very idea of philosophy rests on dogmatic, that is, arbitrary, premises or, more specifically, on premises that are only "historical and relative." For clearly, if philosophy, or the attempt to replace opinions by knowledge, itself rests on mere opinions, philosophy is absurd.

The most influential attempts to establish the dogmatic and hence arbitrary or historically relative character of philosophy proper proceed along the following lines. Philosophy, or the attempt to replace opinions about the whole by knowledge of the whole, presupposes that the whole is knowable, that is, intelligible. This presupposition leads to the consequence that the whole as it is in itself is identified with the whole insofar as it is intelligible or insofar as it can become an object; it leads to the identification of "being" with "intelligible" or "object"; it leads to the dogmatic disregard of everything that cannot become an object, that is, an object for the knowing subject, or the dogmatic disregard of everything that cannot be mastered by the subject. Furthermore, to say that the whole is knowable or intelligible is tantamount to saying that the whole has a permanent structure or that the whole as such is unchangeable or always the same. If this is the case, it is, in principle, possible to predict how the whole will be at any future time: the future of the whole can be anticipated by thought. The presupposition mentioned is said to have its root in the dogmatic identification of "to be" in the highest sense with "to be always," or in the fact that philosophy understands "to be" in such a sense that "to be" in the highest sense must mean "to be always." The dogmatic character of the basic premise of philosophy is said to have been revealed by the discovery of history or of the "historicity" of human life. The meaning of that discovery can be expressed in theses like these: what is called the whole is actually always incomplete and therefore not truly a whole; the whole is essentially changing in such a manner that its future cannot be predicted; the whole as it is in itself can never be grasped, or it is not intelligible; human thought essentially depends on something that cannot be anticipated or that can never be an object or that can never be mastered by the subject; "to be" in the highest sense cannot mean—or, at any rate, it does not necessarily mean—"to be always."

We cannot even attempt to discuss these theses. We must leave them with the following observation. Radical historicism compels us to realize the bearing of the fact that the very idea of natural right presupposes the possibility of philosophy in the full and original meaning of the term. It compels us at the same time to realize the need for unbiased reconsideration of the most elementary premises whose validity is presupposed by philosophy. The question of the validity of these premises cannot be disposed of by adopting or clinging to a more or less persistent tradition of philosophy, for it is of the essence of traditions that they cover or conceal their humble foundations by erecting impressive edifices on them. Nothing ought to be said or done which could create the impression that unbiased reconsideration of the most elementary premises of philosophy is a merely academic or historical affair. Prior to such reconsideration, however, the issue of natural right can only remain an open question.

For we cannot assume that the issue has been finally settled by historicism. The "experience of history" and the less ambiguous experience of the complexity of human affairs may blur, but they cannot extinguish, the evidence of those simple experiences regarding right and wrong which are at the bottom of the philosophic contention that there is a natural right. Historicism either ignores or else distorts these experiences. Furthermore, the most thoroughgoing attempt to establish historicism culminated in the assertion that, if and when there are no human beings, there may be *entia,** but there cannot be esse,*** that is, that there can be *entia* while there is no *esse.* There is an obvious connection between this assertion and the rejection of the view that "to be" in the highest sense means "to be always." Besides, there has always been a glaring contrast between the way in which historicism understands the thought of the past and genuine understanding of the thought of the past; the undeniable possibility of historical objectivity is explicitly or implicitly denied by historicism in all its forms. Above all, in the transition from early (theoretical) to radical ("existentialist") historicism, the "experience of history" was never submitted to critical analysis. It was taken for granted that it is a genuine experience and not a questionable interpretation of experience. The question was not raised whether what is really experienced does not allow of an entirely different and possibly more adequate interpretation. In particular, the "experience of history" does not make doubtful the view that the fundamental problems, such as the problems of justice, persist or retain their identity in all historical change, however much they may be obscured by the temporary denial of their relevance and however variable or provisional all human solutions to these problems may be. In grasping these problems as problems, the human mind liberates itself from its historical limitations. No more is needed to legitimize philosophy in its original, Socratic sense: philosophy is knowledge that one does not know; that is to say, it is knowledge of what one does not know, or awareness of the fundamental problems and, therewith, of the fundamental alternatives regarding their solution that are coeval with human thought.

If the existence and even the possibility of natural right must remain an open question as long as the issue between historicism and nonhistoricist philosophy is not settled, our most urgent need is to understand that issue. The issue is not understood if it is seen merely in the way in which it

* "beings"
** "to be"

presents itself from the point of view of historicism; it must also be seen in the way in which it presents itself from the point of view of nonhistoricist philosophy. This means, for all practical purposes, that the problem of historicism must first be considered from the point of view of classical philosophy, which is nonhistoricist thought in its pure form. Our most urgent need can then be satisfied only by means of historical studies which would enable us to understand classical philosophy exactly as it understood itself, and not in the way in which it presents itself on the basis of historicism. We need, in the first place, a nonhistoricist understanding of nonhistoricist philosophy. But we need no less urgently a nonhistoricist understanding of historicism, that is, an understanding of the genesis of historicism that does not take for granted the soundness of historicism.

Historicism assumes that modern man's turn toward history implied the divination and eventually the discovery of a dimension of reality that had escaped classical thought, namely, of the historical dimension. If this is granted, one will be forced in the end into extreme historicism. But if historicism cannot be taken for granted, the question becomes inevitable whether what was hailed in the nineteenth century as a discovery was not, in fact, an invention, that is, an arbitrary interpretation of phenomena which had always been known and which had been interpreted much more adequately prior to the emergence of "the historical consciousness" than afterward. We have to raise the question whether what is called the "discovery" of history is not, in fact, an artificial and makeshift solution to a problem that could arise only on the basis of very questionable premises.

I suggest this line of approach. "History" meant throughout the ages primarily political history. Accordingly, what is called the "discovery" of history is the work, not of philosophy in general, but of political philosophy. It was a predicament peculiar to eighteenth-century political philosophy that led to the emergence of the historical school.

The political philosophy of the eighteenth century was a doctrine of natural right. It consisted in a peculiar interpretation of natural right, namely, the specifically modern interpretation. Historicism is the ultimate outcome of the crisis of modern natural right. The crisis of modern natural right or of modern political philosophy could become a crisis of philosophy as such only because in the modern centuries philosophy as such had become thoroughly politicized. Originally, philosophy had been the humanizing quest for the eternal order, and hence it had been a pure source of humane inspiration and aspiration. Since the seventeenth century, philosophy has become a weapon, and hence an instrument. It was this politicization of philosophy that was discerned as the root of our troubles by an intellectual who denounced the treason of the intellectuals. He committed the fatal mistake, however, of ignoring the essential difference between intellectuals and philosophers. In this he remained the dupe of the delusion which he denounced. For the politicization of philosophy consists precisely in this, that the difference between intellectuals and philosophers—a difference formerly known as the difference between gentlemen and philosophers, on the one hand, and the difference between sophists or rhetoricians and philosophers, on the other—becomes blurred and finally disappears.

An Epilogue

What one may call the new science of politics emerged shortly before World War I; it became preponderant and at the same time reached its mature or final form before, during, and after World War II. It need not be a product or a symptom of the crisis of the modern Western world— of a world which could boast of being distinguished by ever broadening freedom and humanitarianism; it is surely contemporary with that crisis.

The new political science shares with the most familiar ingredients of our world in its crisis the quality of being a mass phenomenon. That it is a mass phenomenon is compatible with the fact that it possesses its heights and its depths, the handful of opinion leaders, the men responsible for the breakthroughs on the top, and the many who drive on the highways projected by the former at the bottom. It wields very great authority in the West, above all in this country. It controls whole departments of political science in great and in large universities. It is supported by foundations of immense wealth with unbounded faith and unbelievably large grants. In spite of this one runs little risk in taking issue with it. For its devotees are fettered by something like a Hippocratic oath to subordinate all considerations of safety, income, and deference to concern with the truth. The difficulty lies elsewhere. It is not easy to free

one's mind from the impact of any apparently beneficent
authority, for such freeing requires that one step outside of
the circle warmed and charmed by the authority to be
questioned.

Yet it is necessary to make the effort. The new political
science itself must demand it. One might say that precisely
because it is an authority operating within a democracy it
owes an account of itself to those who are subjected, or are
to be subjected, to it. However sound it may be, it is a
novelty. That it emerged so late is probably no accident:
deep-seated resistances had to be overcome step by step in a
process of long duration. Precisely if the new political science constitutes the mature approach to political things, it
presupposes the experience of the failure of earlier approaches. We ourselves no longer have that experience:
"George" has had it for us. Yet to leave it at that is un-
becoming for men of science; men of science cannot leave
it at hearsay or at vague remembrances. To this one might
reply that the resistances to the new political science have
not entirely vanished: the old Adam is still alive. But precisely because this is so, the new political science, being a
rational enterprise, must be able to lead the old Adam by
a perfectly lucid, coherent, and sound argument from his
desert which he mistakes for a paradise to its own green
pastures. It must cease to demand from us, in the posture
of a noncommissioned officer, a clean and unmediated break
with our previous habits, that is, with common sense; it
must supply us with a ladder by which we can ascend, in
full clarity as to what we are doing, from common sense to
science. It must begin to learn to look with sympathy at the
obstacles to it if it wishes to win the sympathy of the best
men of the coming generation—those youths who possess
the intellectual and the moral qualities which prevent men
from simply following authorities, to say nothing of fashions.

The fairly recent change within political science has its
parallels in the other social sciences. Yet the change within

political science appears to be both more pronounced and more limited. The reason is that political science is the oldest of the social sciences and therefore willy-nilly a carrier of old traditions which resist innovation. Political science as we find it now consists of more heterogeneous parts than any other social science. "Public law" and "international law" were established themes centuries before "politics and parties" and "international relations," nay, sociology, emerged. If we look around us, we may observe that the political science profession contains a strong minority of the right, consisting of the strict adherents of the new political science or the "behavioralists," a small minority of the left, consisting of those who reject the new political science root and branch, and a center, consisting of the old-fashioned political scientists, men who are concerned with understanding political things without being much concerned with "methodological" questions but many of whom seem to have given custody of their "methodological" conscience to the strict adherents of the new political science and who thus continue their old-fashioned practice with a somewhat uneasy conscience. It may seem strange that I called the strict adherents of the new political science the right wing and their intransigent opponents the left wing, seeing that the former are liberals almost to a man and the latter are in the odor of conservatism. Yet since I have heard the intransigent opponents of the new political science described as unorthodox I inferred that the new political science is the orthodoxy in the profession, and the natural place of an orthodoxy is on the right.

A rigorous adherent of the new political science will dismiss the preceding remarks as quasi-statistical or sociological irrelevancies which have no bearing whatever on the only important issue, that issue being the soundness of the new political science. To state that issue means to bring out the fundamental difference between the new political science and the old. To avoid ambiguities, irrelevancies, and beatings around the bush, it is best to contrast the new political science directly with the "original" of the old, that is, with Aristotelian political science.

For Aristotle, political science is identical with political philosophy because science is identical with philosophy. Science or philosophy consists of two kinds, theoretical and practical or political; theoretical science is subdivided into mathematics, physics (natural science), and metaphysics; practical science is subdivided into ethics, economics (management of the household), and political science in the narrower sense; logic does not belong to philosophy or science proper, but is, as it were, the prelude to philosophy or science. The distinction between philosophy and science or the separation of science from philosophy was a consequence of the revolution which occurred in the seventeenth century. This revolution was primarily not the victory of science over metaphysics, but what one may call the victory of the new philosophy or science over Aristotelian philosophy or science. Yet the new philosophy or science was not equally successful in all its parts. Its most successful part was physics (and mathematics). Prior to the victory of the new physics, there was not the science of physics simply: there were Aristotelian physics, Platonic physics, Epicurean physics, Stoic physics; to speak colloquially, there was no metaphysically neutral physics. The victory of the new physics led to the emergence of a physics which seemed to be as metaphysically neutral as, say, mathematics, medicine, or the art of shoemaking. The emergence of a metaphysically neutral physics made it possible for "science" to become independent of "philosophy" and in fact an authority for the latter. It paved the way for an economic science which is independent of ethics, for sociology as the study of nonpolitical associations as not inferior in dignity to the political association, and, last but not least, for the separation of political science from political philosophy as well as the separation of economics and sociology from political science.

Second, the Aristotelian distinction between theoretical and practical sciences implies that human action has principles of its own which are known independently of theoretical science (physics and metaphysics), and therefore that the practical sciences do not depend on the theoretical sciences or are not derivative from them. The principles of action are the natural ends toward which man is by nature inclined and of which he has by nature some awareness. This awareness is the necessary condition for his seeking and finding appropriate means for his ends, or for his becoming practically wise or prudent. Practical science, in contradistinction to practical wisdom, itself sets forth coherently the principles of action and the general rules of prudence ("proverbial wisdom"). Practical science raises questions which within practical or political experience, or at any rate on the basis of such experience, reveal themselves to be the most important questions and which are not stated, let alone answered, with sufficient clarity by practical wisdom itself. The sphere governed by prudence is then in principle self-sufficient or closed. Yet prudence is always endangered by false doctrines about the whole of which man is a part, by false theoretical opinions; prudence is therefore always in need of defense against such opinions, and that defense is necessarily theoretical. The theory defending prudence is, however, misunderstood if it is taken to be the basis of prudence. This complication—the fact that the sphere of prudence is, as it were, only de jure but not de facto wholly independent of theoretical science— makes understandable, although it does not by itself justify, the view underlying the new political science according to which no awareness inherent in practice, and in general no natural awareness is genuine knowledge, or, in other words, only "scientific" knowledge is genuine knowledge. This view implies that there cannot be practical sciences proper or that the distinction between practical and theoretical sciences must be replaced by the distinction between theoretical and applied sciences, applied sciences being sciences which are based on theoretical sciences that precede the applied sciences in time and in order. It implies above all that the sciences dealing with human affairs are essentially dependent on the theoretical sciences—especially on psychology which in the Aristotelian scheme is the highest theme of physics, not to say that it constitutes the transition from physics to metaphysics—or become themselves theoretical sciences to be supplemented by such applied sciences as the policy sciences or the sciences of social engineering. The new political science is then no longer based on political experience, but on what is called scientific psychology.

Third, according to the Aristotelian view, the awareness of the principles of action shows itself primarily to a higher degree in public or authoritative speech, particularly in law and legislation, rather than in merely private speech. Hence Aristotelian political science views political things in the perspective of the citizen. Since there is of necessity a variety of citizen perspectives, the political scientist or political philosopher must become the umpire, the impartial judge; his perspective encompasses the partisan perspectives because he possesses a more comprehensive and a clearer grasp of man's natural ends and their natural order than do the partisans. The new political science on the other hand looks at political things from without, in the perspective of the neutral observer, in the same perspective in which one would look at triangles or fish, although or because it may wish to become "manipulative"; it views human beings as an engineer would view materials for building bridges. It follows that the language of Aristotelian political science is identical with the language of political man; it hardly uses a term which did not originate in the marketplace and is not in common use there; but the new political science cannot begin to speak without having elaborated an extensive technical vocabulary.

Fourth, Aristotelian political science necessarily evaluates political things; the knowledge in which it culminates has the character of categoric advice and of exhortation.

The new political science, on the other hand, conceives of the principles of action as "values" which are merely "subjective"; the knowledge which it conveys has the character of prediction and only secondarily that of hypothetical advice.

Fifth, according to the Aristotelian view, man is a being sui generis, with a dignity of its own: man is the rational and political animal. Man is the only being which can be concerned with self-respect; man can respect himself because he can despise himself; he is "the beast with red cheeks," the only being possessing a sense of shame. His dignity is then based on his awareness of what he ought to be or how he should live. Since there is a necessary connection between morality (how man should live) and law, there is a necessary connection between the dignity of man and the dignity of the public order: the political is sui generis and cannot be understood as derivative from the subpolitical. The presupposition of all this is that man is radically distinguished from nonman, from brutes as well as from gods, and this presupposition is ratified by common sense, by the citizen's understanding of things; when the citizen demands or rejects, say, "freedom from want for all," he does not mean freedom from want for tigers, rats, or lice. This presupposition points to a more fundamental presupposition according to which the whole consists of essentially different parts. The new political science, on the other hand, is based on the fundamental premise that there are no essential or irreducible differences: there are only differences of degree; in particular there is only a difference of degree between men and brutes or between men and robots. In other words, according to the new political science, or the universal science of which the new political science is a part, to understand a thing means to understand it in terms of its genesis or its conditions and hence, humanly speaking, to understand the higher in terms of the lower: the human in terms of the subhuman, the rational in terms of the subrational, the political in terms of the subpolitical. In particular, the new political science cannot admit that the common good is something that is.

Prior to the emergence of the new political science, political science had already moved very far from Aristotelian political science in the general direction of the new political science. Nevertheless, it was accused of paying too great attention to the law or to the Ought and of paying too little attention to the Is or to the actual behavior of men. For instance, it seemed to be exclusively concerned with the legal arrangements regarding universal suffrage and its justification and not to consider at all how the universal right to vote is exercised; yet democracy, as it is, is characterized by the manner in which that right is exercised. We may grant that not so long ago there was a political science which was narrowly legalistic—which, for example, took the written constitution of the U.S.S.R. very seriously —but we must add immediately that that error had been corrected, as it were in advance, by an older political science, the political science of Montesquieu, of Machiavelli, or of Aristotle himself. Besides, the new political science, in its justified protest against a merely legalistic political science, is in danger of disregarding the important things known to those legalists: "voting behavior" as it is now studied would be impossible if there were not in the first place the universal right to vote, and this right, even if not exercised by a large minority for very long periods, must be taken into consideration in any long-range prediction since it may be exercised by all in future elections taking place in unprecedented and therefore particularly interesting circumstances. That right is an essential ingredient of democratic "behavior," for it partly explains "behavior" in democracies (for instance, the prevention by force or fraud of certain people from voting). The new political science does not simply deny these things, but it literally relegates them to the background, to "the habit background"; in so doing it puts the cart before the horse. Similar considerations apply, for instance, to the alleged discovery by the new political science of the importance of "propaganda"; that discovery is in fact only a partial rediscovery of the need for vulgar rhetoric, a need that had become somewhat obscured from a few generations which were comforted by faith in universal enlightenment as the inevitable by-product of the diffusion of science, which in its turn was thought to be the inevitable by-product of science. Generally speaking, one may wonder whether the new political science has brought to light anything of political importance which intelligent political practitioners with a deep knowledge of history, nay, intelligent and educated journalists, to say nothing of the old political science at its best, did not know at least as well beforehand.

The main substantive reason, however, for the revolt against the old political science would seem to be the consideration that our political situation is entirely unprecedented and that it is unreasonable to expect earlier political thought to be of any help in coping with our situation; the unprecedented political situation calls for an unprecedented political science, perhaps for a judicious mating of dialectical materialism and psychoanalysis to be consummated on a bed supplied by logical positivism. Just as classical physics had to be superseded by nuclear physics so that the atomic age could come in via the atomic bomb, the old political science has to be superseded by a sort of nuclear political science so that we may be enabled to cope with the extreme dangers threatening atomic man; the equivalent in political science of the nuclei is probably the most minute events in the smallest groups of humans if not in the life of infants; the small groups in question are certainly not of the kind exemplified by the small group which Lenin gathered around himself in Switzerland during World War I. In making this comparison we are not oblivious of the fact that the nuclear physicists show a greater respect for classical physics than the nuclear political scientists show for classical politics. Nor do we forget that, while the nuclei proper are simply prior to macrophysical phenomena, the "political" nuclei which are meant to supply explanations for the political things proper are already molded, nay, constituted, by the political order or the regime within which they occur: an American small group is not a Russian small group.

We may grant that our political situation has nothing in common with any earlier political situation except that it is a political situation. The human race is still divided into a number of the kind of societies which we have come to call states and which are separated from one another by unmistakable and sometimes formidable frontiers. Those states still differ from one another not only in all conceivable other respects, but above all in their regimes, and hence in the things to which the preponderant part of those societies is dedicated or in the spirit which more or less effectively pervades those societies. They have very different images of the future so that for all of them to live together, in contradistinction to uneasily coexisting, is altogether impossible. Each of them, receiving its character from its regime, is still in need of specific measures for preserving itself and its regime and hence is uncertain of its future. Acting willy-nilly through their governments (which may be governments in exile), those societies still move as if on an uncharted sea, and surely without the benefit of tracks, toward a future which is veiled from everyone and which is pregnant with surprises. Their governments still try to determine the future of their societies with the help partly of knowledge, partly of guesses, the recourse to guesses still being partly necessitated by the secrecy in which their most important opponents shroud their most important plans or projects. The new political science which is so eager to predict is, as it admits, as unable to predict the outcome of the unprecedented conflict peculiar to our age as the crudest soothsayer of the most benighted tribe. In former times, people thought that the outcome of serious conflicts is unpredictable because one cannot know how long this or that outstanding leader in war or counsel will live, or how the opposed armies will act in the test of battle, or similar things. We have been brought to believe that chance can be controlled or does not seriously affect the fate of societies. Yet the science which is said to have rendered possible the control of chance has itself become the refuge of chance: man's fate depends now more than ever on science or technology, hence on discoveries or inventions, hence on events whose precise occurrence is by their very nature not predictable. A simply unprecedented political situation would be a situation of no political interest, that is, not a political situation. Now, if the essential character of all political situations was grasped by the old political science, there seems to be no reason why it must be superseded by a new political science. In case the new political science should tend to understand political things in nonpolitical terms, the old political science, wise to many ages, would even be superior to the new political science in helping us to find our bearings in our unprecedented situation, in spite or rather because of the fact that only the new political science can boast of being the child of the atomic age.

But one will never understand the new political science if one does not start from that reason advanced on its behalf which has nothing whatever to do with any true or alleged blindness of the old political science to any political things as such. That reason is a general notion of science. According to that notion, only scientific knowledge is genuine knowledge. From this it follows immediately that all awareness of political things which is not scientific is cognitively worthless. Serious criticism of the old political science is a waste of time; for we know in advance that it could only have been a pseudo science, although perhaps including a few remarkably shrewd hunches. This is not to deny that the adherents of the new political science sometimes engage in apparent criticism of the old, but that criticism is characterized by a constitutional inability to understand the criticized doctrines on their own terms. What science is, is supposed to be known from the practice of the other sciences, of sciences which are admittedly in existence, and not mere desiderata, and the clearest examples of such sciences are the natural sciences. What science is, is supposed to be known, above all, from the science of science, that is, logic.

The basis of the new political science is then logic—a particular kind of logic; the logic in question is not, for instance, Aristotelian or Kantian or Hegelian logic. This means, however, that the new political science rests on what for the political scientist as such is a mere assumption which he is not competent to judge on its own terms—namely, as a logical theory—for that theory is controversial among the people who must be supposed to be competent in such matters, the professors of philosophy. He is, however, competent to judge it by its fruits; he is competent to judge whether his understanding of political things as political things is helped or hindered by the new political science which derives from the logic in question. He is perfectly justified in regarding as an imposition the demand that he comply with "logical positivism" or else plead guilty to being a "metaphysician." He is perfectly justified in regarding this epithet as not "objective," because it is terrifying and unintelligible, like the war cries of savages.

What strikes a sympathetic chord in every political scientist is less the demand that he proceed "scientifically"— for mathematics also proceeds scientifically, and political science surely is not a mathematical discipline—than the demand that he proceed "empirically." This is a demand of common sense. No one in his senses ever dreamt that he could know anything, say, of American government as such or of the present political situation as such except by looking at American government or at the present political situation. The incarnation of the empirical spirit is the man from Missouri, who has to be shown. For he knows that he, as well as everyone else who is of sound mind and whose sight is not defective, can see things and people as they are with his eyes and that he is capable of knowing how his neighbors feel; he takes it for granted that he lives with other human beings of all descriptions in the same world and that because they are all human beings, they all understand one another somehow; he knows that if this were not so, political life would be altogether impossible. If someone would offer him speculations based on extrasensory perception, he would turn his back on him more or less politely. The old political science would not quarrel in these respects with the man from Missouri. It did not claim to know better or differently than he such things as that the Democratic and Republican parties are now, and have been for some time, the preponderant parties in this country and that there are presidential elections every fourth year. By admitting that facts of this kind are known independently of political science, it admitted that empirical knowledge is not necessarily scientific knowledge or that a statement can be true and known to be true without being scientific, and, above all, that political science stands or falls by the truth of the prescientific awareness of political things.

Yet one may raise the question as to how one can be certain of the truth of empirical statements which are prescientific. If we call an elaborate answer to this question an epistemology, we may say that an empiricist, in contradistinction to an empirical, statement is based on the explicit assumption of a specific epistemology. Yet every epistemology presupposes the truth of empirical statements. Our perceiving things and people is more manifest and more reliable than any "theory of knowledge"—any explanation of how our perceiving things and people is possible—can be; the truth of any "theory of knowledge" depends on its ability to give an adequate account of this fundamental reliance. If a logical positivist tries to give an account of "a thing" or a formula for "a thing" in terms of mere sense data and their composition, he is looking, and bids us to look, at the previously grasped "thing"; the previously grasped "thing" is the standard by which we judge of his formula. If an epistemology—for example, solipsism—manifestly fails to give an account of how empirical statements as meant can be true, it fails to carry conviction. To be aware of the necessity of the fundamental reliance which underlies or pervades all empirical statements means to recognize the fundamental riddle, not to have solved it. But no man needs to be ashamed to admit that he does not possess a solution to the fundamental riddle. Surely no man ought to let himself be bullied into the acceptance of an alleged solution—for the denial of the existence of a riddle is a kind of solution of the riddle—by the threat that if he fails to do so he is a "metaphysician." To sustain our weaker brethren against that threat, one might tell them that the belief accepted by the empiricists, according to which science is in principle susceptible of infinite progress, is itself tantamount to the belief that being is irretrievably mysterious.

Let us try to restate the issue by returning first to our man from Missouri. A simple observation seems to be sufficient to show that the man from Missouri is "naïve": he does not see things with his eyes; what he sees with his eyes is only colors, shapes, and the like; he would perceive "things," in contradistinction to "sense data," only if he possessed "extrasensory perception"; his claim—the claim of common sense—implies that there is "extrasensory perception." What is true of "things" is true of "patterns," at any rate of those patterns which students of politics from time to time claim to "perceive." We must leave the man from Missouri scratching his head; by being silent, he remains in his way a philosopher. But others do not leave it at scratching their heads. Transforming themselves from devotees of *empeiria* into empiricists, they contend that what is perceived or "given" is only sense data; the "thing" emerges by virtue of unconscious or conscious "construction": the "things" which to common sense present themselves as "given" are in truth constructs. Common-sense understanding is understanding by means of unconscious construction; scientific understanding is understanding by means of conscious construction. Somewhat more precisely, common-sense understanding is understanding in terms of "things possessing qualities"; scientific understanding is understanding in terms of "functional relations between different series of events." Unconscious constructs are ill made, for their making is affected by all sorts of purely "subjective" influences; only conscious constructs can be well made, perfectly lucid, in every respect the same for everyone, or "objective." Still, one says with greater right that we perceive things than that we perceive human beings as human beings, for at least some of the properties which we ascribe to things are sensually perceived, whereas the soul's actions, passions, or states can never become sense data.

Now, that understanding of things and human beings which is rejected by empiricism is the understanding by which political life, political understanding, political experience, stands or falls. Hence, the new political science, based as it is on empiricism, must reject the results of political understanding and political experience as such, and since the political things are given to us in political understanding and political experience, the new political science cannot be helpful for the deeper understanding of political things: it must reduce the political things to nonpolitical data. The new political science comes into being through an attempted break with common sense. But that break cannot be consistently carried out, as can be seen in a general way from the following consideration. Empiricism cannot be established empiricistically: it is not known through sense data that the only possible objects of perception are sense data. If one tries therefore to establish empiricism empirically, one must make use of that understanding of things which empiricism renders doubtful: the relation of eyes to colors or shapes is established through the same kind of perception through which we perceive things as things rather than sense data or constructs. In other words, sense data as sense data become known only through an act of abstraction or disregard which presupposes the legitimacy of our primary awareness of things as things and of people as people. Hence the only way of overcoming the naïveté of the man from Missouri is in the first place to admit that that naïveté cannot be avoided in any way or that there is no possible human thought which is not in the last analysis dependent on the legitimacy of that naïveté and the awareness or the knowledge going with it.

We must not disregard the most massive or the crudest reason to which empiricism owes much of its attractiveness. Some adherents of the new political science would argue as follows: One can indeed not reasonably deny that prescientific thought about political things contains genuine knowledge; but the trouble is that within prescientific political thought, genuine knowledge of political things is inseparable from prejudices or superstitions; hence one cannot get rid of the spurious elements in prescientific political thought except by breaking altogether with prescientific thought or by acting on the assumption that prescientific thought does not have the character of knowledge at all. Common sense contains indeed genuine knowledge of broomsticks; but the trouble is that this knowledge has in common sense the same status as the alleged knowledge concerning witches; by trusting common sense one is in danger of bringing back the whole kingdom of darkness with Thomas Aquinas at its head. The old political science was not unaware of the imperfections of political opinion, but it did not believe that the remedy lies in the total rejection of common-sense understanding as such. It was critical in the original sense, that is, discerning, regarding political opinion. It was aware that the errors regarding witches were found out without the benefit of empiricism. It was aware that judgments or maxims which were justified by the uncontested experience of decades, and even of centuries or millenniums, may have to be revised because of unforeseen changes; it knew in the words of Burke "that the generality of people are fifty years, at least, behind hand in their politics." Accordingly, the old political science was concerned with political improvement by political means as distinguished from social engineering; it knew that those political means include revolutions and wars, since there may be foreign regimes (Hitler Germany is the orthodox example) which are dangerous to the survival of freedom in this country, and of which it would be criminally foolish to assume that they will transform themselves gradually into good neighbors.

Acceptance of the distinctive premises of the new political science leads to the consequences which have been sufficiently illustrated in the four preceding essays.* In the first place, the new political science is constantly compelled to borrow from common-sense knowledge, thus unwittingly testifying to the truth that there is genuine prescientific knowledge of political things which is the basis of all scientific knowledge of them. Second, the logic on which the new political science is based may provide sufficient criteria of exactness; it does not provide objective criteria of relevance. Criteria of relevance are inherent in the prescientific understanding of political things; intelligent and informed citizens distinguish soundly between important and unimportant political matters. Political men are concerned with what is to be done politically here and now in accordance with principles of preference of which they are aware, although not necessarily in an adequate manner; it is those principles of preference which supply the criteria of relevance in regard to political things. Ordinarily a political man must at least pretend to "look up" to something to which at least the preponderant part of his society looks up. That to which at least everyone who counts politically is supposed to look up, that which is politically the highest, gives a society its character; it constitutes and justifies the regime of the society in question. The "highest" is that

* This essay originally appeared as part of a collection. See acknowledgments, p. iv.

through which a society is "a whole," a distinct whole with a character of its own, just as for common sense "the world" is a whole by being overarched by heaven of which one cannot be aware except by "looking up." There is obviously, and for cause, a variety of regimes and hence of what is regarded as the politically highest, that is, of the purposes to which the various regimes are dedicated.

The qualitatively different regimes, or kinds of regimes, and the qualitatively different purposes constituting and legitimating them by revealing themselves as the most important political things, supply the key to the understanding of all political things and the basis for the reasoned distinction between important and unimportant political things. The regimes and their principles pervade the societies throughout, in the sense that there are no recesses of privacy which are simply impervious to that pervasion, as is indicated by such expressions, coined by the new political science, as "the democratic personality." Nevertheless, there are political things which are not affected by the difference of regimes. In a society which cannot survive without an irrigation system, every regime will have to preserve that system intact. Every regime must try to preserve itself against subversion by means of force. There are both technical things and politically neutral things (things which are common to all regimes) which necessarily are the concern of political deliberation without ever being as such politically controversial. The preceding remarks are a very rough sketch of the view of political things that was characteristic of the old political science. According to that view, what is most important for political science is identical with what is most important politically. To illustrate this by the present-day example, for the old-fashioned political scientists today, the most important concern is the Cold War, or the qualitative difference, which amounts to a conflict, between liberal democracy and Communism.

The break with the common-sense understanding of political things compels the new political science to abandon the criteria of relevance which are inherent in political understanding. Hence, the new political science lacks orientation regarding political things; it has no protection whatever except by surreptitious recourse to common sense against losing itself in the study of irrelevancies. It is confronted by a chaotic mass of data into which it must bring an order alien to those data and originating in the demands of political science as a science anxious to comply with the demands of logical positivism. The universals in the light of which the old political science viewed the political phenomena (the various regimes and their purposes) must be replaced by a different kind of universals. The first step toward the finding of the new kind of universals may be said to take this form: what is equally present in all regimes (the politically neutral) must be the key to the different regimes (the political proper, the essentially controversial); what is equally present in all regimes is, say, coercion and freedom; the scientific analysis of a given regime will then indicate exactly—in terms of percentages—the amount of coercion and the amount of freedom peculiar to it. That is to say, as political scientists we must express the political phenomena par excellence, the essential differences or the heterogeneity of regimes, in terms of the homogeneous elements which pervade all regimes. What is important for us as political scientists is not the politically important. Yet we cannot forever remain blind to the fact that what claims to be a purely scientific or theoretical enterprise has grave political consequences—consequences which are so little accidental that they appeal for their own sake to the new political scientists: everyone knows what follows from the demonstration, which presupposes the begging of all important questions, that there is only a difference of degree between liberal democracy and Communism in regard to coercion and freedom. The Is necessarily leads to an Ought, all sincere protestations to the contrary notwithstanding.

The second step toward the finding of the new kind of universals consists in the following reasoning: all political societies, whatever their regimes, surely are groups of some kind; hence, the key to the understanding of political things must be a theory of groups in general. Groups must have some cohesion, and groups change; we are then in need of a universal theory which tells us why or how groups cohere and why or how they change. Seeking for those why's or how's we shall discover n factors and m modes of their interaction. The result of this reduction of the political to the sociological—of a reduction for which it is claimed that it will make our understanding of political things more "realistic"—is in fact a formalism unrivaled in any scholasticism of the past. All peculiarities of political societies, and still more of the political societies with which we are concerned as citizens, become unrecognizable if restated in terms of the vague generalities which hold of every conceivable group; at the end of the dreary and boring process we understand what we are interested in not more but less than we understood it at the beginning. What in political language is called the rulers and the ruled (to say nothing of oppressors and oppressed) becomes through this process nothing but different parts of a social system, of a mechanism, each part acting on the other and being acted upon by it; there may be a stronger part, but there cannot be a ruling part; the relation of parts of a mechanism supersedes the political relation.

We need not dwell on the next, but not necessarily last, step of the reasoning which we are trying to sketch, namely, the requirement that the researches regarding groups must be underpinned, nay, guided, by "a general theory of personality" or the like: we know nothing of the political wisdom or the folly of a statesman's actions until we know everything about the degree of affection which he received from each of his parents, if any. The last step might be thought to be the use by the new political science of observations regarding rats: can we not observe human beings as we observe rats, are decisions which rats make not much simpler than the decisions which humans frequently make, and is not the simpler always the key to the more complex? We do not doubt that we can observe, if we try hard enough, the overt behavior of humans as we observe the overt behavior of rats. But we ought not to forget that in the case of rats we are limited to observing overt behavior because they do not talk, and they do not talk because they have nothing to say or because they have no inwardness. Yet to return from these depths to the surface, an important example of the formalism in question is supplied by the well-known theory regarding the principles of legitimacy which substitutes formal characteristics (traditional, rational, charismatic) for the substantive principles which are precisely the purposes to which the various regimes are dedicated and by which they are legitimated. The universals for which the new political science seeks are "laws of human behavior"; those laws are to be discovered by means of "empirical" research. There is an amazing disproportion between the apparent breadth of the goal (say, a general theory of social change) and the true pettiness of the researches undertaken in order to achieve that goal (say, a change in a hospital when one head nurse is replaced by another). This is no accident. Since we lack objective criteria of relevance, we have no reason to be more interested in a world-shaking revolution which affects directly or indirectly all men than in the most trifling "social changes." Moreover, if the laws sought are to be "laws of human behavior," they cannot be restricted to human behavior as it is affected by this or that regime. But human behavior as studied by "empirical" research always occurs within a peculiar regime. More precisely, the most cherished techniques of "empirical" research in the social sciences can be applied only to human beings living now in countries in which the government tolerates research of this kind. The new political science is therefore constantly tempted (and as a rule it does not resist the temptation) to absolutize the relative or peculiar, that is, to be parochial. We have read statements about "the revolutionary" or "the conservative" which did not even claim to have any basis other than observations made in the United States at the present moment; if those statements had any relations to facts at all, they might have some degree of truth regarding revolutionaries or conservatives in certain parts of the United States today, but they reveal themselves immediately as patently wrong if taken as they were meant—namely, as descriptions of the revolutionary or the conservative as such; the error in question was due to the parochialism inevitably fostered by the new political science.

At the risk of some repetition we must say a few words about the language of the new political science. The break with the political understanding of political things necessitates the making of a language different from the language used by political men. The new political science rejects the latter language as ambiguous and imprecise and claims that its own language is unambiguous and precise. Yet this claim is not warranted. The language of the new political science is not less vague, but more vague, than the language used in political life. Political life would be altogether impossible if its language were unqualifiedly vague; that language is capable of the utmost unambiguity and precision, as in a declaration of war or in an order given to a firing squad. If available distinctions like that between war, peace, and armistice prove to be insufficient, political life finds, without the benefit of political science, the right new expression (Cold War as distinguished from Hot or Shooting War) which designates the new phenomenon with unfailing precision. The alleged vagueness of political language is primarily due to the fact that it corresponds to the complexity of political life or that it is nourished by long experience with political things in a great variety of circumstances. By simply condemning prescientific language, instead of deviating from usage in particular cases because of the proved inadequacy of usage in the cases in question, one simply condemns oneself to irredeemable vagueness. No thoughtful citizen would dream of equating politics with something as vague and empty as "power" or "power relations." The thinking men who are regarded as the classic interpreters of power—Thucydides and Machiavelli—did not need these expressions; these expressions as now used originate, not in political life, but in the academic reaction to the understanding of political life in terms of law alone: these expressions signify nothing but that academic reaction.

Political language does not claim to be perfectly clear and distinct; it does not claim that it is based on a full understanding of the things which it designates unambiguously enough; it is suggestive: it leaves those things in the penumbra in which they come to sight. The purge effected by "scientific" definitions of those things has the character of sterilization. The language of the new political science claims to be perfectly clear and distinct and at the same time entirely provisional; its terms are meant to imply hypotheses about political life. But this claim to undogmatic openness is a mere ceremonial gesture. When one speaks of "conscience," one does not claim that one has fathomed the phenomenon indicated by that term. But when the new political scientist speaks of the "Super-Ego," he is certain that anything meant by "conscience" which is not covered by the "Super-Ego" is a superstition. As a consequence he cannot distinguish between a bad conscience, which may induce a man to devote the rest of his life to compensating another man to the best of his powers for an irreparable damage, and "guilt feelings" which one ought to get rid of as fast and as cheaply as possible. Similarly he is certain to have understood the trust which induces people to vote for a candidate for high office by speaking of the "father image"; he does not have to inquire whether and to what extent the candidate in question deserves that trust—a trust different from the trust which children have in their father. The allegedly provisional or hypothetical terms are never questioned in the process of research, for their implications channel the research in such directions that the "data" which might reveal the inadequacy of the hypotheses never turn up. We conclude that to the extent to which the new political science is not formalistic it is vulgarian. This vulgarianism shows itself particularly in the "value-free" manner in which it uses and thus debases terms that originally were meant only for indicating things of a noble character—terms like "culture," "personality," "values," "charismatic," and "civilization."

The most important example of the dogmatism to which we have alluded is supplied by the treatment of religion in the new political or social science. The new science uses sociological or psychological theories regarding religion which exclude, without considering it, the possibility that religion rests ultimately on God's revealing Himself to man; hence those theories are mere hypotheses which can never be confirmed. Those theories are in fact the hidden basis of the new science. The new science rests on a dogmatic atheism which presents itself as merely methodological or hypothetical. For a few years, logical positivism tried with much noise and little thought to dispose of religion by asserting that religious assertions are "meaningless statements." This trick seems to have been abandoned without noise. Some adherents of the new political science might rejoin with some liveliness that their posture toward religion is imposed on them by intellectual honesty: not being able to believe, they cannot accept belief as the basis of their science. We gladly grant that, other things being equal, a frank atheist is a better man than an alleged theist who conceives of God as a symbol. But we must add that intellectual honesty is not enough. Intellectual honesty is not love of truth. Intellectual honesty, a kind of self-denial, has taken the place of love of truth because truth has come to be believed to be repulsive, and one cannot love the repulsive. Yet just as our opponents refuse respect to unreasoned belief, we on our part, with at least equal right, must refuse respect to unreasoned unbelief; honesty with oneself regarding one's unbelief is in itself not more than unreasoned unbelief, probably accompanied by a vague confidence that the issue of unbelief versus belief has long since been settled once and for all. It is hardly necessary to add that the dogmatic exclusion of religious awareness proper renders questionable all long-range predictions concerning the future of societies.

The reduction of the political to the subpolitical is the reduction of primarily given wholes to elements which are relatively simple, that is, sufficiently simple for the research purpose at hand, yet necessarily susceptible of being analyzed into still simpler elements *in infinitum*. It implies that there cannot be genuine wholes. Hence it implies that there cannot be a common good. According to the old political science, there is necessarily a common good, and the common good in its fullness is the good society and what is required for the good society. The consistent denial of the common good is as impossible as every other consistent manifestation of the break with common sense. The empiricists who reject the notion of wholes are compelled to speak sooner or later of such things as "the open society," which is their definition of the good society. The alternative (if it is an alternative) is to deny the possibility of a substantive public interest, but to admit the possibility of substantive group interests; yet it is not difficult to see that what is granted to the goose "group" cannot be consistently denied to the gander "country." In accordance with this, the new political science surreptitiously reintroduces the common good in the form of "the rules of the game" with which all conflicting groups are supposed to comply because those rules, reasonably fair to every group, can reasonably be admitted by every group. The "group politics" approach is a relic of Marxism, which more reasonably denied that there can be a common good in a society consisting of classes that are locked in a life-and-death struggle, overt or hidden, and therefore found the common good in a classless and hence stateless society comprising the whole human race, or the surviving part of it. The consistent denial of the common good requires a radical "individualism." In fact, the new political science appears to teach that there cannot be a substantive public interest because there is not, and cannot be, a single objective which is approved by all members of society: murderers show by their action that not even the prohibition against murder is strictly speaking to the public interest. We are not so sure whether the murderer wishes that murder cease to be a punishable action and not rather that he himself get away with murder. Be this as it may, this denial of the common good is based on the premise that even if an objective is to the interest of the overwhelming majority, it is not to the interest of all: no minority, however small, no individual, however perverse, must be left out. More precisely, even if an objective is to the interest of all, but not believed by all to be to the interest of all, it is not to the public interest: everyone is by nature the sole judge of what is to his interest: his judgment regarding his interest is not subject to anybody else's examination on the issue whether his judgment is sound.

This premise is not the discovery or invention of the new political science; it was stated with the greatest vigor by Hobbes, who opposed it to the opposite premise which had been the basis of the old political science proper. But Hobbes still saw that his premise entails the war of everybody against everybody and hence drew the conclusion that everyone must cease to be the sole judge of what is to his interest if there is to be human life; the individual's reason must give way to the public reason. The new political science denies in a way that there is a public reason: government may be a broker, if a broker possessing "the monopoly of violence," but it surely is not the public reason. The true public reason is the new political science, which judges in a universally valid, or objective, manner of what is to the interest of each, for it shows to everyone what means he must choose in order to attain his attainable ends, whatever those ends may be. It has been shown earlier in this volume* what becomes of the new political science, or of the only kind of rationality which the new political science still admits, if its Hobbesian premise is not conveniently forgotten: the new form of public reason goes the way of the old.**

The denial of the common good presents itself today as a direct consequence of the distinction between facts and values, according to which only factual judgments, not value judgments, can be true or objective. The new political science leaves the justification of values or of preferences to "political philosophy" or more precisely to ideology on the ground that any justification of preferences would have to derive values from facts, and such derivation is not legitimately possible. Preferences are not strictly speaking opinions and hence cannot be true or false, whereas ideologies are opinions and, for the reason given, false opinions. Whereas acting man has necessarily chosen values, the new political scientist as pure spectator is not committed to any value; in particular, he is neutral in the conflict between liberal democracy and its enemies. The traditional value systems antedate the awareness of the difference between facts and values; they claimed to be derived from facts—from Divine Revelation or from similar sources—in general, from superior or perfect beings which as such unite in themselves fact and value; the discovery of the difference between facts and values amounts therefore to a refutation of the traditional value systems as originally meant. It is at least doubtful whether those value systems can be divorced from what present themselves as their factual bases. At any rate, it follows from the difference between facts and values that men can live without ideology: they can adopt, posit, or proclaim values without making the illegitimate attempt to derive their values from facts or without

* See note, p. 115.
** See *Essays on the Scientific Study of Politics* (New York: Holt, Rinehart and Winston, 1962).

relying on false or at least unevident assertions regarding what is. One thus arrives at the notion of the rational society or of the nonideological regime: a society which is based on the understanding of the character of values. Since this understanding implies that before the tribunal of reason all values are equal, the rational society will be egalitarian or democratic, and permissive or liberal: the rational doctrine regarding the difference between facts and values rationally justifies the preference for liberal democracy—contrary to what is intended by that distinction itself. In other words, whereas the new political science ought to deny the proposition that there can be no society without an ideology, it asserts that proposition.

One is thus led to wonder whether the distinction between facts and values, or the assertion that no Ought can be derived from an Is, is well founded. Let us assume that a man's "values" (that is, what he values) are fully determined by his heredity and environment (that is, by his Is), or that there is a one-to-one relation between value *a* and Is *A*. In this case the Ought would be determined by the Is or derivative from it. But the very issue as commonly understood presupposes that this assumption is wrong: man possesses a certain latitude; he can choose not only from among various ways of overt behavior (like jumping or not jumping into a river in order to escape death at the hands of a stronger enemy who may or may not be able to swim), but from among various values; this latitude, this possibility, has the character of a fact. A man lacking this latitude—for example, a man for whom every stimulus is a value or who cannot help giving in to every desire—is a defective man, a man with whom something is wrong. The fact that someone desires something does not yet make that something his value; he may successfully fight his desire, or if his desire overpowers him, he may blame himself for this as for a failure on his part; only choice, in contradistinction to mere desire, makes something a man's value. The distinction between desire and choice is a distinction among facts. Choice does not mean here the choice of means to pregiven ends; choice here means the choice of ends, the positing of ends, or rather of values.

Man is then understood as a being which differs from all other known beings because he posits values; this positing is taken to be a fact. In accordance with this, the new political science denies that man has natural ends—ends toward which he is by nature inclined; it denies more specifically the premise of modern natural right according to which self-preservation is the most important natural end; man can choose death in preference to life, not in a given situation, out of despair, but simply: he can posit death as his value. The view that the pertinent Is is our positing of values in contradistinction to the yielding to mere desires necessarily leads to Oughts of a radically different character from the so-called Oughts corresponding to mere desires. We conclude that the "relativism" accepted by the new political science, according to which values are nothing but objects of desire, is based on an insufficient analysis of the Is, that is, of the pertinent Is, and furthermore that one's opinion regarding the character of the Is settles one's opinion regarding the character of the Ought. We must leave it open here whether a more adequate analysis of the pertinent Is, that is, of the nature of man, does not lead to a more adequate determination of the Ought or beyond a merely formal characterization of the Ought. At any rate, if a man is of the opinion that as a matter of fact all desires are of equal dignity, since we know of no factual consideration which would entitle us to assign different dignities to different desires, he cannot but be of the opinion, unless he is prepared to become guilty of gross arbitrariness, that all desires ought to be treated as equal within the limits of the possible, and this opinion is what is meant by permissive egalitarianism.

There is, then, more than a mysterious pre-established harmony between the new political science and a certain version of liberal democracy. The alleged value-free analysis of political phenomena is controlled by an unavowed commitment built into the new political science to that version of liberal democracy. That version of liberal democracy is not discussed openly and impartially, with full consideration of all relevant pros and cons. We call this characteristic of the new political science its democratism. The new political science looks for laws of human behavior to be discovered by means of data supplied through certain techniques of research which are believed to guarantee the maximum of objectivity; it therefore puts a premium on the study of things which occur frequently now in democratic societies: neither those in their graves nor those behind the Curtains can respond to questionnaires or interviews. Democracy is then the tacit presupposition of the data; it does not have to become a theme; it can easily be forgotten: the wood is forgotten for the trees; the laws of human behavior are in fact laws of the behavior of human beings more or less molded by democracy; man is tacitly identified with democratic man. The new political science puts a premium on observations which can be made with the utmost frequency, and therefore by people of the meanest capacities. It therefore frequently culminates in observations made by people who are not intelligent about people who are not intelligent. While the new political science becomes ever less able to see democracy or to hold a mirror to democracy, it ever more reflects the most dangerous proclivities of democracy. It even strengthens those proclivities. By teaching in effect the equality of literally all desires, it teaches in effect that there is nothing of which a man ought to be ashamed; by destroying the possibility of self-contempt, it destroys with the best of intentions the possibility of self-respect. By teaching the equality of all values, by denying that there are things which are intrinsically high and others which are intrinsically low, as well as by denying that there is an essential difference between men and brutes, it unwittingly contributes to the victory of the gutter.

Yet the same new political science came into being through the revolt against what one may call the democratic orthodoxy of the immediate past. It had learned certain lessons which were hard for that orthodoxy to swallow regarding the irrationality of the masses and the necessity of elites; if it had been wise, it would have learned those lessons from the galaxy of antidemocratic thinkers of the remote past. It believed, in other words, it had learned that, contrary to the belief of the orthodox democrats, no compelling case can be made for liberalism (for example, for 'the unqualified freedom of such speech as does not constitute a clear and present danger) nor for democracy (free elections based on universal suffrage). But it succeeded in reconciling those doubts with the unfaltering commitment to liberal democracy by the simple device of declaring that no value judgments, including those supporting liberal democracy, are rational and hence that an ironclad argument in favor of liberal democracy ought in reason not even to be expected. The very complex pros and cons regarding liberal democracy have thus become entirely obliterated by the poorest formalism. The crisis of liberal democracy has become concealed by a ritual which calls itself methodology or logic. This almost willful blindness to the crisis of liberal democracy is part of that crisis. No wonder then that the new political science has nothing to say against those who unhesitatingly prefer surrender, that is the abandonment of liberal democracy, to war.

Only a great fool would call the new political science diabolic: it has no attributes peculiar to fallen angels. It is not even Machiavellian, for Machiavelli's teaching was graceful, subtle, and colorful. Nor is it Neronian. Nevertheless one may say of it that it fiddles while Rome burns. It is excused by two facts: it does not know that it fiddles, and it does not know that Rome burns.

Part Two

Introduction to
History of Political Philosophy

Today "political philosophy" has become almost synonymous with "ideology," not to say "myth." It surely is understood in contradistinction to "political science." The distinction between political philosophy and political science is a consequence of the fundamental distinction between philosophy and science. Even this fundamental distinction is of relatively recent origin. Traditionally, philosophy and science were not distinguished: natural science was one of the most important parts of philosophy. The great intellectual revolution of the seventeenth century which brought to light modern natural science was a revolution of a new philosophy *or* science against traditional (chiefly Aristotelian) philosophy *or* science. But the new philosophy or science was only partly successful. The most successful part of the new philosophy or science was the new natural science. By virtue of its victory, the new natural science became more and more independent of philosophy, at least apparently, and even, as it were, became an authority for philosophy. In this way the distinction between philosophy and science became generally accepted, and eventually also the distinction between political philosophy and political science as a kind of natural science of political things. Traditionally, however, political philosophy and political science were the same.

Political philosophy is not the same as political thought in general. Political thought is coeval with political life. Political philosophy, however, emerged within a particular political life, in Greece, in that past of which we have written records. According to the traditional view, the Athenian Socrates (469–399 B.C.) was the founder of political philosophy. Socrates was the teacher of Plato, who in his turn was the teacher of Aristotle. The political works of Plato and Aristotle are the oldest works devoted to political philosophy which have come down to us. The kind of political philosophy which was originated by Socrates is called classical political philosophy. Classical political philosophy was the predominant political philosophy until the emergence of modern political philosophy in the sixteenth and seventeenth centuries. Modern political philosophy came into being through the conscious break with the principles established by Socrates. By the same token classical political philosophy is not limited to the political teaching of Plato and Aristotle and their schools; it includes also the political teaching of the Stoics as well as the political teachings of the church fathers and the Scholastics, in so far as these teachings are not based exclusively on Divine revelation. The traditional view according to which Socrates was the founder of political philosophy is in need of some qualifications, or rather explanations; yet it is less misleading than any alternative view.

Socrates surely was not the first philosopher. This means that political philosophy was preceded by philosophy. The first philosophers are called by Aristotle "those who discourse on nature"; he distinguishes them from those "who discourse on the gods." The primary theme of philosophy, then, is "nature." What is nature? The first Greek whose work has come down to us, Homer himself, mentions "nature" only a single time; this first mention of "nature" gives us a most important hint as to what the Greek philosophers understood by "nature." In the tenth book of the *Odyssey*, Odysseus tells of what befell him on the island of the sorceress-goddess Circe. Circe had transformed many of his comrades into swine and locked them in sties. On his way to Circe's house to rescue his poor comrades, Odysseus is met by the god Hermes who wishes to preserve him. He promises Odysseus an egregious herb which will make him safe against Circe's evil arts. Hermes "drew a herb from the earth and showed me its *nature*. Black at the root it was, like milk its blossom; and the gods call it moly. Hard is it to dig for mortal men, but the gods can do everything." Yet the gods' ability to dig the herb with ease would be of no avail if they did not know the nature of the herb—its looks and its power—in the first place. The gods are thus omnipotent because they are, not indeed omniscient, but the knowers of the natures of the things—of natures which they have not made. "Nature" means here the character of a thing, or of a kind of thing, the way in which a thing or a kind of thing looks and acts, and the thing, or the kind of thing, is taken not to have been made by gods or men. If we were entitled to take a poetic utterance literally, we could say that the first man we know who spoke of nature was the Wily Odysseus who had seen the towns of many men and had thus come to know how much the thoughts of men differ from town to town or from tribe to tribe.

It seems that the Greek word for nature (*physis*) means primarily "growth" and therefore also that into which a thing grows, the term of the growth, the character a thing has when its growth is completed, when it can do what only the fully grown thing of the kind in question can do or do well. Things like shoes or chairs do not "grow" but are "made": they are not "by nature" but "by art." On the other hand, there are things which are "by nature" without having "grown" and even without having come into being in any way. They are said to be "by nature" because they have not been made and because they are the

"first things," out of which or through which all other natural things have come into being. The atoms to which the
philosopher Democritus traced everything are by nature in
the last sense.

Nature, however understood, is not known by nature.
Nature had to be discovered. The Hebrew Bible, for example, does not have a word for nature. The equivalent in
biblical Hebrew of "nature" is something like "way" or
"custom." Prior to the discovery of nature, men knew that
each thing or kind of thing has its "way" or its "custom"
—its form of "regular behavior." There is a way or custom of fire, of dogs, of women, of madmen, of human
beings: fire burns, dogs bark and wag their tails, women
ovulate, madmen rave, human beings can speak. Yet there
are also ways or customs of the various human tribes
(Egyptians, Persians, Spartans, Moabites, Amalekites, and
so on). Through the discovery of nature the radical
difference between these two kinds of "ways" or "customs" came to the center of attention. The discovery of
nature led to the splitting up of "way" or "custom" into
"nature" (*physis*) on the one hand and "convention" or
"law" (*nomos*) on the other. For instance, that human
beings can speak is natural, but that this particular tribe
uses this particular language is due to convention. The distinction implies that the natural is prior to the conventional. The distinction between nature and convention is
fundamental for classical political philosophy and even for
most of modern political philosophy, as can be seen most
simply from the distinction between natural right and positive right.

Once nature was discovered and understood primarily in
contradistinction to law or convention, it became possible
and necessary to raise this question: Are the political
things natural, and if they are, to what extent? The very
question implied that the laws are not natural. But obedience to the laws was generally considered to be justice.
Hence one was compelled to wonder whether justice is

merely conventional or whether there are things which are by nature just. Are even the laws merely conventional or do they have their roots in nature? Must the laws not be "according to nature," and especially according to the nature of man, if they are to be good? The laws are the foundation or the work of the political community: is the political community by nature? In the attempts to answer these questions it was presupposed that there are things which are by nature good for man as man. The precise question therefore concerns the relation of what is by nature good for man, on the one hand, to justice or right on the other. The simple alternative is this: all right is conventional or there is some natural right. Both opposed answers were given and developed prior to Socrates. For a variety of reasons it is not helpful to present here a summary of what can be known of these pre-Socratic doctrines. We shall get some notion of the conventionalist view (the view that all right is conventional) when we turn to Plato's *Republic*, which contains a summary of that view. As for the opposite view, it must suffice here to say that it was developed by Socrates and classical political philosophy in general much beyond the earlier views.

What then is meant by the assertion that Socrates was the founder of political philosophy? Socrates did not write any books. According to the most ancient reports, he turned away from the study of the divine or natural things and directed his inquiries entirely to the human things, i.e., the just things, the noble things, and the things good for man as man; he always conversed about "what is pious, what is impious, what is noble, what is base, what is just, what is unjust, what is sobriety, what is madness, what is courage, what is cowardice, what is the city, what is the statesman, what is rule over men, what is a man able to rule over men," and similar things.[1] It seems that Socrates was induced to turn away from the study of the divine or natural things by his piety. The gods do not approve of

1. Xenophon *Memorabilia* I. 1. 11–16.

man's trying to seek out what they do not wish to reveal, especially the things in heaven and beneath the earth. A pious man will therefore investigate only the things left to men's investigation, i.e., the human things. Socrates pursued his investigations by means of conversations. This means that he started from generally held opinions. Among the generally held opinions the most authoritative ones are those sanctioned by the city and its laws—by the most solemn convention. But the generally held opinions contradict one another. It therefore becomes necessary to transcend the whole sphere of the generally held opinions, or of opinion as such, in the direction of knowledge. Since even the most authoritative opinions are only opinions, even Socrates was compelled to go the way from convention or law to nature, to ascend from law to nature. But now it appears more clearly than ever before that opinion, convention, or law, contains truth, or is not arbitrary, or is in a sense natural. One may say that the law, the human law, thus proves to point to a divine or natural law as its origin. This implies, however, that the human law, precisely because it is not identical with the divine or natural law, is not unqualifiedly true or just: only natural right, justice itself, the "idea" or "form" of justice, is unqualifiedly just. Nevertheless, the human law, the law of the city, is unqualifiedly obligatory for the men subject to it provided they have the right to emigrate with their property, i.e., provided their subjection to the laws of their city was voluntary.[2]

The precise reason why Socrates became the founder of political philosophy appears when one considers the character of the questions with which he dealt in his conversations. He raised the question "What is . . . ?" regarding everything. This question is meant to bring to light the nature of the kind of thing in question, that is, the form or the character of the thing. Socrates presupposed that knowledge of the whole is, above all, knowledge of the

2. Plato *Crito* 51[d–e].

character, the form, the "essential" character of every part of the whole, as distinguished from knowledge of that out of which or through which the whole may have come into being. If the whole consists of essentially different parts, it is at least possible that the political things (or the human things) are essentially different from the nonpolitical things—that the political things form a class by themselves and therefore can be studied by themselves. Socrates, it seems, took the primary meaning of "nature" more seriously than any of his predecessors: he realized that "nature" is primarily "form" or "idea." If this is true, he did not simply turn away from the study of the natural things, but originated a new kind of the study of the natural things—a kind of study in which, for example, the nature or idea of justice, or natural right, and surely the nature of the human soul or man, is more important than, for example, the nature of the sun.

One cannot understand the nature of man if one does not understand the nature of human society. Socrates as well as Plato and Aristotle assumed that the most perfect form of human society is the *polis*. The *polis* is today frequently taken to be the Greek city-state. But for the classical political philosophers it was accidental that the *polis* was more common among Greeks than among non-Greeks. One would then have to say that the theme of classical political philosophy was, not the Greek city-state, but the city-state. This presupposes, however, that the city-state is one particular form of "the state." It presupposes therefore the concept of the state as comprising the city-state among other forms of the state. Yet classical political philosophy lacked the concept of "the state." When people speak today of "the state," they ordinarily understand "state" in contradistinction to "society." This distinction is alien to classical political philosophy. It is not sufficient to say that *polis* (city) comprises both state and society, for the concept "city" antedates the distinction between state and society; therefore one does not understand "the city" by saying the city comprises state and society. The modern equivalent to "the city" on the level of the citizen's understanding is "the country." For when a man says, for example, that "the country is in danger," he also has not yet made a distinction between state and society. The reason why the classical political philosophers were chiefly concerned with the city was not that they were ignorant of other forms of societies in general and of political societies in particular. They knew the tribe (the nation) as well as such structures as the Persian Empire. They were chiefly concerned with the city because they preferred the city to those other forms of political society. The grounds of this preference may be said to have been these: tribes are not capable of a high civilization, and very large societies cannot be free societies. Let us remember that the authors of the *Federalist Papers* were still under a compulsion to prove that it is possible for a large society to be republican or free. Let us also remember that the authors of the *Federalist Papers* signed themselves "Publius": republicanism points back to classical antiquity and therefore also to classical political philosophy.

Plato
427–347 B.C.

Thirty-five dialogues and thirteen letters have come down to us as Platonic writings, not all of which are now regarded as genuine. Some scholars go so far as to doubt that any of the letters is genuine. In order not to encumber our presentation with polemics, we shall disregard the letters altogether. We must then say Plato never speaks to us in his own name, for in his dialogues only his characters speak. Strictly, there is then no Platonic teaching; at most there is the teaching of the men who are the chief characters in his dialogues. Why Plato proceeded in this manner is not easy to say. Perhaps he was doubtful whether there can be a philosophic teaching proper. Perhaps he, too, thought like his master Socrates that philosophy is in the last analysis knowledge of ignorance. Socrates is indeed the chief character in most of the Platonic dialogues. One could say that Plato's dialogues as a whole are less the presentation of a teaching than a monument to the life of Socrates—to the core of his life: they all show how Socrates engaged in his most important work, the awakening of his fellow men and the attempting to guide them toward the good life which he himself was living. Still, Socrates is not always the chief character in Plato's dialogues; in a few he does hardly more than listen while others speak, and in one dialogue (the *Laws*) he is not even present. We mention these strange facts because they show how difficult it is to speak of Plato's teaching.

All Platonic dialogues refer more or less directly to the political question. Yet there are only three dialogues which indicate by their very titles that they are devoted to political philosophy: the *Republic,* the *Statesman,* and the *Laws.* The political teaching of Plato is accessible to us chiefly through these three works.

The Republic

In the *Republic,* Socrates discusses the nature of justice with a fairly large number of people. The conversation about this general theme takes place, of course, in a particular setting: in a particular place, at a particular time, with men each of whom has his particular age, character, abilities, position in society, and appearance. While the place of the conversation is made quite clear to us, the time, i.e., the year, is not. Hence we lack certain knowledge of the political circumstances in which this conversation about the principles of politics takes place. We may assume, however, that it takes place in an era of political decay of Athens, that at any rate Socrates and the chief interlocutors (the brothers Glaukon and Adeimantos) were greatly concerned with that decay and were thinking of the restoration of political health. Certain it is that Socrates makes very radical proposals of "reform" without encountering serious resistance. But there are also a few indications in the *Republic* to the effect that the longed-for reformation is not likely to succeed on the political plane or that the only possible reformation is that of the individual man.

The conversation opens with Socrates' addressing a question to the oldest man present, Kephalos, who is respectable on account of his piety as well as his wealth. Socrates' question is a model of propriety. It gives Kephalos an opportunity to speak of everything good which he possesses, to display his happiness, as it were, and it concerns the only subject about which Socrates could conceivably learn something from him: about how it feels to be very old. In the course of his answer Kephalos comes to speak of injustice and justice. He seems to imply that justice is identical with telling the truth and paying back what one has received from anyone. Socrates shows him that telling the truth and returning another man's property are not always just. At this point Kephalos' son and heir, Polemarchos, rising in defense of his father's opinion, takes the place of his father in the conversation. But the opinion which he defends is not exactly the same as his father's; if we may make use of a joke of Socrates', Polemarchos inherits only half, and perhaps even less than a half, of his father's intellectual property. Polemarchos no longer maintains that telling the truth is essential to justice. Without knowing it, he thus lays down one of the principles of the *Republic*. As appears later in the work, in a well-ordered society it is necessary that one tell untruths of a certain kind to children and even to the adult subjects.[1] This example reveals the character of the discussion which occurs in the first book of the *Republic*, where Socrates refutes a number of false opinions about justice. This negative or destructive work, however, contains within itself the constructive assertions of the bulk of the *Republic*. Let us consider from this point of view the three opinions on justice discussed in the first book.

Kephalos' opinion as taken up by Polemarchos (after his father had left to perform an act of piety) is to the effect that justice consists in returning deposits. More generally stated, Kephalos holds that justice consists in returning, leaving, or giving to everyone what belongs to him. But he also holds that justice is good, i.e., salutary, not only to the giver but also to the receiver. Now it is obvious that in some cases giving to a man what belongs to him is harmful to him. Not all men make a good or wise use of what

---

1. Plato, *Republic* 377 ff., 389b–c, 414b–415d, 459c–d.

belongs to them, of their property. If we judge very strictly, we might be driven to say that very few people make a wise use of their property. If justice is to be salutary, we might be compelled to demand that everyone should own only what is "fitting" for him, what is good for him, and for as long as it is good for him. In brief, we might be compelled to demand the abolition of private property or the introduction of communism. To the extent to which there is a connection between private property and the family, we would even be compelled to demand abolition of the family or the introduction of absolute communism, i.e., of communism not only regarding property but regarding women and children as well. Above all, extremely few people will be able to determine wisely which things and which amounts of them are good for the use of each individual—or at any rate for each individual who counts; only men of exceptional wisdom are able to do this. We would then be compelled to demand that society be ruled by simply wise men, by philosophers in the strict sense, wielding absolute power. The refutation of Kephalos' view of justice thus contains the proof of the necessity of absolute communism in the sense defined, as well as of the absolute rule of the philosophers. This proof, it is hardly necessary to say, is based on the disregard of, or the abstraction from, a number of most relevant things; it is "abstract" in the extreme. If we wish to understand the *Republic,* we must find out what these disregarded things are and why they are disregarded. The *Republic* itself, carefully read, supplies the answers to these questions.

Before going any further, we must dispose of a misunderstanding which is at present very common. The theses of the *Republic* summarized in the two preceding paragraphs clearly show that Plato, or at any rate Socrates, was not a liberal democrat. They also suffice to show that Plato was not a Communist in the sense of Marx, or a Fascist: Marxist communism and fascism are incompatible with the rule of philosophers, whereas the scheme of the *Republic* stands or falls by the rule of philosophers. But let us hasten back to the *Republic*.

Whereas the first opinion on justice was only implied by Kephalos and stated by Socrates, the second opinion is stated by Polemarchos, although not without Socrates' assistance. Furthermore, Kephalos' opinion is linked in his mind with the view that injustice is bad because it is punished by the gods after death. This view forms no part of Polemarchos' opinion. He is confronted with the contradiction between the two opinions according to which justice must be salutary to the receiver and justice consists in giving to each what belongs to him. Polemarchos overcomes the contradiction by dropping the second opinion. He also modifies the first. Justice, he says, consists in helping one's friends and harming one's enemies. Justice thus understood would seem to be unqualifiedly good for the giver and for those receivers who are good to the giver. This difficulty, however, arises: If justice is taken to be giving to others what belongs to them, the only thing which the just man must know is what belongs to anyone with whom he has any dealing; this knowledge is supplied by the law, which in principle can be easily known by mere listening. But if the just man must give to his friends what is good for them, he himself must judge; he himself must be able correctly to distinguish friends from enemies; he himself must know what is good for each of his friends. Justice must include knowledge of a high order. To say the least, justice must be an art comparable to medicine, the art which knows and produces what is good for human bodies. Polemarchos is unable to identify the knowledge or the art which goes with justice or which is justice. He is therefore unable to show how justice can be salutary. The discussion points to the view that justice is the art which gives to each man what is good for his soul, i.e., that justice is identical with, or at least inseparable from, philosophy, the medicine of the soul. It points to the view that there cannot be justice among men unless the philosophers rule. But Socrates does not yet state this view. Instead he makes clear to Pole-marchos that the just man will help just men rather than his "friends," and he will harm no one. He does not say that the just man will help everyone. Perhaps he means that there are human beings whom he cannot benefit. But he surely also means something more. Polemarchos' thesis may be taken to reflect a most potent opinion regarding justice—the opinion according to which justice means pub-lic-spiritedness, full dedication to one's city as a particular society which as such is potentially the enemy of other cities. Justice so understood is patriotism, and consists in-deed in helping one's friends, i.e., one's fellow citizens, and harming one's enemies, i.e., foreigners. Justice thus under-stood cannot be entirely dispensed with in any city however just, for even the most just city is a city, a particular or closed or exclusive society. Therefore Socrates himself de-mands later in the dialogue that the guardians of the city be by nature friendly to their own people and harsh or nasty to strangers.[2] He also demands that the citizens of the just city cease to regard all human beings as their brothers and limit the feelings and actions of fraternity to their fellow citizens alone.[3] The opinion of Polemarchos properly understood is the only one among the generally known views of justice discussed in the first book of the *Republic* which is entirely preserved in the positive or con-structive part of the *Republic*. This opinion, to repeat, is to the effect that justice is full dedication to the common good; it demands that man withhold nothing of his own from his city; it demands therefore by itself—i.e., if we ab-stract from all other considerations—absolute communism.

The third and last opinion discussed in the first book of the *Republic* is the one maintained by Thrasymachos. He is the only speaker in the work who exhibits anger and behaves discourteously and even savagely. He is highly in-dignant over the result of Socrates' conversation with Pole-

2. *Ibid.*, 375b–376c.
3. *Ibid.*, 414d–e.

marchos. He seems to be particularly shocked by Socrates' contention that it is not good for oneself to harm anyone or that justice is never harmful to anyone. It is most important, both for the understanding of the *Republic* and generally, that we do not behave toward Thrasymachos as Thrasymachos behaves, i.e., angrily, fanatically, or savagely. If we look then at Thrasymachos' indignation without indignation, we must admit that his violent reaction is to some extent a revolt of common sense. Since the city as city is a society which from time to time must wage war, and war is inseparable from harming innocent people,[4] the unqualified condemnation of harming human beings would be tantamount to the condemnation of even the justest city. Apart from this, it seems to be entirely fitting that the most savage man present should maintain a most savage thesis on justice. Thrasymachos contends that justice is the advantage of the stronger. Still, this thesis proves to be only the consequence of an opinion which is not only not manifestly savage but is even highly respectable. According to that opinion, the just is the same as the lawful or legal, i.e., what the customs or laws of the city prescribe. Yet this opinion implies that there is nothing higher to which one can appeal from the man-made laws or conventions. This is the opinion now known by the name of "legal positivism," but in its origin it is not academic; it is the opinion on which all political societies tend to act. If the just is identical with the legal, the source of justice is the will of the legislator. The legislator in each city is the regime—the man or body of men that rules the city: the tyrant, the common people, the men of excellence, and so on. According to Thrasymachos, each regime lays down the laws with a view to its own preservation and well-being, in a word, to its own advantage and to nothing else. From this it follows that obedience to the laws or justice is not necessarily advantageous to the ruled and may even be bad for them.

4. *Ibid.*, 471a–b.

And as for the rulers, justice simply does not exist: they lay down the laws with exclusive concern for their own advantage.

Let us concede for a moment that Thrasymachos' view of law and of rulers is correct. The rulers surely may make mistakes. They may command actions which are in fact disadvantageous to themselves and advantageous to the ruled. In that case the just or law-abiding subjects will in fact do what is disadvantageous to the rulers and advantageous to the subjects. When this difficulty is pointed out to him by Socrates, Thrasymachos declares after some hesitation that the rulers are not rulers if and when they make mistakes: the ruler in the strict sense is infallible, just as the artisan in the strict sense is infallible. It is this Thrasymachean notion of "the artisan in the strict sense" which Socrates uses with great felicity against Thrasymachos. For the artisan in the strict sense proves to be concerned, not with his own advantage, but with the advantage of the others whom he serves: the shoemaker makes shoes for others and only accidentally for himself; the physician prescribes things to his patients with a view to their advantage; hence if ruling is, as Thrasymachos admitted, something like an art, the ruler serves the ruled, i.e., rules for the advantage of the ruled. The artisan in the strict sense is infallible, i.e., does his job well, and he is only concerned with the well-being of others. This, however, means that art strictly understood is justice—justice in deed, and not merely in intention as law-abidingness is. "Art is justice"—this proposition reflects the Socratic assertion that virtue is knowledge. The suggestion emerging from Socrates' discussion with Thrasymachos leads to the conclusion that the just city will be an association where everyone is an artisan in the strict sense, a city of craftsmen or artificers, of men (and women) each of whom has a single job which he does well and with full dedication, i.e., without minding his own advantage and only for the good of others or for the common good. This conclusion pervades the whole teaching of the *Republic*.

The city constructed there as a model is based on the principle of "one man one job." The soldiers in it are "artificers" of the freedom of the city; the philosophers in it are "artificers" of the whole common virtue; there is an "artificer" of heaven; even God is presented as an artisan—as the artificer even of the eternal ideas.[5] It is because citizenship in the just city is craftsmanship of one kind or another, and the seat of craftsmanship or art is in the soul and not in the body, that the difference between the two sexes loses its importance, or the equality of the two sexes is established.[6]

Thrasymachos could have avoided his downfall if he had left matters at the common-sense view according to which rulers are of course fallible, or if he had said that all laws are framed by the rulers with a view to their apparent (and not necessarily true) advantage. Since he is not a noble man, we are entitled to suspect that he chose the alternative which proved fatal to him with a view to his own advantage. Thrasymachos was a famous teacher of rhetoric, the art of persuasion. (Hence, incidentally, he is the only man possessing an art who speaks in the *Republic.*) The art of persuasion is necessary for persuading rulers and especially ruling assemblies, at least ostensibly, of their true advantage. Even the rulers themselves need the art of persuasion in order to persuade their subjects that the laws, which are framed with exclusive regard to the benefit of the rulers, serve the benefit of the subjects. Thrasymachos' own art stands or falls by the view that prudence is of the utmost importance for ruling. The clearest expression of this view is the proposition that the ruler who makes mistakes is no longer a ruler at all.

Thrasymachos' downfall is caused not by a stringent refutation of his view of justice, nor by an accidental slip on his part, but by the conflict between his depreciation of justice or his indifference to justice and the implication

5. *Ibid.,* 395c; 500d; 530a; 507c, 597.
6. *Ibid.,* 454c–455a; cf. 452a.

of his art: there is some truth in the view that art is justice. One could say—and as a matter of fact Thrasymachos himself says—that Socrates' conclusion, namely, that no ruler or other artisan ever considers his own advantage, is very simpleminded: Socrates seems to be a babe in the woods. As regards the artisans proper, they of course consider the compensation which they receive for their work. It may be true that, to the extent to which the physician is concerned with what is characteristically called his honorarium, he does not exercise the art of the physician but the art of money-making; but since what is true of the physician is true of the shoemaker and any other craftsman as well, one would have to say that the only universal art, the art accompanying all arts, the art of arts, is the art of money-making; one must therefore further say that serving others or being just becomes good for the artisan only through his practicing the art of money-making, or that no one is just for the sake of justice, or that no one likes justice as such. But the most devastating argument against Socrates' reasoning is supplied by the arts which are manifestly concerned with the most ruthless and calculating exploitation of the ruled by the rulers. Such an art is the art of the shepherd—the art wisely chosen by Thrasymachos in order to destroy Socrates' argument, especially since kings and other rulers have been compared to shepherds since the oldest times. The shepherd is surely concerned with the well-being of his flock—so that the sheep will supply men with the juiciest lamb chops. As Thrasymachos puts it, the shepherds are exclusively concerned with the good of the owners and of themselves.[7] But there is obviously a difference between the owners and the shepherds: the juiciest lamb chops are for the owner and not for the shepherd, unless the shepherd is dishonest. Now, the position of Thrasymachos or of any man of his kind with regard to both rulers and ruled is precisely that of the shepherd with re-

7. *Ibid.,* 343b.

gard to both the owners and the sheep: Thrasymachos can securely derive benefit from the assistance which he gives to the rulers (regardless of whether they are tyrants, common people, or men of excellence) only if he is loyal to them, if he does his job for them well, if he keeps his part of the bargain, if he is just. Contrary to his assertion, he must grant that a man's justice is salutary, not only to others and especially to the rulers, but also to himself. It is partly because he has become aware of this necessity that he changes his manners so remarkably in the last part of the first book. What is true of the helpers of rulers is true of the rulers themselves and all other human beings (including tyrants and gangsters) who need the help of other men in their enterprises, however unjust: no association can last if its members do not practice justice among themselves.[8] This, however, amounts to an admission that justice may be a mere means, if an indispensable means, for injustice—for the exploitation of outsiders. Above all, it does not dispose of the possibility that the city is a community held together by collective selfishness and nothing else, or that there is no fundamental difference between the city and a gang of robbers. These and similar difficulties explain why Socrates regards his refutation of Thrasymachos as insufficient: he says at its conclusion that he has tried to show that justice is good without having made clear what justice is.

The adequate defense or praise of justice presupposes not only knowledge of what justice is, but also an adequate attack on justice. At the beginning of the second book, Glaukon attempts to present such an attack; he claims that he restates Thrasymachos' thesis, in which he does not believe, with greater vigor than Thrasymachos had done. Glaukon also takes it for granted that the just is the same as the legal or conventional, but he attempts to show how convention emerges out of nature. By nature each man is concerned only with his own good and wholly unconcerned

8. *Ibid.*, 351c–352a.

with any other man's good to the point that he has no
hesitation whatever about harming his fellows. Since everyone acts accordingly, they all bring about a situation which
is unbearable for most of them; the majority, i.e., the weak-
lings, figure out that every one of them would be better off
if they agreed among themselves as to what each of them
may or may not do. What they agree upon is not stated by
Glaukon, but part of it can easily be guessed: they will
agree that no one may violate the life and limb, the honor,
the liberty, and the property of any of the associates, i.e.,
the fellow citizens, and that everyone must do his best to
protect his associates against outsiders. Both the abstention
from such violations and the service of protection are in
no way desirable in themselves but only necessary evils, yet
lesser evils than universal insecurity. But what is true of
the majority is not true of "the real man" who can take
care of himself and who is better off if he does not submit
to law or convention. Yet even the others do violence to
their nature by submitting to law and justice: they submit
to it only from fear of the consequences of the failure to
submit, i.e., from fear of punishment of one kind or another, not voluntarily and gladly. Therefore every man
would prefer injustice to justice if he could be sure of escaping detection: justice is preferable to injustice only with
a view to possible detection, to one's becoming known as
just to others, i.e., to good repute or other rewards. Therefore since, as Glaukon hopes, justice is choiceworthy for its
own sake, he demands from Socrates a proof that the life
of the just man is preferable to that of the unjust man,
even if the just man is thought to be unjust in the extreme
and suffers all kinds of punishment or is in the depth of
misery, and the unjust man is thought to be of consummate
justice and receives all kinds of reward or is at the peak of
happiness: the height of injustice, i.e., of the conduct according to nature, is the tacit exploitation of law or convention for one's own benefit alone, the conduct of the
supremely shrewd and manly tyrant. In the discussion with

Thrasymachos, the issue had become blurred by the suggestion that there is a kinship between justice and art. Glaukon makes the issue manifest by comparing the perfectly
unjust man to the perfect artisan, whereas he conceives of
the perfectly just man as a simple man who has no quality
other than justice. With a view to the teaching of the
Republic as a whole, one is tempted to say that Glaukon
understands pure justice in the light of pure fortitude; his
perfectly just man reminds one of the unknown soldier
who undergoes the most painful and most humiliating
death for no other purpose whatsoever except in order to
die bravely and without any prospect of his noble deed ever
becoming known to anyone.

Glaukon's demand on Socrates is strongly supported by
Adeimantos. It becomes clear from Adeimantos' speech that
Glaukon's view according to which justice is choiceworthy
entirely for its own sake is altogether novel, for in the traditional view justice was regarded as choiceworthy chiefly,
if not exclusively, because of the divine rewards for justice
and the divine punishments for injustice, and various other
consequences. Adeimantos' long speech differs from Glaukon's because it brings out the fact that if justice is to be
choiceworthy for its own sake, it must be easy or pleasant.[9]
Glaukon's and Adeimantos' demands establish the standard
by which one must judge Socrates' praise of justice; they
force one to investigate whether or to what extent Socrates
has proved in the *Republic* that justice is choiceworthy for
its own sake or pleasant or even by itself sufficient to make
a man perfectly happy in the midst of what is ordinarily
believed to be the most extreme misery.

In order to defend the cause of justice, Socrates turns to
founding, together with Glaukon and Adeimantos, a city in
speech. The reason why this procedure is necessary can be
stated as follows. Justice is believed to be law-abidingness or
the firm will to give to everyone what belongs to him, i.e.,

9. Cf. *ibid.*, 364a, c–d, 365c with 357b and 358a.

what belongs to him according to law; yet justice is also
believed to be good or salutary; but obedience to the laws
or giving to everyone what belongs to him according to law
is not unqualifiedly salutary since the laws may be bad;
justice will be simply salutary only when the laws are good,
and this requires that the regime from which the laws flow
is good: justice will be fully salutary only in a good city.
Socrates' procedure implies, furthermore, that he knows of
no actual city which is good; this is the reason why he is
compelled to found a good city. He justifies his turning
to the city by the consideration that justice can be detected
more easily in the city than in the human individual because the former is larger than the latter; he thus implies
that there is a parallelism between the city and the human
individual or, more precisely, between the city and the soul
of the human individual. This means that the parallelism
between the city and the human individual is based upon
a certain abstraction from the human body. To the extent
to which there is a parallelism between the city and the
human individual or his soul, the city is at least similar to
a natural being. Yet that parallelism is not complete. While
the city and the individual seem equally to be able to be
just, it is not certain that they can be equally happy (cf.
the beginning of the fourth book). The distinction between
the justice of the individual and his happiness was prepared
by Glaukon's demand on Socrates that justice should be
praised regardless of whether or not it has any extraneous
attractions. It is also prepared by the common opinion
according to which justice requires complete dedication of
the individual to the common good.

The founding of the good city takes place in three stages:
the healthy city or the city of pigs, the purified city or the
city of the armed camp, and the City of Beauty or the city
ruled by philosophers.

The founding of the city is preceded by the remark that
the city has its origin in human need: every human being,
just or unjust, is in need of many things, and at least for

this reason in need of other human beings. The healthy city satisfies properly the primary needs, the needs of the body. The proper satisfaction requires that each man exercise only one art. This means that everyone does almost all his work for others but also that the others work for him. All will exchange with one another their own products as their own products: there will be private property; by working for the advantage of others everyone works for his own advantage. The reason why everyone will exercise only one art is that men differ from one another by nature, i.e., different men are gifted for different arts. Since everyone will exercise that art for which he is by nature fitted, the burden will be easier on everyone. The healthy city is a happy city: it knows no poverty, no coercion or government, no war and eating of animals. It is happy in such a way that every member of it is happy: it does not need government because there is perfect harmony between everyone's service and his reward; no one encroaches on anyone else. It does not need government because everyone chooses by himself the art for which he is best fitted; there is no disharmony between natural gifts and preferences. There is also no disharmony between what is good for the individual (his choosing the art for which he is best fitted by nature) and what is good for the city: nature has so arranged things that there is no surplus of blacksmiths or deficit of shoemakers. The healthy city is happy because it is just, and it is just because it is happy; in the healthy city, justice is easy or pleasant and free from any tincture of self-sacrifice. It is just without anyone's concerning himself with its justice; it is just by nature. Nevertheless, it is found wanting. It is impossible for the same reason that anarchism in general is impossible. Anarchism would be possible if men could remain innocent, but it is of the essence of innocence that it is easily lost; men can be just only through knowledge, and men cannot acquire knowledge without effort and without antagonism. Differently stated, while the healthy city is just in a sense, it lacks virtue or excellence: such justice as it possesses is not virtue. Virtue is impossible without toil, effort, or repression of the evil in oneself. The healthy city is a city in which evil is only dormant. Death is mentioned only when the transition from the healthy city to the next stage has already begun.[10] The healthy city is called a city of pigs not by Socrates but by Glaukon. Glaukon does not quite know what he says. Literally speaking, the healthy city is a city without pigs.[11]

Before the purified city can emerge or rather be established, the healthy city must have decayed. Its decay is brought about by the emancipation of the desire for unnecessary things, i.e., for things which are not necessary for the well-being or health of the body. Thus the luxurious or feverish city emerges, the city characterized by the striving for the unlimited acquisition of wealth. One can expect that in such a city the individuals will no longer exercise the single art for which each is meant by nature but any art or combination of arts which is most lucrative, or that there will no longer be a strict correspondence between service and reward: hence there will be dissatisfaction and conflicts and therefore need for government which will restore justice; hence there will be need for something else which also was entirely absent from the healthy city, i.e., education at least of the rulers, and more particularly education to justice. There will certainly be need for additional territory and hence there will be war, war of aggression. Building on the principle "one man one art," Socrates demands that the army consist of men who have no art other than that of warriors. It appears that the art of the warriors or of the guardians is by far superior to the other arts. Hitherto it looked as if all arts were of equal rank and the only universal art, or the only art accompanying all arts, was the art of money-making.[12] Now we receive the first glimpse of the true order of arts. That order is hier-

10. *Ibid.,* 372d.
11. *Ibid.,* 370d–e, 373c.
12. *Ibid.,* 342a–b, 346c.

archic; the universal art is the highest art, the art directing all other arts, which as such cannot be practiced by the practitioners of arts other than the highest. This art of arts will prove to be philosophy. For the time being we are told only that the warrior must have a nature resembling the nature of that philosophic beast, the dog. For the warriors must be spirited, and hence irascible and harsh, on the one hand and gentle on the other, since they must be harsh toward strangers and gentle to their fellow citizens. They must have a disinterested liking for their fellow citizens and a disinterested dislike for foreigners. The men possessing such special natures need in addition a special education. With a view to their work they need training in the art of war. But this is not the education with which Socrates is chiefly concerned. They will be by nature the best fighters and the only ones armed and trained in arms: they will inevitably be the sole possessors of political power. Besides, the age of innocence having gone, evil is rampant in the city and therefore also in the warriors. The education which the warriors more than anyone else need is therefore above all education in civic virtue. That education is "music" education, education especially through poetry and music. Not all poetry and music is apt to make men good citizens in general and good warriors or guardians in particular. Therefore the poetry and music not conducive to this moral-political end must be banished from the city. Socrates is very far from demanding that Homer and Sophocles should be replaced by the makers of edifying trash; the poetry which he demands for the good city must be genuinely poetic. He demands particularly that the gods be presented as models of human excellence, i.e., of the kind of human excellence to which the guardians can and must aspire. The rulers will be taken from among the elite of the guardians. Yet the prescribed education, however excellent and effective, is not sufficient if it is not buttressed by the right kind of institutions, i.e., by absolute communism or by the completest possible abolition of privacy: everyone may enter everyone else's dwelling at will. As reward for their service to the craftsmen proper, the guardians do not receive money of any kind but only a sufficient amount of food, and, we may suppose, of the other necessities.

Let us see in what way the good city as hitherto described reveals that justice is good or even attractive for its own sake. That justice, or the observing of the just proportion between service and reward, between working for others and one's own advantage, is necessary was shown in the discussion with Thrasymachos by the example of the gang of robbers. The education of the guardians as agreed upon between Socrates and Adeimantos is not education to justice.[13] It is education to courage and moderation. The music education in particular, as distinguished from the gymnastic education, is education to moderation, and this means to love of the beautiful, i.e., of what is by nature attractive in itself. Justice in the narrow and strict sense may be said to flow from moderation or from the proper combination of moderation and courage. Socrates thus silently makes clear the difference between the gang of robbers and the good city: the essential difference consists in the fact that the armed and ruling part of the good city is animated by love of the beautiful, by the love of everything praiseworthy and graceful. The difference is not to be sought in the fact that the good city is guided in its relations to other cities, Greek or barbarian, by considerations of justice: the size of the territory of the good city is determined by that city's own moderate needs and by nothing else.[14] The difficulty appears perhaps more clearly from what Socrates says when speaking of the rulers. In addition to the other required qualities, the rulers must have the quality of caring for the city or loving the city; but a man is most likely to love that whose interest he believes to be identical with his own interest or whose happiness he believes to be the condition of his own happiness. The love

13. *Ibid.,* 392a–c.
14. *Ibid.,* 423b; cf. also 398a and 422d.

here mentioned is not obviously disinterested in the sense that the ruler loves the city, or his serving the city, for its own sake. This may explain why Socrates demands that the rulers be honored both while they live and after their death.[15] At any rate the highest degree of caring for the city and for one another will not be forthcoming unless everyone is brought to believe in the falsehood that all fellow citizens, and only they, are brothers.[16] To say the least, the harmony between self-interest and the interest of the city, which was lost with the decay of the healthy city, has not yet been restored. No wonder then that at the beginning of the fourth book Adeimantos expresses his dissatisfaction with the condition of the soldiers in the city of the armed camp. Read within the context of the whole argument, Socrates' reply is to this effect: only as a member of a happy city can a man be happy; only within these limits can a man, or any other part of the city, be happy; complete dedication to the happy city is justice. It remains to be seen whether complete dedication to the happy city is, or can be, happiness of the individual.

After the founding of the good city is in the main completed, Socrates and his friends turn to seeking where in it justice and injustice are, and whether the man who is to be happy must possess justice or injustice.[17] They look first for the three virtues other than justice (wisdom, courage, and moderation). In the city which is founded according to nature, wisdom resides in the rulers and in the rulers alone, for the wise men are by nature the smallest part of any city, and it would not be good for the city if they were not the only ones at its helm. In the good city, courage resides in the warrior class, for political courage, as distinguished from brutish fearlessness, arises only through education in those by nature fitted for it. Moderation on the other hand is to be found in all parts of the good city. In the present

15. *Ibid.,* 414a, 465d–466c; cf. 346e ff.
16. *Ibid.,* 415b.
17. *Ibid.,* 427d.

context, moderation does not mean exactly what it meant when the education of the warriors was discussed, but rather the control of what is by nature worse by that which is by nature better—that control through which the whole is in harmony. In other words, moderation is the agreement of the naturally superior and inferior as to which of the two ought to rule in the city. Since controlling and being controlled differ, one must assume that the moderation of the rulers is not identical with the moderation of the ruled. While Socrates and Glaukon found the three virtues mentioned in the good city with ease, it is difficult to find justice in it because, as Socrates says, justice is so obvious in it. Justice consists in everyone's doing the one thing pertaining to the city for which his nature is best fitted or, simply, in everyone's minding his own business: it is by virtue of justice thus understood that the other three virtues are virtues.[18] More precisely, a city is just if each of its three parts (the money-makers, the warriors, and the rulers) does its own work and only its own work.[19] Justice is then, like moderation and unlike wisdom and courage, not a preserve of a single part but required of every part. Hence justice, like moderation, has a different character in each of the three classes. One must assume, for instance, that the justice of the wise rulers is affected by their wisdom and the justice of the money-makers is affected by their lack of wisdom, for if even the courage of the warriors is only political or civic courage, and not courage pure and simple,[20] it stands to reason that their justice too—to say nothing of the justice of the money-makers—will not be justice pure and simple. In order to discover justice pure and simple, it then becomes necessary to consider justice in the individual man. This consideration would be easiest if justice in the individual were identical with justice in the city; this would require that the individual or rather his

18. *Ibid.,* 433a–b.
19. *Ibid.,* 434c.
20. *Ibid.,* 430c; cf. *Phaedo* 82a.

soul consist of the same three kinds of "natures" as the city. A very provisional consideration of the soul seems to establish this requirement: the soul contains desire, spiritedness or anger,[21] and reason, just as the city consists of the money-makers, the warriors, and the rulers. Hence we may conclude that a man is just if each of these three parts of his soul does its own work and only its own work, i.e., if his soul is in a state of health. But if justice is health of the soul, and conversely injustice is disease of the soul, it is obvious that justice is good and injustice is bad, regardless of whether or not one is known to be just or unjust.[22] A man is just if the rational part in him is wise and rules,[23] and if the spirited part, being the subject and ally of the rational part, assists it in controlling the multitude of desires which almost inevitably become desires for more and ever more money. This means, however, that only the man in whom wisdom rules the two other parts, i.e., only the wise man, can be truly just.[24] No wonder then that the just man eventually proves to be identical with the philosopher.[25] The money-makers and the warriors are not truly just even in the just city because their justice derives exclusively from habituation of one kind or another as distinguished from philosophy; hence in the deepest recesses of their souls they long for tyranny, i.e., for complete injustice.[26] We see then how right Socrates was when he expected to find injustice in the good city.[27] This is not to deny, of course, that as members of the good city the non-philosophers will act much more justly than they would as members of inferior cities.

The justice of those who are not wise appears in a different light when justice in the city is being considered,

21. *Republic* 441a–c.
22. *Ibid.*, 444d–445b.
23. *Ibid.*, 441e.
24. Cf. *ibid.*, 442c.
25. *Ibid.*, 580d–583b.
26. *Ibid.*, 619b–d.
27. *Ibid.*, 427d.

on the one hand, and justice in the soul on the other. This fact shows that the parallelism between the city and the soul is defective. This parallelism requires that, just as in the city the warriors occupy a higher rank than the money-makers, so in the soul spiritedness occupy a higher rank than desire. It is very plausible that those who uphold the city against foreign and domestic enemies and who have received a music education deserve higher respect than those who lack public responsibility as well as a music education. But it is much less plausible that spiritedness as such should deserve higher respect than desire as such. It is true that "spiritedness" includes a large variety of phenomena ranging from the most noble indignation about injustice, turpitude, and meanness down to the anger of a spoiled child who resents being deprived of anything that he desires, however bad. But the same is also true of "desire": one kind of desire is *eros,* which ranges in its healthy forms from the longing for immortality, via offspring through the longing for immortality via immortal fame, to the longing for immortality via participation by knowledge in the things which are unchangeable in every respect. The assertion that spiritedness is higher in rank than desire as such is then questionable. Let us never forget that while there is a philosophic *eros,* there is no philosophic spiritedness;[28] or in other words that Thrasymachos is much more visibly spiritedness incarnate than desire incarnate. The assertion in question is based on a deliberate abstraction from *eros*—an abstraction characteristic of the *Republic.*

This abstraction shows itself most strikingly in two facts: when Socrates mentions the fundamental needs which give rise to human society, he is silent about the need for procreation, and when he describes the tyrant, Injustice incarnate, he presents him as *Eros* incarnate.[29] In the thematic discussion of the respective rank of spiritedness and desire,

28. Cf. *ibid.,* 366c.
29. *Ibid.,* 573b–e, 574e–575a.

he is silent about *eros*.[30] It seems that there is a tension between *eros* and the city and hence between *eros* and justice: only through the depreciation of *eros* can the city come into its own. *Eros* obeys its own laws, not the laws of the city however good; in the good city, *eros* is simply subjected to what the city requires. The good city requires that all love of one's own—all spontaneous love of one's own parents, one's own children, one's own friends and beloved —be sacrificed to the common love of the common. As far as possible, the love of one's own must be abolished except as it is love of the city as this particular city, as one's own city. As far as possible, patriotism takes the place of *eros,* and patriotism has a closer kinship to spiritedness, eagerness to fight, "waspishness," anger, and indignation than to *eros*.

While it is harmful to one's soul to jump at Plato's throat because he is not a liberal democrat, it is also bad to blur the difference between Platonism and liberal democracy, for the premises "Plato is admirable" and "liberal democracy is admirable" do not legitimately lead to the conclusion that Plato was a liberal democrat. The founding of the good city started from the fact that men are by nature different, and this proved to mean that men are by nature of unequal rank. They are unequal particularly with regard to their ability to acquire virtue. The inequality which is due to nature is increased and deepened by the different kinds of education or habituation and the different ways of life (communistic or noncommunistic) which the different parts of the good city enjoy. As a result, the good city comes to resemble a caste society. A Platonic character who hears an account of the good city of the *Republic* is reminded by it of the caste system established in ancient Egypt, although it is quite clear that in Egypt the rulers were priests and not philosophers.[31] Certainly in

30. Cf. *ibid.*, 439d.
31. *Timaeus* 24a–b.

the good city of the *Republic,* not descent but, in the first
place, everyone's own natural gifts determine to which class
he belongs. But this leads to a difficulty. The members of
the upper class, which lives communistically, are not supposed to know who their natural parents are, for they are
supposed to regard all men and women belonging to the
older generation as their parents. On the other hand, the
gifted children of the noncommunist lower class are to
be transferred to the upper class (and vice versa); since their
superior gifts are not necessarily recognizable at the moment of their birth, they are likely to come to know their
natural parents and even to become attached to them; this
would seem to unfit them for transfer to the upper class.
There are two ways in which this difficulty can be removed.
The first is to extend absolute communism to the lower
class; and, considering the connection between way of life
and education, also to extend music education to that
class.[32] According to Aristotle,[33] Socrates has left it undecided whether in the good city absolute communism is limited to the upper class or extends also to the lower class.
To leave this question undecided would be in agreement
with Socrates' professed low opinion of the importance of
the lower class.[34] Still, there can be only little doubt that
Socrates wishes to limit both communism and music education to the upper class.[35] Therefore, in order to remove
the difficulty mentioned, he can hardly avoid making an
individual's membership in the upper or lower class hereditary and thus violating one of the most elementary principles of justice. Apart from this, one may wonder whether a
perfectly clear line between those gifted and those not
gifted for the profession of warriors can be drawn, hence
whether a perfectly just assignment of individuals to the
upper or lower class is possible, and hence whether the

32. *Republic* 401b–c, 421e–422d, 460a, 543a.
33. *Politics* 1264a 13–17.
34. *Republic* 421a, 434a.
35. *Ibid.,* 415e, 431b–c, 456d.

good city can be perfectly just.[36] But be this as it may, if communism is limited to the upper class, there will be privacy both in the money-making class and among the philosophers as philosophers, for there may very well be only a single philosopher in the city and surely never a herd: the warriors are the only class which is entirely political or public or entirely dedicated to the city; the warriors alone present therefore the clearest case of the just life in one sense of the word "just."

It is necessary to understand the reason why communism is limited to the upper class or what the natural obstacle to communism is. That which is by nature private or a man's own is the body and only the body.[37] The needs or desires of the body induce men to extend the sphere of the private, of what is each man's own, as far as they can. This most powerful striving is countered by music education which brings about moderation, i.e., a most severe training of the soul of which, it seems, only a minority of men is capable. Yet this kind of education does not extirpate the natural desire of each for things or human beings of his own: the warriors will not accept absolute communism if they are not subject to the philosophers. It thus becomes clear that the striving for one's own is countered ultimately only by philosophy, by the quest for the truth which, as such, cannot be anyone's private possession. Whereas the private par excellence is the body, the common par excellence is the mind, the pure mind rather than the soul in general. The superiority of communism to noncommunism as taught in the *Republic* is intelligible only as a reflection of the superiority of philosophy to nonphilosophy. This clearly contradicts the result of the preceding paragraph. The contradiction can and must be resolved by the distinction between two meanings of justice. This distinction cannot become clear before one has understood the teaching of

36. Reconsider *ibid.*, 427d.
37. *Ibid.*, 464d; cf. *Laws* 739c.

the *Republic* regarding the relation of philosophy and the city. We must therefore make a new beginning.

At the end of the fourth book, it look as if Socrates had completed the task which Glaukon and Adeimantos had imposed on him, for he had shown that justice as health of the soul is desirable not only because of its consequences but above all for its own sake. But then, at the beginning of the fifth book, we are suddenly confronted by a new start, by the repetition of a scene which had occurred at the very beginning. Both at the very beginning and at the beginning of the fifth book (and nowhere else), Socrates' companions make a decision, nay, take a vote, and Socrates, who had no share in the decision, obeys it.[38] Socrates' companions behave in both cases like a city (an assembly of the citizens), if the smallest possible city.[39] But there is this decisive difference between the two scenes: whereas Thrasymachos was absent from the first scene, he has become a member of the city in the second scene. It could seem that the foundation of the good city requires that Thrasymachos be converted into one of its citizens.

At the beginning of the fifth book, Socrates' companions force him to take up the subject of communism in regard to women and children. They do not object to the proposal itself in the way in which Adeimantos had objected to the communism regarding property at the beginning of the fourth book, for even Adeimantos is no longer the same man he was at that time. They only wish to know the precise manner in which the communism regarding women and children is to be managed. Socrates replaces that question by these more incisive questions: (1) Is that communism possible? (2) Is it desirable? It appears that the communism regarding women is the consequence or presupposition of the equality of the two sexes concerning the work they must do: the city cannot afford to lose half of its adult population from its working and fighting force, and there is no

38. Cf. *Republic* 449b–450a with 327b–328b.
39. Cf. *ibid.*, 369d.

essential difference between men and women regarding natural gifts for the various arts. The demand for equality of the two sexes requires a complete upheaval of custom, an upheaval which is here presented less as shocking than as laughable; the demand is justified on the ground that only the useful is fair or noble and that only what is bad, i.e., against nature, is laughable: the customary difference of conduct between the two sexes is rejected as being against nature, and the revolutionary change is meant to bring about the order according to nature.[40] For justice requires that every human being should practice the art for which he or she is fitted by nature, regardless of what custom or convention may dictate. Socrates shows first that the equality of the two sexes is possible, i.e., in agreement with the nature of the two sexes as their nature appears when viewed with regard to aptitude for the practice of the various arts, and then he shows that it is desirable. In proving this possibility, he explicitly abstracts from the difference between the two sexes in regard to procreation.[41] This means that the argument of the *Republic* as a whole, according to which the city is a community of male and female artisans, abstracts to the highest degree possible from the highest activity essential to the city which takes place "by nature" and not "by art."

Socrates then turns to the communism regarding women and children and shows that it is desirable because it will make the city more "one," and hence more perfect, than a city consisting of separate families would be: the city should be as similar as possible to a single human being or to a single living body, i.e., to a natural being.[42] At this point we understand somewhat better why Socrates started his discussion of justice by assuming an important parallelism between the city and the individual: he was thinking ahead of the greatest possible unity of the city. The abolition of

40. *Ibid.*, 455d–e, 456b–c.
41. *Ibid.*, 455c–e.
42. *Ibid.*, 462c–d, 464b.

the family does not mean, of course, the introduction of license or promiscuity; it means the most severe regulation of sexual intercourse from the point of view of what is useful for the city or what is required for the common good. The consideration of the useful, one might say, supersedes the consideration of the holy or sacred:[43] human males and females are to be coupled with exclusive regard to the production of the best offspring, in the spirit in which the breeders of dogs, birds, and horses proceed; the claims of *eros* are simply silenced. The new order naturally affects the customary prohibitions against incest, the most sacred rules of customary justice.[44] In the new scheme, no one will know any more his natural parents, children, brothers, and sisters, but everyone will *regard* all men of the older generation as his fathers and mothers, of his own generation as his brothers and sisters, and of the younger generation as his children.[45] This means, however, that the city constructed according to nature lives in a most important respect more according to convention than according to nature. For this reason we are disappointed to see that, while Socrates takes up the question of whether communism regarding women and children is possible, he drops it immediately.[46] Since the institution under consideration is indispensable for the good city, Socrates thus leaves open the question of the possibility of the good city, i.e., of the just city, as such. And this happens to his listeners and to the readers of the *Republic* after they have made the greatest sacrifices—such as the sacrifice of *eros* as well as of the family—for the sake of the just city.

Socrates is not for long allowed to escape from his awesome duty to answer the question regarding the possibility of the just city. The manly Glaukon compels him to face that question. Perhaps we should say that by apparently

43. Cf. *ibid.*, 458e.
44. Cf. *ibid.*, 461b–e.
45. *Ibid.*, 463c.
46. *Ibid.*, 466d.

escaping to the subject of war—a subject both easier in itself and more attractive to Glaukon than the communism of women and children—yet treating that subject according to the stern demands of justice and thus depriving it of much of its attractiveness, he compels Glaukon to compel him to return to the fundamental question. Be this as it may, the question to which Socrates and Glaukon return is not the same one which they left. The question which they left was whether the good city is possible in the sense that it is in agreement with human nature. The question to which they return is whether the good city is possible in the sense that it can be brought into being by the transformation of an actual city.[47] The latter question might be thought to presuppose the affirmative answer to the first question, but this is not quite correct. As we learn now, our whole effort to discover what justice is (so that we would be enabled to see how it is related to happiness) was a quest for "justice itself" as a "pattern." By seeking for justice itself as a pattern we implied that the just man and the just city will not be perfectly just but will indeed approximate justice itself with particular closeness;[48] only justice itself is perfectly just.[49] This implies that not even the characteristic institutions of the just city (absolute communism, equality of the sexes, and the rule of the philosophers) are simply just. Now justice itself is not "possible" in the sense that it is capable of coming into being, because it "is" always without being capable of undergoing any change whatever. Justice is an "idea" or "form," one of many "ideas." Ideas are the only things which strictly speaking "are," i.e., are without any admixture of nonbeing, because they are beyond all becoming, and whatever is becoming is between being and nonbeing. Since the ideas are the only things which are beyond all change, they are in a sense the cause of all change and all changeable things.

47. *Ibid.*, 473b–c.
48. *Ibid.*, 472b–c.
49. *Ibid.*, 479a; cf. 538c ff.

For example, the idea of justice is the cause for anything (human beings, cities, laws, commands, actions) becoming just. They are self-subsisting beings which subsist always. They are of utmost splendor. For instance, the idea of justice is perfectly just. But their splendor escapes the eyes of the body. The ideas are "visible" only to the eye of the mind, and the mind as mind perceives nothing but ideas. Yet, as is indicated by the facts that there are many ideas and that the mind which perceives the ideas is radically different from the ideas themselves, there must be something higher than the ideas: "the good" or "the idea of the good" which is in a sense the cause of all ideas as well as of the mind perceiving them.[50] It is only through perception of "the good" on the part of the human beings who are by nature equipped for perceiving it that the good city can come into being and subsist for a while.

The doctrine of ideas which Socrates expounds to Glaukon is very hard to understand; to begin with, it is utterly incredible, not to say that it appears to be fantastic. Hitherto we have been given to understand that justice is fundamentally a certain character of the human soul, or of the city, i.e., something which is not self-subsisting. Now we are asked to believe that it is self-subsisting, being at home as it were in an entirely different place than human beings and everything else that participates in justice.[51] No one has ever succeeded in giving a satisfactory or clear account of this doctrine of ideas. It is possible, however, to define rather precisely the central difficulty. "Idea" means primarily the looks or shape of a thing; it means then a kind or class of things which are united by the fact that they all possess the same "looks," i.e., the same character and power, or the same "nature"; therewith it means the class-character or the nature of the things belonging to the class in question: the "idea" of a thing is that which we mean by trying to find out the "what" or the "nature" of a thing or a class

---

50. *Ibid.*, 517c.
51. Cf. *ibid.*, 509b–510a.

of things. The connection between "idea" and "nature" appears in the *Republic* from the facts that "the idea of justice" is called "that which is just by nature," and that the ideas, in contradistinction to the things which are not ideas or to the sensibly perceived things, are said to be "in nature."[52] This does not explain, however, why the ideas are presented as "separated" from the things which are what they are by participating in an idea or, in other words, why "dogness" (the class character of dogs) should be "the true dog." It seems that two kinds of phenomena lend support to Socrates' assertion. In the first place the mathematical things as such can never be found among sensible things: no line drawn on sand or paper is a line as meant by the mathematician. Secondly and above all, what we mean by justice and kindred things is not as such, in its purity or perfection, necessarily found in human beings or societies; it rather seems that what is meant by justice transcends everything which men can ever achieve; precisely the justest men were and are the ones most aware of the shortcomings of their justice. Socrates seems to say that what is patently true of mathematical things and of the virtues is true universally: there is an idea of the bed or the table just as of the circle and of justice. Now while it is obviously reasonable to say that a perfect circle or perfect justice transcends everything which can ever be seen, it is hard to say that the perfect bed is something on which no man can ever rest. However this may be, Glaukon and Adeimantos accept this doctrine of ideas with relative ease, with greater ease than absolute communism. This paradoxical fact does not strike us with sufficient force because we somehow believe that these able young men study philosophy under Professor Socrates and have heard him expound the doctrine of ideas on innumerable occasions, if we do not believe that the *Republic* is a philosophic treatise addressed to readers familiar with more elementary (or "earlier") dialogues. Yet Plato ad-

52. *Ibid.,* 501b; 597b–d.

dresses the readers of the *Republic* only through the medium of Socrates' conversation with Glaukon and the other interlocutors in the *Republic,* and Plato as the author of the *Republic* does not suggest that Glaukon—to say nothing of Adeimantos and the rest—has seriously studied the doctrine of ideas.[53] Yet while Glaukon and Adeimantos cannot be credited with a genuine understanding of the doctrine of ideas, they have heard, and in a way they know, that there are gods like *Dike* or Right,[54] and *Nike* or Victory, who is not this or that victory or this or that statue of Nike but a self-subsisting being which is the cause of every victory and which is of unbelievable splendor. More generally, they know that there are gods—self-subsisting beings which are the causes of everything good, which are of unbelievable splendor, and which cannot be apprehended by the senses since they never change their "form."[55] This is not to deny that there is a profound difference between the gods as understood in the "theology"[56] of the *Republic* and the ideas, or that in the *Republic* the gods are in a way replaced by the ideas. It is merely to assert that those who accept that theology and draw all conclusions from it are likely to arrive at the doctrine of ideas.

We must now return to the question of the possibility of the just city. We have learned that justice itself is not "possible" in the sense that anything which comes into being can ever be perfectly just. We learn immediately afterward that not only justice itself but also the just city is not "possible" in the sense indicated. This does not mean that the just city as meant and as sketched in the *Republic* is an idea like "justice itself," and still less that it is an "ideal": "ideal" is not a Platonic term. The just city is not a self-subsisting being like the idea of justice, located so to speak

53. Cf. *ibid.,* 507a–c with 596a and 532c–d, contrast with *Phaedo* 65d and 74a–b.
54. *Republic* 536b; cf. 487a.
55. Cf. *ibid.,* 379a–b and 380d ff.
56. *Ibid.,* 379a.

in a superheavenly place. Its status is rather like that of a painting of a perfectly beautiful human being, i.e., it is only by virtue of the painter's painting; more precisely, the just city is only "in speech": it "is" only by virtue of having been figured out with a view to justice itself or to what is by nature right on the one hand and the human all-too-human on the other. Although the just city is decidedly of lower rank than justice itself, even the just city as a pattern is not capable of coming into being as it has been blue-printed; only approximations to it can be expected in cities which are in deed and not merely in speech.[57] What this means is not clear. Does it mean that the best feasible solution will be a compromise so that we must become reconciled to a certain degree of private property (e.g., that we must permit every warrior to keep his shoes and the like as long as he lives) and a certain degree of inequality of the sexes (e.g., that certain military and administrative functions will remain the preserve of the male warriors)? There is no reason to suppose that this is what Socrates meant. In the light of the succeeding part of the conversation, the following suggestion would seem to be more plausible. The assertion according to which the just city cannot come into being as blueprinted is provisional, or prepares the assertion that the just city, while capable of coming into being, is very unlikely to come into being. At any rate, immediately after having declared that only an approximation to the good city can reasonably be expected, Socrates raises the question: What feasible change in the actual cities will be the necessary and sufficient condition of their transformation into good cities? His answer is, the "coincidence" of political power and philosophy: the philosophers must rule as kings, or the kings must genuinely and adequately philosophize. As we have shown in our summary of the first book of the *Republic,* this answer is not altogether surprising. If justice is less the giving or leaving to each what the law assigns to him than the giving or

57. *Ibid.,* 472c–473a; cf. 500c–501c with 484c–d and 592b.

leaving to each what is good for his soul, but what is good for his soul is the virtues, it follows that no one can be truly just who does not know "the virtues themselves," or, generally, the ideas, or who is not a philosopher.

By answering the question of how the good city is possible, Socrates introduces philosophy as a theme of the *Republic*. This means that in the *Republic,* philosophy is not introduced as the end of man, the end for which man should live, but as a means for realizing the just city, the city as armed camp which is characterized by absolute communism and equality of the sexes in the upper class, the class of warriors. Since the rule of philosophers is not introduced as an ingredient of the just city but only as a means for its realization, Aristotle is justified in disregarding this institution in his critical analysis of the *Republic (Politics* II). At any rate, Socrates succeeds in reducing the question of the possibility of the just city to the question of the possibility of the coincidence of philosophy and political power. That such a coincidence should be possible is, to begin with, most incredible: everyone can see that the philosophers are useless if not even harmful in politics. Socrates, who had some experiences of his own with the city of Athens—experiences to be crowned by his capital punishment—regards this accusation of the philosophers as well-founded, although in need of deeper exploration. He traces the antagonism of the cities toward the philosophers primarily to the cities: the present cities, i.e., the cities not ruled by philosophers, are like assemblies of madmen which corrupt most of those fit to become philosophers, and on which those who have succeeded against all odds in becoming philosophers rightly turn their back in disgust. But Socrates is far from absolving the philosophers altogether. Only a radical change on the part of both the cities and the philosophers can bring about that harmony between them for which they seem to be meant by nature. The change consists precisely in this: that the cities cease to be unwilling to be ruled by philosophers and the philosophers cease to be unwilling to rule the cities. This coincidence of philosophy and political power is very difficult to achieve, very improbable, but not impossible. To bring about the needed change on the part of the city, of the nonphilosophers or the multitude, the right kind of persuasion is necessary and sufficient. The right kind of persuasion is supplied by the art of persuasion, the art of Thrasymachos directed by the philosopher and in the service of philosophy. No wonder then that in our context Socrates declares that he and Thrasymachos have just become friends. The multitude of the nonphilosophers is good-natured and therefore persuadable by the philosophers.[58] But if this is so, why did not the philosophers of old, to say nothing of Socrates himself, succeed in persuading the multitude of the supremacy of philosophy and the philosophers, and thus bring about the rule of philosophers and therewith the salvation and the happiness of their cities? Strange as it may sound, in this part of the argument it appears to be easier to persuade the multitude to accept the rule of the philosophers than to persuade the philosophers to rule the multitude: the philosophers cannot be persuaded—they can only be compelled to rule the cities.[59] Only the nonphilosophers could compel the philosophers to take care of the cities. But, given the prejudice against the philosophers, this compulsion will not be forthcoming if the philosophers do not in the first place persuade the nonphilosophers to compel the philosophers to rule over them, and this persuasion will not be forthcoming, given the philosophers' unwillingness to rule. We arrive then at the conclusion that the just city is not possible because of the philosophers' unwillingness to rule.

Why are the philosophers unwilling to rule? Being dominated by the desire for knowledge as the one thing needful, or knowing that philosophy is the most pleasant and blessed possession, the philosophers have no leisure for looking

58. *Ibid.*, 498c–502a.
59. *Ibid.*, 499b–c, 500d, 520a–d, 521b, 539e.

down at human affairs, let alone for taking care of them.[60] The philosophers believe that while still alive they are already firmly settled, far away from their cities, in the Isles of the Blessed.[61] Hence only compulsion could induce them to take part in political life in the just city, i.e., in the city which regards the proper upbringing of the philosophers as its most important task. Having perceived the truly grand, the human things appear to the philosophers to be paltry. The very justice of the philosophers—their abstaining from wronging their fellow human beings—flows from contempt for the things for which the nonphilosophers hotly contest.[62] They know that the life not dedicated to philosophy and therefore in particular the political life is like life in a cave, so much so that the city can be identified with the Cave.[63] The cave dwellers (i.e., the nonphilosophers) see only the shadows of artifacts.[64] That is to say, whatever they perceive they understand in the light of their opinions, sanctified by the fiat of legislators, regarding the just and noble things, i.e., of conventional opinions, and they do not know that these their most cherished convictions possess no higher status than that of opinions. For if even the best city stands or falls by a fundamental falsehood, although a noble falsehood, it can be expected that the opinions on which the imperfect cities rest, or in which they believe, will not be true. Precisely the best of the nonphilosophers, the good citizens, are passionately attached to these opinions and therefore violently opposed to philosophy,[65] which is the attempt to go beyond opinion toward knowledge: the multitude is not as persuadable by the philosophers as we sanguinely assumed in an earlier round of the argument. This is the true reason why the coincidence

60. *Ibid.,* 485a, 501b–c, 517c.
61. *Ibid.,* 519c.
62. *Ibid.,* 486a–b.
63. *Ibid.,* 539e.
64. *Ibid.,* 514b–515c.
65. *Ibid.,* 517a.

of philosophy and political power is, to say the least, extremely improbable: philosophy and the city tend away from one another in opposite directions.

The difficulty of overcoming the natural tension between the city and the philosophers is indicated by Socrates' turning from the question of whether the just city is "possible" in the sense of being conformable to human nature to the question of whether the just city is "possible" in the sense of being capable of being brought to light by the transformation of an actual city. The first question, understood in contradistinction to the second, points to the question whether the just city could not come into being through the settling together of men who had been wholly unassociated before. It is to this question that Socrates tacitly gives a negative answer by turning to the question of whether the just city could be brought into being by the transformation of an actual city. The good city cannot be brought to light out of human beings who have not yet undergone any human discipline, out of "primitives" or "stupid animals" or "savages," gentle or cruel; its potential members must already have acquired the rudiments of civilized life. The long process through which primitive men become civilized men cannot be the work of the founder or legislator of the good city but is presupposed by him.[66] But on the other hand, if the potential good city must be an old city, its citizens will have been thoroughly molded by their city's imperfect laws or customs, hallowed by old age, and will have become passionately attached to them. Socrates is therefore compelled to revise his original suggestion according to which the rule of philosophers is the necessary and sufficient condition of the coming into being of the just city. Whereas he had originally suggested that the good city will come into being if the philosophers become kings, he finally suggests that the good city will come into being if, when the philosophers have become kings, they expel every-

66. Cf. *ibid.*, 376e.

one older than ten from the city, i.e., separate the children completely from their parents and their parents' ways and bring them up in the entirely novel ways of the good city.[67] By taking over a city, the philosophers make sure that their subjects will not be savages; by expelling everyone older than ten, they make sure that their subjects will not be enslaved by traditional civility. The solution is elegant. It leaves one wondering, however, how the philosophers can compel everyone older than ten to obey submissively the expulsion decree, since they cannot yet have trained a warrior class absolutely obedient to them. This is not to deny that Socrates could persuade many fine young men, and even some old ones, to believe that the multitude could be, not indeed compelled, but persuaded by the philosophers to leave their city and their children and to live in the fields so that justice will be done.

The part of the *Republic* which deals with philosophy is the most important part of the book. Accordingly, it transmits the answer to the question regarding justice to the extent to which that answer is given in the *Republic*. The explicit answer to the question of what justice is had been rather vague: justice consists in each part of the city or of the soul "doing the work for which it is by nature best fitted," or in a "kind" of doing that work; a part is just if it does its work or minds its own business "in a certain manner." The vagueness is removed if one replaces "in a certain manner" by "in the best manner" or "well": justice consists in each part doing its work well.[68] Hence the just man is the man in whom each part of the soul does its work well. Since the highest part of the soul is reason, and since this part cannot do its work well if the two other parts too do not do their work well, only the philosopher can be truly just. But the work which the philosopher does well is intrinsically attractive and in fact the most pleasant

67. *Ibid.,* 540d–541a; cf. 499b, 501a,e.

68. *Ibid.,* 433a–b and 443d; cf. Aristotle, *Nicomachean Ethics* 1098a 7–12.

work, wholly regardless of its consequences.[69] Hence only in philosophy do justice and happiness coincide. In other words, the philosopher is the only individual who is just in the sense in which the good city is just: he is self-sufficient, truly free, or his life is as little devoted to the service of other individuals as the life of the city is devoted to the service of other cities. But the philosopher in the good city is just also in the sense that he serves his fellow men, his fellow citizens, his city, or that he obeys the law. That is to say, the philosopher is just also in the sense in which all members of the just city, and in a way all just members of any city, regardless of whether they are philosophers or nonphilosophers, are just. Yet justice in this second sense is not intrinsically attractive or choiceworthy for its own sake, but is good only with a view to its consequences, or is not noble but necessary: the philosopher serves his city, even the good city, not, as he seeks the truth, from natural inclination, from *eros,* but under compulsion.[70] It is hardly necessary to add that compulsion does not cease to be compulsion if it is self-compulsion. According to a notion of justice which is more common than that suggested by Socrates' definition, justice consists in not harming others; justice thus understood proves to be in the highest case merely a concomitant of the philosopher's greatness of soul. But if justice is taken in the larger sense, according to which it consists in giving to each what is good for his soul, one must distinguish between the cases in which this giving is intrinsically attractive to the giver (these will be the cases of potential philosophers) and those in which it is merely a duty or compulsory. This distinction, incidentally, underlies the difference between the voluntary conversations of Socrates (the conversations which he spontaneously seeks) and the compulsory ones (those which he cannot with propriety avoid). This clear distinction between the justice which is choiceworthy for its own sake, wholly regardless of

69. Plato, *Republic* 583a.
70. *Ibid.,* 519e–520b; 540b,e.

its consequences, and identical with philosophy, and the justice which is merely necessary and identical in the highest case with the political activity of the philosopher is rendered possible by the abstraction from *eros* which is characteristic of the *Republic*. For one might well say that there is no reason why the philosopher should not engage in political activity out of that kind of love of one's own which is patriotism.[71]

By the end of the seventh book justice has come to sight fully. Socrates has in fact performed the duty laid upon him by Glaukon and Adeimantos to show that justice properly understood is choiceworthy for its own sake regardless of its consequences and therefore that justice is unqualifiedly preferable to injustice. Nevertheless the conversation continues, for it seems that our clear grasp of justice does not include a clear grasp of injustice, but must be supplemented by a clear grasp of the wholly unjust city and the wholly unjust man: only after we have seen the wholly unjust city and the wholly unjust man with the same clarity with which we have seen the wholly just city and the wholly just man will we be able to judge whether we ought to follow Socrates' friend Thrasymachos, who chooses injustice, or Socrates himself, who chooses justice.[72] This in its turn requires that the fiction of the possibility of the just city be maintained. As a matter of fact, the *Republic* never abandons the fiction that the just city as a society of human beings, as distinguished from a society of gods or sons of gods, is possible.[73] When Socrates turns to the study of injustice, it even becomes necessary for him to reaffirm this fiction with greater force than ever before. The unjust city will be uglier and more condemnable in proportion as the just city will be more possible. But the possibility of the just city will remain doubtful if the just city was never actual. Accordingly Socrates now asserts that

71. Consider *Apology of Socrates* 30a.
72. *Republic* 545a–b; cf. 498c–d.
73. *Laws* 739b–e.

the just city was once actual. More precisely, he makes the Muses assert it or rather imply it. The assertion that the just city was once actual is, as one might say, a mythical assertion which agrees with the mythical premise that the best is the oldest. Socrates asserts then through the mouth of the Muses that the good city was actual in the beginning, prior to the emergence of the inferior kinds of cities;[74] the inferior cities are decayed forms of the good city, soiled fragments of the pure city which was entire; hence the nearer in time a kind of inferior city is to the just city, the better it is, or vice versa. It is more proper to speak of the good and inferior regimes than of the good and inferior cities (observe the transition from "cities" to "regimes" in 543d–544a). "Regime" is our translation of the Greek *politeia*. The book which we call *Republic* is in Greek entitled *Politeia*. *Politeia* is commonly translated by "constitution." The term designates the form of government understood as the form of the city, i.e., as that which gives the city its character by determining the end which the city in question pursues or what it looks up to as the highest, and simultaneously the kind of men who rule the city. For instance, oligarchy is the kind of regime in which the rich rule and therefore admiration for wealth and for the acquisition of wealth animates the city as a whole, and democracy is the kind of regime in which all free men rule and therefore freedom is the end which the city pursues. According to Socrates, there are five kinds of regime: (1) kingdom or aristocracy, the rule of the best man or the best men, that is directed toward goodness or virtue, the regime of the just city; (2) timocracy, the rule of lovers of honor or of the ambitious men, which is directed toward superiority or victory; (3) oligarchy, or the rule of the rich, in which wealth is most highly esteemed; (4) democracy, the rule of free men, in which freedom is most highly esteemed; (5) tyranny, the rule of the completely unjust man, in which unqualified and unashamed injustice holds sway.

74. Cf. *Republic* 547b.

The descending order of the five kinds of regime is modeled on Hesiod's descending order of the five races of men: the races of gold, of silver, of bronze, the divine race of heroes, the race of iron.[75] We see at once that the Platonic equivalent of Hesiod's divine race of heroes is democracy. We shall soon see the reason for this seemingly strange correspondence.

The *Republic* is based on the assumption that there is a strict parallelism between the city and the soul. Accordingly Socrates asserts that, just as there are five kinds of regime, so there are five kinds of characters of men, the timocratic man, for instance, corresponding to timocracy. The distinction which for a short while was popular in present-day political science between the authoritarian and the democratic "personalities," as corresponding to the distinction between authoritarian and democratic societies, was a dim and crude reflection of Socrates' distinction between the royal or aristocratic, the timocratic, the oligarchic, the democratic, and the tyrannical soul or man, as corresponding to the aristocratic, timocratic, oligarchic, democratic, and tyrannical regimes. In this connection it should be mentioned that in describing the regimes, Socrates does not speak of "ideologies" belonging to them; he is concerned with the character of each kind of regime and with the end which it manifestly and explicitly pursues, as well as with the political justification of the end in question in contradistinction to any transpolitical justification stemming from cosmology, theology, metaphysics, philosophy of history, myth, and the like. In his study of the inferior regimes Socrates examines in each case first the regime and then the corresponding individual or soul. He presents both the regime and the corresponding individual as coming into being out of the preceding one. We shall consider here only his account of democracy, both because this subject is most important to citizens of a democracy and because of its intrinsic importance. Democracy arises from oligarchy,

75. Cf. *ibid.*, 546e–547a and Hesiod, *Works and Days* 106 ff.

which in its turn arises from timocracy, the rule of the insufficiently musical warriors who are characterized by the supremacy of spiritedness. Oligarchy is the first regime in which desire is supreme. In oligarchy the ruling desire is that for wealth or money, or unlimited acquisitiveness. The oligarchic man is thrifty and industrious, controls all his desires other than the desire for money, lacks education, and possesses a superficial honesty derivative from the crudest self-interest. Oligarchy must give to each the unqualified right to dispose of his property as he sees fit. It thus renders inevitable the emergence of "drones," i.e., of members of the ruling class who are either burdened with debt or already bankrupt, and hence disfranchised—of beggars who hanker after their squandered fortune and hope to restore their fortune and political power through a change of regime ("Catilinarian existences"). Besides, the correct oligarchs themselves, being both rich and unconcerned with virtue and honor, render themselves and especially their sons fat, spoiled, and soft. They thus become despised by the lean and tough poor. Democracy comes into being when the poor, having become aware of their superiority to the rich and perhaps being led by some drones who act as traitors to their class and possess the skills which ordinarily only members of a ruling class possess, make themselves at an opportune moment masters of the city by defeating the rich, killing and exiling a part of them, and permitting the rest to live with them in the possession of full citizen rights. Democracy itself is characterized by freedom, which includes the right to say and do whatever one wishes: everyone can follow the way of life which pleases him most. Hence democracy is the regime which fosters the greatest variety: every way of life, every regime can be found in it. Hence, we must add, democracy is the only regime other than the best in which the philosopher can lead his peculiar way of life without being disturbed: it is for this reason that with some exaggeration one can compare democracy to Hesiod's age of the divine race of heroes, which comes closer to the golden age than any other. Certainly in a democracy the citizen who is a philosopher is under no compulsion to participate in political life or to hold office.[76] One is thus led to wonder why Socrates did not assign to democracy the highest place among the inferior regimes, or rather the highest place simply, seeing that the best regime is not possible. One could say that he showed his preference for democracy "by deed": by spending his whole life in democratic Athens, by fighting for her in her wars, and by dying in obedience to her laws. However this may be, he surely did not prefer democracy to all other regimes "in speech." The reason is that, being a just man, he thought of the well-being not merely of the philosophers but of the nonphilosophers as well, and he held that democracy is not designed for inducing the nonphilosophers to attempt to become as good as they possibly can, for the end of democracy is not virtue but freedom, i.e., the freedom to live either nobly or basely according to one's liking. Therefore he assigns to democracy a rank even lower than to oligarchy, since oligarchy requires some kind of restraint whereas democracy, as he presents it, abhors every kind of restraint. One could say that, adapting himself to his subject matter, Socrates abandons all restraint when speaking of the regime which loathes restraint. In a democracy, he asserts, no one is compelled to rule or to be ruled if he does not like it; he can live in peace while his city is at war; capital punishment does not have the slightest consequence for the condemned man: he is not even jailed; the order of rulers and ruled is completely reversed: the father behaves as if he were a boy and the son has neither respect nor fear of the father, the teacher fears his pupils while the pupils pay no attention to the teacher, and there is complete equality of the sexes; even horses and donkeys no longer step aside when encountering human beings. Plato writes as if the Athenian democracy had not carried out Socrates' execution, and Socrates speaks as if the Athenian

76. *Republic* 557d–e.

democracy had not engaged in an orgy of bloody persecution of guilty and innocent alike when the Hermes statues were mutilated at the beginning of the Sicilian expedition.[77] Socrates' exaggeration of the licentious mildness of democracy is matched by an almost equally strong exaggeration of the intemperance of democratic man. He could indeed not avoid the latter exaggeration if he did not wish to deviate in the case of democracy from the procedure which he follows in his discussion of the inferior regimes. That procedure consists in understanding the man corresponding to an inferior regime as the son of a father corresponding to the preceding regime. Hence democratic man had to be presented as the son of an oligarchic father, as the degenerate son of a wealthy father who is concerned with nothing but making money: the democratic man is the drone, the fat, soft, and prodigal playboy, the lotus-eater who, assigning a kind of equality to equal and unequal things, lives one day in complete surrender to his lowest desires and the next ascetically, or who, according to Karl Marx's ideal, "goes hunting in the morning, fishes in the afternoon, raises cattle in the evening, devotes himself to philosophy after dinner," i.e., does at every moment what he happens to like at that moment: the democratic man is not the lean, tough, and thrifty craftsman or peasant who has a single job.[78] Socrates' deliberately exaggerated blame of democracy becomes intelligible to some extent once one considers its immediate addressee, the austere Adeimantos, who is not a friend of laughter and who had been the addressee of the austere discussion of poetry in the section on the education of the warriors: by his exaggerated blame of democracy Socrates lends words to Adeimantos' "dream" of democracy.[79] One must also not forget that the sanguine account of the multitude which was provisionally required in order to prove the harmony between the city

---

77. See Thucydides, VI. 27–29 and 53–61.
78. Cf. Plato, *Republic* 564c–565a and 575c.
79. Cf. *ibid.*, 563d with 389a.

and philosophy is in need of being redressed; the exaggerated blame of democracy reminds us with greater force than was ever before used of the disharmony between philosophy and the people.[80]

After Socrates had brought to light the entirely unjust regime and the entirely unjust man and then compared the life of the entirely unjust man with that of the perfectly just man, it became clear beyond the shadow of a doubt that justice is preferable to injustice. Nevertheless the conversation continues. Socrates suddenly returns to the question of poetry, to a question which had already been answered at great length when he discussed the education of the warriors. We must try to understand this apparently sudden return. In an explicit digression from the discussion of tyranny, Socrates had noted that the poets praise tyrants and are honored by tyrants (and also by democracy), whereas they are not honored by the three better regimes.[81] Tyranny and democracy are characterized by surrender to the sensual desires, including the most lawless ones. The tyrant is *Eros* incarnate, and the poets sing the praise of *Eros*. They pay very great attention and homage precisely to that phenomenon from which Socrates abstracts in the *Republic* to the best of his powers. The poets therefore foster injustice. So does Thrasymachos. But just as Socrates, in spite of this, could be a friend of Thrasymachos, so there is no reason why he could not be a friend of the poets and especially of Homer. Perhaps Socrates needs the poets in order to restore, on another occasion, the dignity of *Eros:* the *Banquet,* the only Platonic dialogue in which Socrates is shown to converse with poets, is devoted entirely to *Eros*.

The foundation for the return to poetry was laid at the very beginning of the discussion of the inferior regimes and of the inferior souls. The transition from the best regime to the inferior regimes was explicitly ascribed to the Muses speaking "tragically," and the transition from the best man

80. Cf. *ibid.,* 577c–d with 428d–e and 422a,c.
81. *Ibid.,* 568a–d.

to the inferior men has in fact a somewhat "comical" touch:[82] poetry takes the lead when the descent from the highest theme—justice understood as philosophy—begins. The return to poetry, which is preceded by the account of the inferior regimes and the inferior souls, is followed by a discussion of "the greatest rewards for virtue," i.e., the rewards not inherent in justice or philosophy itself.[83] The return to poetry constitutes the center of that part of the *Republic* in which the conversation descends from the highest theme. This cannot be surprising, for philosophy as quest for the truth is the highest activity of man, and poetry is not concerned with the truth.

In the first discussion of poetry, which preceded by a long time the introduction of philosophy as a theme, poetry's unconcern with the truth was its chief recommendation, for at that time it was untruth that was needed.[84] The most excellent poets were expelled from the just city, not because they teach untruth, but because they teach the wrong kind of untruth. But in the meantime it has become clear that only the life of the philosophizing man insofar as he philosophizes is the just life, and that that life, so far from needing untruth, utterly rejects it.[85] The progress from the city, even the best city, to the philosopher requires, it seems, a progress from the qualified acceptance of poetry to its unqualified rejection.

In the light of philosophy, poetry reveals itself to be the imitation of imitations of the truth, i.e., of the ideas. The contemplation of the ideas is the activity of the philosopher, the imitation of the ideas is the activity of the ordinary artisan, and the imitation of the works of artisans is the activity of poets and other "imitative" artisans. To begin with, Socrates presents the order of rank in these terms: the maker of the ideas (e.g., of the idea of the bed) is the

82. *Ibid.,* 545d–e, 549c–e.
83. *Ibid.,* 608c, 614a.
84. *Ibid.,* 377a.
85. *Ibid.,* 485c–d.

God, the maker of the imitation (of the bed which can be used) is the artisan, and the maker of the imitation of the imitation (of the painting of a bed) is the imitative artisan. Later on he restates the order of rank in these terms: first the user, then the artisan, and finally the imitative artisan. The idea of the bed originates in the user who determines the "form" of the bed with a view to the end for which it is to be used. The user is then the one who possesses the highest or most authoritative knowledge: the highest knowledge is not that possessed by any artisans as such at all; the poet who stands at the opposite pole from the user does not possess any knowledge, not even right opinion.[86] In order to understand this seemingly outrageous indictment of poetry one must first identify the artisan whose work the poet imitates. The poets' themes are above all the human things referring to virtue and vice; the poets see the human things in the light of virtue, but the virtue toward which they look is an imperfect and even distorted image of virtue.[87] The artisan whom the poet imitates is the nonphilosophic legislator who is an imperfect imitator of virtue itself.[88] In particular, justice as understood by the city is necessarily the work of the legislator, for the just as understood by the city is the legal. No one expressed Socrates' suggestion more clearly than Nietzsche, who said that "the poets were always the valets of some morality. . . ."[89] But according to the French saying, for a valet there is no hero: Are the artists and in particular the poets not aware of the secret weakness of their heroes? This is indeed the case according to Socrates. The poets bring to light, for instance, the full force of the grief which a man feels for the loss of someone dear to him—of a feeling to which a respectable man would not give adequate utterance except when he is alone, because its adequate utterance in the presence of

86. *Ibid.*, 601c–602a.
87. *Ibid.*, 598e, 599c–e, 600e.
88. Cf. *ibid.*, 501a.
89. *The Gay Science*, No. 1.

others is not becoming and lawful: the poets bring to light that in our nature which the law forcibly restrains.[90] If this is so, if the poets are perhaps the men who understand best the nature of the passions which the law restrains, they are very far from being merely the servants of the legislators; they are also the men from whom the prudent legislator will learn. The genuine "quarrel between philosophy and poetry"[91] concerns, from the philosopher's point of view, not the worth of poetry as such, but the order of rank of philosophy and poetry. According to Socrates, poetry is legitimate only as ministerial to the "user" par excellence, to the king who is the philosopher, and not as autonomous. For autonomous poetry presents human life as autonomous, i.e., as not directed toward the philosophic life, and therefore it never presents the philosophic life itself except in its comical distortion; hence autonomous poetry is necessarily either tragedy or comedy since the nonphilosophic life understood as autonomous has either no way out of its fundamental difficulty or only an inept one. But ministerial poetry presents the nonphilosophic life as ministerial to the philosophic life and therefore, above all, it presents the philosophic life itself.[92] The greatest example of ministerial poetry is the Platonic dialogue.

The *Republic* concludes with a discussion of the greatest rewards for justice and the greatest punishments for injustice. The discussion consists of three parts: (1) proof of the immortality of the soul; (2) the divine and human rewards and punishments for men while they are alive; (3) the rewards and punishments after death. The central part is silent about the philosophers: rewards for justice and punishments for injustice during life are needed for the nonphilosophers whose justice does not have the intrinsic attractiveness which the justice of the philosophers has. The account of the rewards and punishments after death is

---

90. *Republic* 603e–604a, 606a,c, 607a.
91. *Ibid.,* 607b.
92. Cf. *ibid.,* 604e.

given in the form of a myth. The myth is not baseless, since it is based on the proof of the immortality of the souls. The soul cannot be immortal if it is composed of many things, unless the composition is most perfect. But the soul as we know it from our experience lacks that perfect harmony. In order to find the truth, one would have to recover by reasoning the original or true nature of the soul.[93] This reasoning is not achieved in the *Republic*. That is to say, Socrates proves the immortality of the soul without having brought to light the nature of the soul. The situation at the end of the *Republic* corresponds precisely to the situation at the end of the first book of the *Republic,* where Socrates makes clear that he has proved that justice is salutary without knowing the "what" or nature of justice. The discussion following the first book does bring to light the nature of justice as the right order of the soul, yet how can one know the right order of the soul if one does not know the nature of the soul? Let us remember here also the fact that the parallelism between soul and city, which is the premise of the doctrine of the soul stated in the *Republic,* is evidently questionable and even untenable. The *Republic* cannot bring to light the nature of the soul because it abstracts from *eros* and from the body. If we are genuinely concerned with finding out precisely what justice is, we must take "another longer way around" in our study of the soul than the way which is taken in the *Republic*.[94] This does not mean that what we learn from the *Republic* about justice is not true or is altogether provisional. The teaching of the *Republic* regarding justice, although not complete, can yet be true insofar as the nature of justice depends decisively on the nature of the city—for even the transpolitical cannot be understood as such except if the city is understood—and the city is completely intelligible because its limits can be made perfectly manifest: to see these limits, one need not have answered the question regarding

93. *Ibid.,* 611b–612a.
94. *Ibid.,* 504b, 506d.

the whole; it is sufficient to have raised the question regarding the whole. The *Republic* then indeed makes clear what justice is. However, as Cicero has observed, the *Republic* does not bring to light the best possible regime but rather the nature of political things—the nature of the city.[95] Socrates makes clear in the *Republic* what character the city would have to have in order to satisfy the highest needs of man. By letting us see that the city constructed in accordance with this requirement is not possible, he lets us see the essential limits, the nature, of the city.

The Statesman

The *Statesman* is preceded by the *Sophist,* which in its turn is preceded by the *Theaitetos*. The *Theaitetos* presents a conversation between Socrates and the young mathematician Theaitetos, which takes place in the presence of the mature and renowned mathematician Theodoros, as well as of Theaitetos' young companion named Socrates, and which is meant to make clear what knowledge or science is. The conversation does not lead to a positive result: Socrates by himself only knows that he does not know, and Theaitetos is not like Glaukon or Adeimantos, who can be assisted by Socrates (or can assist him) in bringing forth a positive teaching. On the day following Socrates' conversation with Theaitetos, Socrates again meets with Theodoros, the younger Socrates, and Theaitetos, but this time there is also present a nameless philosopher designated only as a stranger from Elea. Socrates asks the stranger whether his fellows regard the sophist, the statesman, and the philosopher as one and the same or as two or as three. It could seem that the question regarding the identity or nonidentity of the sophist, the statesman, and the philosopher takes the place of the question, or is a more articulate version of the question: What is knowledge? The stranger replies that his fellows regard the sophist, the statesman or king,

95. Cicero, *Republic* II.52.

and the philosopher as different from one another. The fact that the philosopher is not identical with the king was recognized in the central thesis of the *Republic,* according to which the coincidence of philosophy and kingship is the condition for the salvation of cities and indeed of the human race: identical things do not have to coincide. But the *Republic* did not make sufficiently clear the cognitive status of kingship or statesmanship. From the *Republic* we can easily receive the impression that the knowledge required of the philosopher-king consists of two heterogeneous parts: the purely philosophic knowledge of the ideas which culminates in the vision of the idea of the good, on the one hand, and the merely political experience which does not have the status of knowledge at all, but which enables one to find one's way in the Cave and to discern the shadows on its walls, on the other. But the indispensable supplement to philosophic knowledge also seemed to be a kind of art or science.[96] The Eleatic stranger seems to take the second and higher view of the nonphilosophic awareness peculiar to the statesman. Yet in the dialogues *Sophist* and *Statesman* he makes clear the nature of the sophist and of the statesman, i.e., the difference between the sophist and the statesman, without making clear the difference between the statesman and the philosopher. We are promised by Theodoros that the Eleatic stranger will also expound (in a sequel to the *Statesman*) what the philosopher is, but Plato does not keep his Theodoros' promise. Do we then understand what the philosopher is once we have understood what the sophist and the statesman are? Is statesmanship not, as it appeared from the *Republic,* a mere supplement to philosophy, but an ingredient of philosophy? That is to say, is statesmanship, the art or knowledge peculiar to the statesman, far from being merely the awareness necessary for finding one's way in the Cave and far from being itself independent of the vision of the idea of the good, a condition or rather an ingredient of the vision

96. Cf. Plato, *Republic* 484d and 539e with 501a–c.

of the idea of the good? If it were so, then "politics" would be much more important according to the *Statesman* than it is according to the *Republic*. Surely the conversation about the king or statesman takes place when Socrates is already accused of a capital crime for the commission of which he was shortly thereafter condemned and executed (see the end of the *Theaitetos*): the city seems to be much more powerfully present in the *Statesman* than in the *Republic*, where the antagonist of Socrates, Thrasymachos, only plays the city. On the other hand, however, whereas in the *Republic* Socrates founds a city, if only in speech, with the help of two brothers who are passionately concerned with justice and the city, in the *Statesman* Socrates listens silently to a nameless stranger (a man lacking political responsibility) bringing to light what the statesman is in the cool atmosphere of mathematics: the concern with finding out what the statesman is seems to be philosophic rather than political.[97] The *Statesman* seems to be much more sober than the *Republic*.

We may say that the *Statesman* is more scientific than the *Republic*. By "science" Plato understands the highest form of knowledge, or rather the only kind of awareness which deserves to be called knowledge. He calls that form of knowledge "dialectics." "Dialectics" means primarily the art of conversation and then the highest form of that art, that art as practiced by Socrates, that art of conversation which is meant to bring to light the "whats" of things, or the ideas. Dialectics is then the knowledge of the ideas—a knowledge which makes no use whatever of sense experience: it moves from idea to idea until it has exhausted the whole realm of the ideas, for each idea is a part and therefore points to other ideas.[98] In its completed form dialectics would descend from the highest idea, the idea ruling the realm of ideas, step by step to the lowest ideas. The movement proceeds "step by step," i.e., it follows the articula-

97. Cf. *Statesman* 285d.
98. *Republic* 511a–d, 531a–533d, 537c.

tion, the natural division of the ideas. The *Statesman* as well as the *Sophist* present an imitation of dialectics thus understood; both are meant to give an inkling of dialectics thus understood; the imitation which they present is playful. Yet the play is not mere play. If the movement from idea to idea without recourse to sense experience should be impossible, if in other words the *Republic* should be utopian not only in what it states about the city at its best but also in what it says about philosophy or dialectics at its best, dialectics at its best, not being possible, will not be serious. The dialectics which is possible will remain dependent on experience.[99] There is a connection between this feature of the *Statesman* and the fact that the ideas as treated in the *Statesman* are classes, or comprise all individuals "participating" in the idea in question, and therefore do not subsist independently of the individuals or "beyond" them. However this may be, in the *Statesman* the Eleatic stranger tries to bring to light the nature of the statesman by descending from "art" or "knowledge" step by step to the art of the statesman or by dividing "art" step by step until he arrives at the art of the statesman. For a number of reasons we cannot here follow his "methodical" procedure.

Shortly after the beginning of the conversation, the Eleatic stranger makes young Socrates agree to what one may call the abolition of the distinction between the public and the private. He achieves this result in two steps. Since statesmanship or kingship is essentially a kind of knowledge, it is of no importance whether the man possessing that knowledge is clothed in the vestments of high office by virtue of having been elected, for example, or whether he lives in a private station. Second, there is no essential difference between the city and the household and hence between the statesman or king, on the one hand, and the householder or master (i.e., the master of slaves), on the

99. Cf. *Statesman* 264c.

other. Law and freedom, the characteristically political phenomena, which are inseparable from one another, are disposed of at the very beginning because statesmanship is understood as a kind of knowledge or art, or because abstraction is made from that which distinguishes the political from the arts. The Eleatic stranger abstracts here from the fact that sheer bodily force is a necessary ingredient of the rule of men over men. This abstraction is partly justified by the fact that statesmanship or kingship is a cognitive rather than a manual (or brachial) art. It is, however, not simply cognitive like arithmetic; it is an art which gives commands to human beings. But all arts which give commands do so for the sake of the coming into being of something. Some of these arts give commands for the sake of the coming into being of living beings or animals, i.e., they are concerned with the breeding and nurture of animals. The kingly art is a kind of this genus of art. For the proper understanding of the kingly art it does not suffice to divide the genus "animal" into the species "brutes" and "men." This distinction is as arbitrary as the distinction of the human race into Greeks and barbarians, as distinguished from the distinction into men and women; it is not a natural distinction but a distinction originating in pride.[100] The stranger's training of young Socrates in dialectics, or in the art of dividing kinds or ideas or classes, goes hand in hand with training in modesty or moderation. According to the stranger's division of the species of animals, man's nearest kin is even lower than it is according to Darwin's doctrine of the origin of the species. But what Darwin meant seriously and literally, the stranger means playfully.[101] Man must learn to see the lowliness of his estate in order to turn from the human to the divine, i.e., in order to be truly human.

The division of "art" leads to the result that the art of the statesman is the art concerned with the breeding and

100. *Ibid.*, 262c–263d, 266d.
101. Cf. *ibid.*, 271e, 272b–c.

nurture of, or with the caring for, herds of the kind of animal called man. This result is manifestly insufficient, for there are many arts—e.g., medicine and matchmaking—which claim as justly to be concerned with a caring for human herds as does the political art. The error was due to the fact that the human herd was taken to be a herd of the same kind as the herds of other animals. But human herds are a very special kind of herd: the bipartition of "animal" into brutes and men originates not merely in pride. The error is removed by a myth. According to the myth now told in its fullness for the first time, there is once a time (the age of Kronos) when the god guides the whole and then a time (the age of Zeus) when the god lets the whole move by its own motion. In the age of Kronos, the god ruled and took care of the animals by assigning the different species of animals to the rule and care of different gods, who acted like shepherds and thus secured universal peace and affluence: there were no political societies, no private property, and no families. This does not necessarily mean that men lived happily in the age of Kronos; only if they used the then available peace and affluence for philosophizing can they be said to have lived happily. At any rate, in the present age the god does not take care of man: in the present age there is no divine providence; men must take care of themselves. Bereft of divine care, the world abounds with disorder and injustice; men must establish order and justice as well as they can, with the understanding that in this age of scarcity, communism, and hence also absolute communism, is impossible. The *Statesman* may be said to bring into the open what the *Republic* had left unsaid, namely, the impossibility of the best regime presented in the *Republic*.

The myth of the *Statesman* is meant to explain the error committed by the Eleatic stranger and young Socrates in the initial definition of the *Statesman:* by looking for a single art of caring for human herds they were unwittingly looking toward the age of Kronos or toward divine caring;

with the disappearance of divine caring, i.e., of a caring by
beings which in the eyes of everyone are superior to men,
it became inevitable that every art or every man should
believe itself or himself to be as much entitled to rule as
every other art or every other man,[102] or that at least many
arts should become competitors of the kingly art. The inevitable first consequence of the transition from the age of
Kronos to the age of Zeus was the delusion that all arts and
all men are equal. The mistake consisted in assuming that
the kingly art is devoted to the total caring for human
herds (which total caring would include the feeding and
mating of the ruled) and not to a partial or limited caring.
In other words, the mistake consisted in the disregard of
the fact that in the case of all arts of herding other than
the human art of herding human beings, the herder belongs to a different species than the members of the herd.
We must then divide the whole "caring for herds" into
two parts: caring for herds in which the herder belongs to
the same species as the members of the herd and caring for
herds in which the herder belongs to a different species
than the members of the herd (human herders of brutes
and divine herders of human beings). We must next divide
the first of these two kinds into parts, so that we can discover which partial herding of herds in which the herder
belongs to the same species as the members of the herd is
the kingly art. Let us assume that the partial caring sought
is "ruling cities." Ruling cities is naturally divided into
ruling not willed by the ruled (ruling by sheer force) and
ruling willed by the ruled; the former is tyrannical, and
the latter is kingly. Here we receive the first glimpse of
freedom as the specifically political theme. But at the very
moment in which the stranger alludes to this difficulty, he
turns away from it. He finds the whole previous procedure
unsatisfactory.

The method which proves to be helpful, where the divi-

102. *Ibid.*, 274e–275c.

sion of classes and into classes as well as the myth have
failed, is the use of an example. The stranger illustrates
the usefulness of examples by an example. The example is
meant to illustrate man's situation in regard to knowledge
—to the phenomenon which is the guiding theme of the
trilogy *Theaitetos-Sophist-Statesman*. The example chosen
is children's knowledge of reading. Starting from knowledge
of the letters (the "elements"), they proceed step by step
to the knowledge of the shortest and easiest syllables (the
combination of "elements"), and then to the knowledge of
long and difficult ones. Knowledge of the whole is not possible if it is not similar to the art of reading: knowledge
of the elements must be available, the elements must be
fairly small in number, and not all elements must be com-
binable.[103] But can we say that we possess knowledge of the
"elements" of the whole or that we can ever start from an
absolute beginning? Did we in the *Statesman* begin from
an adequate understanding of "art" or "knowledge"? Is it
not true that, while we necessarily long for knowledge of
the whole, we are condemned to rest satisfied with partial
knowledge of parts of the whole and hence never truly to
transcend the sphere of opinion? Is therefore philosophy,
and hence human life, not necessarily Sisyphean? Could this
be the reason why the demand for freedom is not so evidently sound as many present-day lovers of freedom believe
on the basis of very similar thoughts? (Perhaps this could
induce one to consider Dostoyevsky's *Grand Inquisitor* in
the light of Plato's *Statesman*.) After having compelled us
to raise these and kindred questions, the stranger turns to
his example, which is meant to throw light, not on knowledge in general or on philosophy as such, but on the kingly
art. The example chosen by him is the art of weaving: he
illustrates the political art by an emphatically domestic art
and not by such "outgoing" arts as herding and piloting;
he illustrates the most virile art by a characteristically

103. Cf. *Sophist* 252d–e.

feminine art. In order to find out what weaving is, one must divide "art," but divide it differently than they divided it at first. The analysis of the art of weaving which is made on the basis of the new division enables the stranger to elucidate art in general and the kingly art in particular before he applies explicitly the result of that analysis to the kingly art. Perhaps the most important point made in this context is the distinction between two kinds of the art of measurement: one kind which considers the greater and less in relation to one another, and another kind which considers the greater and less (now understood as excess and defect) in relation to the mean or, say, the fitting, or something similar. All arts, and especially the kingly art, make their measurements with a view to the right mean or the fitting, i.e., they are not mathematical.

By explicitly applying to the kingly art the results of his analysis of the art of weaving, the stranger is enabled to make clear the relation of the kingly art to all other arts and especially to those arts which claim with some show of justice to compete with the kingly art for the rule of the city. The most successful and clever competitors are those outstanding sophists who pretend to possess the kingly art, and these are the rulers of cities, i.e., the rulers lacking the kingly or statesmanly art, or practically all political rulers that were, are, and will be. Of this kind of political rule there are three sorts: the rule of one, the rule of a few, and the rule of many; but each of these three kinds is divided into two parts with a view to the difference between violence and voluntariness or between lawfulness and lawlessness; thus monarchy is distinguished from tyranny, and aristocracy from oligarchy, whereas the name of democracy is applied to the rule of the multitude regardless of whether the multitude of the poor rules over the rich with the consent of the rich and in strict obedience to the laws or with violence and more or less lawlessly. (The distinction of regimes sketched by the stranger is almost identical with the distinction developed by Aristotle in the third book of his *Politics;* but consider the difference.) None of these regimes bases its claim on the knowledge or art of the rulers, i.e., on the only claim which is unqualifiedly legitimate. It follows that the claims based on the willingness of the subjects (on consent or freedom) and on lawfulness are dubious. This judgment is defended with reference to the example of the other arts and especially of medicine. A physician is a physician whether he cures us with our will or against our will, whether he cuts us, burns us, or inflicts upon us any other pain, and whether he acts in accordance with written rules or without them; he is a physician if his ruling redounds to the benefit of our bodies. Correspondingly, the only regime which is correct or which is truly a regime is that in which the possessors of the kingly art rule, regardless of whether they rule according to laws or without laws and whether the ruled consent to their rule or not, provided their rule redounds to the benefit of the body politic; it does not make any difference whether they achieve this end by killing some or banishing them, and thus reduce the bulk of the city, or by bringing in citizens from abroad, and thus increase its bulk.

Young Socrates, who is not shocked by what the stranger says about killing and banishing, is rather shocked by the suggestion that rule without laws (absolute rule) can be legitimate. To understand fully the response of young Socrates, one must pay attention to the fact that the stranger does not make a distinction between human laws and natural laws. The stranger turns the incipient indignation of young Socrates into a desire on the latter's part for discussion. Rule of law is inferior to the rule of living intelligence because laws, owing to their generality, cannot determine wisely what is right and proper in all circumstances given the infinite variety of circumstances: only the wise man on the spot could correctly decide what is right and proper in the circumstances. Nevertheless laws are necessary. The few wise men cannot sit beside each of the many unwise men and tell him exactly what it is becoming for him to do. The few wise men are almost always absent from the innumerable unwise men. All laws, written or unwritten, are poor substitutes but indispensable substitutes for the individual rulings by wise men. They are crude rules of thumb which are sufficient for the large majority of cases: they treat human beings as if they were members of a herd. The freezing of crude rules of thumb into sacred, inviolable, unchangeable prescriptions which would be rejected by everyone as ridiculous if done in the sciences and the arts is a necessity in the ordering of human affairs; this necessity is the proximate cause of the ineradicable difference between the political and the suprapolitical spheres. But the main objection to laws is not that they are not susceptible of being individualized but that they are assumed to be binding on the wise man, on the man possessing the kingly art.[104] Yet even this objection is not entirely valid. As the stranger explains through images,[105] the wise man is subjected to the laws, whose justice and wisdom is inferior to his, because the unwise men cannot help distrusting the wise man, and this distrust is not entirely indefensible given the fact that they cannot understand him. They cannot believe that a wise man who would deserve to rule as a true king without laws would be willing and able to rule over them. The ultimate reason for their unbelief is the fact that no human being has that manifest superiority, in the first place regarding the body and then regarding the soul, which would induce everybody to submit to his rule without any hesitation and without any reserve.[106] The unwise men cannot help making themselves the judges of the wise man. No wonder then that the wise men are unwilling to rule over them. The unwise men must even demand of the wise man that he regard the law as simply authoritative, i.e., that he not even doubt that the established laws are perfectly just and wise; if he fails to do so, he will become

104. *Statesman* 295b–c.
105. *Ibid.*, 297a ff.
106. *Ibid.*, 301c–e.

guilty of corrupting the young, a capital offense; they must forbid free inquiry regarding the most important subjects. All these implications of the rule of laws must be accepted, since the only feasible alternative is the lawless rule of selfish men. The wise man must bow to the law which is inferior to him in wisdom and justice, not only in deed but in speech as well. (Here we cannot help wondering whether there are no limits to the wise man's subjection to the laws. The Platonic illustrations are these: Socrates obeyed without flinching the law which commanded him to die because of his alleged corruption of the young; yet he would not have obeyed a law formally forbidding him the pursuit of philosophy. Read the *Apology of Socrates* together with the *Crito*.) The rule of law is preferable to the lawless rule of unwise men since laws, however bad, are in one way or another the outcome of some reasoning. This observation permits the ranking of the incorrect regimes, i.e., of all regimes other than the absolute rule of the true king or statesman. Law-abiding democracy is inferior to the law-abiding rule of the few (aristocracy) and to the law-abiding rule of one (monarchy), but lawless democracy is superior to the lawless rule of a few (oligarchy) and to the lawless rule of one (tyranny). "Lawless" does not mean here the complete absence of any laws or customs. It means the habitual disregard of the laws by the government and especially of those laws which are meant to restrain the power of the government: a government which can change every law, or is "sovereign," is lawless. From the sequel it appears that, according to the stranger, even in the city ruled by the true king there will be laws (the true king is the true legislator), but that the true king, in contradistinction to all other rulers, may justly change the laws or act against the laws. In the absence of the true king, the stranger would probably be satisfied if the city were ruled by a code of laws framed by a wise man, one which can be changed by the unwise rulers only in extreme cases.

After the true kingly art has been separated from all

other arts, it remains for the stranger to determine the peculiar work of the king. Here the example of the art of weaving takes on decisive importance. The king's work resembles a web. According to the popular view all parts of virtue are simply in harmony with one another. In fact, however, there is a tension between them. Above all, there is a tension between courage or manliness and moderation, gentleness, or concern with the seemly. This tension explains the tension and even hostility between the preponderantly manly and the preponderantly gentle human beings. The true king's task is to weave together these opposite kinds of human beings, for the people in the city who are completely unable to become either manly or moderate cannot become citizens at all. An important part of the kingly weaving together consists in intermarrying the children of preponderantly manly families and those of preponderantly gentle families. The human king must then approximate the divine shepherd by enlarging the art of ruling cities strictly understood so as to include in it the art of mating or matchmaking. The matchmaking practiced by the king is akin to the matchmaking practiced by Socrates,[107] which means that it is not identical with the latter. If we were to succeed in understanding the kinship between the king's matchmaking and Socrates' matchmaking, we would have made some progress toward the understanding of the kinship between the king and the philosopher. This much can be said safely: While it is possible and even necessary to speak of "the human herd" when trying to define the king, the philosopher has nothing to do with "herds."

The *Statesman* belongs to a trilogy whose theme is knowledge. For Plato, knowledge proper or striving for knowledge proper is philosophy. Philosophy is striving for knowledge of the whole, for contemplation of the whole. The whole consists of parts; knowledge of the whole is knowledge of all parts of the whole as parts of the whole. Philosophy is

107. Cf. *Theaitetos* 151b.

the highest human activity, and man is an excellent, perhaps the most excellent, part of the whole. The whole is not a whole without man, without man's being whole or complete. But man becomes whole not without his own effort, and this effort presupposes knowledge of a particular kind: knowledge which is not contemplative or theoretical but prescriptive or commanding[108] or practical. The *Statesman* presents itself as a theoretical discussion of practical knowledge. In contradistinction to the *Statesman*, the *Republic* leads up from practical or political life to philosophy, to the theoretical life; the *Republic* presents a practical discussion of theory: it shows to men concerned with the solution of the human problem that that solution consists in the theoretical life; the knowledge which the *Republic* sets forth is prescriptive or commanding. The theoretical discussion of the highest practical knowledge (the kingly art) in the *Statesman*, merely by setting forth the character of the kingly art, takes on a commanding character: it sets forth what the ruler ought to do. While the distinction of theoretical and practical knowledge is necessary, their separation is impossible. (Consider from this point of view the description of the theoretical life in the *Theaitetos* 173b–177c.) The kingly art is one of the arts directly concerned with making men whole or entire. The most obvious indication of every human being's incompleteness, and at the same time of the manner in which it can be completed, is the distinction of the human race into the two sexes: just as the union of men and women, the primary goal of *eros*, makes "man" self-sufficient for the perpetuity, not to say sempiternity, of the human species, all other kinds of incompleteness to be found in men are completed in the species, in the "idea," of man. The whole human race, and not any part of it, is self-sufficient as a part of the whole, and not as the master or conqueror of the whole. It is perhaps for this reason that the *Statesman* ends with a praise of a certain kind of matchmaking.

108. *Statesman* 260a–b.

The Laws

The *Republic* and the *Statesman* transcend the city in different but kindred ways. They show first how the city would have to transform itself if it wishes to maintain its claim to supremacy in the face of philosophy. They show then that the city is incapable of undergoing this transformation. The *Republic* shows silently that the ordinary city —i.e., the city which is not communistic and which is the association of the fathers rather than of the artisans—is the only city that is possible. The *Statesman* shows explicitly the necessity of the rule of laws. The *Republic* and the *Statesman* reveal, each in its own way, the essential limitation and therewith the essential character of the city. They thus lay the foundation for answering the question of the best political order, the best order of the city compatible with the nature of man. But they do not set forth that best possible order. This task is left for the *Laws*. We may then say that the *Laws* is the only political work proper of Plato. It is the only Platonic dialogue from which Socrates is absent. The characters of the *Laws* are old men of long political experience: a nameless Athenian stranger, the Cretan Kleinias, and the Spartan Megillos. The Athenian stranger occupies the place ordinarily occupied in the Platonic dialogues by Socrates. The conversation takes place far away from Athens, on the island of Crete, while the three old men walk from the city of Knossos to the cave of Zeus.

Our first impression is that the Athenian stranger has gone to Crete in order to discover the truth about those Greek laws which in one respect were the most renowned, for the Cretan laws were believed to have had their origin in Zeus, the highest god. The Cretan laws were akin to the Spartan laws, which were even more renowned than the Cretan laws and were traced to Apollo. At the suggestion of the Athenian, the three men converse about laws and regimes. The Athenian learns from the Cretan that the

Cretan legislator has framed all his laws with a view to war: by nature every city is at all times in a state of undeclared war with every other city; victory in war, and hence war, is the condition for all blessings. The Athenian easily convinces the Cretan that the Cretan laws aim at the wrong end: the end is not war but peace. For if victory in war is the condition of all blessings, war is not the end: the blessings themselves belong to peace. Hence the virtue of war, courage, is the lowest part of virtue, inferior to moderation and above all to justice and wisdom. Once we have seen the natural order of the virtues, we know the highest principle of legislation, for that legislation must be concerned with virtue, with the excellence of the human soul, rather than with any other goods, is easily granted by the Cretan gentleman Kleinias, who is assured by the Athenian that the possession of virtue is necessarily followed by the possession of health, beauty, strength, and wealth.[109] It appears that both the Spartan and the Cretan legislators, convinced as they were that the end of the city is war and not peace, provided well for the education of their subjects or fellows to courage, to self-control regarding pains and fears, by making them taste the greatest pains and fears; but they did not provide at all for education to moderation, to self-control regarding pleasures, by making them taste the greatest pleasures. In fact, if we can trust Megillos, at any rate the Spartan legislator discouraged the enjoyment of pleasure altogether.[110] The Spartan and Cretan legislators surely forbade the pleasures of drinking—pleasures freely indulged in by the Athenians. The Athenian contends that drinking, even drunkenness, properly practiced is conducive to moderation, the twin virtue of courage. In order to be properly practiced, drinking must be done in common, i.e., in a sense in public, so that it can be supervised. Drinking, even drunkenness, will be salutary if the drinkers are ruled by the right kind of man. For a man to be a commander of

109. *Laws* 631b–d; cf. 829a–b.
110. *Ibid.*, 636e.

a ship it is not sufficient that he possess the art or science of sailing; he must also be free from seasickness.[111] Art or knowledge is likewise not sufficient for ruling a banquet. Art is not sufficient for ruling any association and in particular the city. The banquet is a more fitting simile of the city than is the ship ("the ship of state"), for just as the banqueteers are drunk from wine, the citizens are drunk from fears, hopes, desires, and aversions and are therefore in need of being ruled by a man who is sober. Since banquets are illegal in Sparta and Crete but legal in Athens, the Athenian is compelled to justify an Athenian institution. The justification is a long speech, and long speeches were Athenian rather than Spartan and Cretan. The Athenian is then compelled to justify an Athenian institution in an Athenian manner. He is compelled to transform his non-Athenian interlocutors to some extent into Athenians. Only in this way can he correct their erroneous views about laws and therewith eventually their laws themselves. From this we understand better the character of the *Laws* as a whole. In the *Republic*[112] the Spartan and Cretan regimes were used as examples of timocracy, the kind of regime inferior only to the best regime but by far superior to democracy, i.e., the kind of regime which prevailed in Athens during most of Socrates' (and Plato's) lifetime. In the *Laws* the Athenian stranger attempts to correct timocracy, i.e., to change it into the best possible regime which is somehow in between timocracy and the best regime of the *Republic*. That best possible regime will prove to be very similar to "the ancestral regime," the predemocratic regime, of Athens.

The Cretan and Spartan laws were found to be faulty because they did not permit their subjects to taste the greatest pleasures. But can drinking be said to afford the greatest pleasures, even the greatest sensual pleasures? Yet the Athenian had in mind those greatest pleasures which

111. *Ibid.*, 639b–c.
112. *Republic* 544c.

people can enjoy in public and to which they must be exposed in order to learn to control them. The pleasures of
banquets are drinking and singing. In order to justify banquets one must therefore discuss also singing, music, and
hence education as a whole:[113] the music pleasures are the
greatest pleasures which people can enjoy in public and
which they must learn to control by being exposed to them.
The Spartan and Cretan laws suffer then from the great
defect that they do not at all, or at least not sufficiently,
expose their subjects to the music pleasures.[114] The reason
for this is that these two societies are not towns but armed
camps, a kind of herd: in Sparta and Crete even those
youths who are by nature fit to be educated as individuals
by private teachers are brought up merely as members of a
herd. In other words, the Spartans and Cretans know only
how to sing in choruses: they do not know the most beautiful song, the most noble music.[115] In the *Republic,* the city
of the armed camp, a greatly improved Sparta, was transcended by the City of Beauty, the city in which philosophy, the highest Muse, is duly honored. In the *Laws,* where
the best possible regime is presented, this transcending does
not take place. The city of the *Laws* is, however, not a city
of the armed camp in any sense. Yet it has certain features
in common with the city of the armed camp of the *Republic.* Just as in the *Republic,* music education proves to be
education toward moderation, and such education proves
to require the supervision of musicians and poets by the
true statesman or legislator. Yet while in the *Republic* education to moderation proves to culminate in the love of
the beautiful, in the *Laws* moderation rather takes on the
colors of sense of shame or of reverence. Education is surely
education to virtue, to the virtue of the citizen or to the
virtue of man.[116]

113. *Laws* 642a.
114. Cf. *ibid.,* 673a–c.
115. *Ibid.,* 666e–667b.
116. *Ibid.,* 643c, 659d–e; 653a–b.

The virtue of man is primarily the proper posture toward pleasures and pains or the proper control of pleasures and pains; the proper control is the control effected by right reasoning. If the result of reasoning is adopted by the city, that result becomes law; law which deserves the name is the dictate of right reasoning primarily regarding pleasures and pains. The kinship but not identity of right reasoning and good laws corresponds to the kinship but not identity of the good man and the good citizen. In order to learn to control the ordinary pleasures and pains, the citizens must be exposed from their childhood to the pleasures afforded by poetry and the other imitative arts, which in turn must be controlled by good or wise laws, by laws which therefore ought never to be changed; the desire for innovation so natural to poetry and the other imitative arts must be suppressed as much as possible; the means for achieving this is the consecration of the correct after it has come to light. The perfect legislator will persuade or compel the poets to teach that justice goes with pleasure and injustice with pain. The perfect legislator will demand that this manifestly salutary doctrine be taught even if it were not true.[117] This doctrine takes the place of the theology of the second book of the *Republic*. In the *Republic* the salutary teaching regarding the relation of justice and pleasure or happiness could not be discussed in the context of the education of the nonphilosophers because the *Republic* did not presuppose, as the *Laws* does, that the interlocutors of the chief character know what justice is.[118] The whole conversation regarding education and therewith also the ends or principles of legislation is subsumed by the Athenian stranger under the theme "wine" and even "drunkenness" because the improvement of old laws can safely be entrusted only to well-bred old men, who as such are averse to every change and who, in order to become willing to

---

117. *Ibid.*, 660e–664b.
118. *Republic* 392a–c.

change the old laws, must undergo some rejuvenation like the one produced by the drinking of wine.

Only after having determined the end which political life is meant to serve (education and virtue) does the stranger turn to the beginning of political life or the genesis of the city in order to discover the cause of political change and in particular of the change of regimes. There have been many beginnings of political life because there have been many destructions of almost all men through floods, plagues, and similar calamities bringing with them the destruction of all arts and tools; only a few human beings survived on mountaintops or in other privileged places; it took many generations until they dared to descend to the lowlands, and during those generations the last recollection of the arts vanished. The condition out of which all cities and regimes, all arts and laws, all vice and virtue emerged is men's lack of all these things; the "out of which" something emerges is one kind of cause of the thing in question; the primary lack of what we may call civilization would seem to be the cause of all political change.[119] If man had had a perfect beginning, there would have been no cause for change, and the imperfection of his beginning is bound to have effects in all stages, however perfect, of his civilization. The stranger shows that this is the case by following the changes which human life underwent from the beginnings when men apparently were virtuous because they were, not indeed wise, but simpleminded or innocent yet in fact savage, until the destruction of the original settlement of Sparta and her sister cities Messene and Argos. He only alludes with delicacy to the Spartans' despotic subjugation of the Messenians. He summarizes the result of his inquiry by enumerating the generally accepted and effective titles to rule. It is the contradiction among the titles or the claims to them which explains the change of regimes. It appears that the title to rule based on wisdom, while the highest, is only one among seven. Among

119. *Laws* 676a,c, 678a.

the others we find the title or claim of the master to rule over his slaves, of the stronger to rule over the weaker, and of those chosen by lot to rule over those not so chosen.[120] Wisdom is not a sufficient title; a viable regime presupposes a blend of the claim based on wisdom with the claims based on the other kinds of superiority; perhaps the proper or wise blend of some of the other titles can act as a substitute for the title deriving from wisdom. The Athenian stranger does not abstract, as the Eleatic stranger does, from bodily force as a necessary ingredient of the rule of man over man. The viable regime must be mixed. The Spartan regime is mixed. But is it mixed wisely? In order to answer this question one must first see the ingredients of the right mixture in isolation. These are monarchy, of which Persia offers the outstanding example, and democracy, of which Athens offers the most outstanding example.[121] Monarchy by itself stands for the absolute rule of the wise man or of the master; democracy stands for freedom. The right mixture is that of wisdom and freedom, of wisdom and consent, of the rule of wise laws framed by a wise legislator and administered by the best members of the city, and of the rule of the common people.

After the end as well as the general character of the best possible regime have been made clear, Kleinias reveals that the present conversation is of direct use to him. The Cretans plan to found a colony, and they have commissioned him together with others to take care of the project and in particular to frame laws for the colony as they see fit; they may even select foreign laws if they appear to them to be superior to the Cretan laws. The people to be settled come from Crete and from the Peloponnesos: they do not come from one and the same city. If they came from the same city, with the same language and the same laws and the same sacred rites and beliefs, they could not easily be persuaded to accept institutions different from those of

120. *Ibid.,* 690a–d.
121. *Ibid.,* 693d.

their home city. On the other hand, heterogeneity of the population of a future city causes dissensions.[122] In the present case the heterogeneity seems to be sufficient to make possible considerable change for the better, i.e., the establishment of the best possible regime, and yet not too great to prevent fusion. We have here the viable alternative to the expulsion of everyone older than ten which would be required for the establishment of the best regime of the *Republic*. The traditions which the various groups of settlers bring with them will be modified rather than eradicated. Thanks to the good fortune which brought about the presence in Crete of the Athenian stranger while the sending out of the colony is in preparation, there is a fair chance that the traditions will be modified wisely. All the greater care must be taken that the new order established under the guidance of the wise man will not be changed afterward by less wise men: it ought to be exposed to change as little as possible, for any change of a wise order seems to be a change for the worse. At any rate, without the chance presence of the Athenian stranger in Crete there would be no prospect of wise legislation for the new city. This makes us understand the stranger's assertion that not human beings but chance legislates: most laws are as it were dictated by calamities. Still, some room is left for the legislative art. Or, inversely, the possessor of the legislative art is helpless without good fortune, for which he can only pray. The most favorable circumstance for which the legislator would pray is that the city for which he is to frame laws be ruled by a young tyrant whose nature is in some respects the same as that of the philosopher, except that he does not have to be graceful or witty, a lover of the truth, and just; his lack of justice (the fact that he is prompted by desire for his own power and glory alone) does not do harm if he is willing to listen to the wise legislator. Given this condition—given a coincidence of the greatest power with wisdom through the cooperation of the tyrant

122. *Ibid.*, 707e–708d.

with the wise legislator—the legislator will effect the quickest and most profound change for the better in the habits of the citizens. But since the city to be founded is to undergo as little change as possible, it is perhaps more important to realize that the regime most difficult to change is oligarchy, the regime which occupies the central place in the order of regimes presented in the *Republic*.[123] Surely, the city to be founded must not be tyrannically ruled. The best regime is that in which a god or demon rules, as in the age of Kronos, the golden age. The nearest imitation of divine rule is the rule of laws. But the laws in their turn depend on the man or men who can lay down and enforce the laws, i.e., the regime (monarchy, tyranny, oligarchy, aristocracy, democracy). In the case of each of these regimes a section of the city rules the rest, and therefore it rules the city with a view to a sectional interest, not to the common interest.[124] We know already the solution to this difficulty: the regime must be mixed as it was in a way in Sparta and Crete,[125] and it must adopt a code framed by a wise legislator.

The wise legislator will not limit himself to giving simple commands accompanied by sanctions, i.e., threats of punishment. This is the way for guiding slaves, not free men. He will preface the laws with preambles or preludes setting forth the reasons of the laws. Yet different kinds of reasons are needed for persuading different kinds of men, and the multiplicity of reasons may be confusing and thus endanger the simplicity of obedience. The legislator must then possess the art of saying simultaneously different things to different kinds of citizens in such a way that the legislator's speech will effect in all cases the same simple result: obedience to his laws. In acquiring this art he will be greatly helped by the poets.[126] Laws must be twofold: they must

123. Cf. *ibid.*, 708e–712a with *Republic* 487a.
124. *Laws* 713c–715b.
125. *Ibid.*, 712c–e.
126. *Ibid.*, 719b–720e.

consist of the "unmixed law," the bald statement of what ought to be done or forborne "or else," i.e., the "tyrannical prescription," and the prelude to the law which gently persuades by appealing to reason.[127] The proper mixture of coercion and persuasion, of "tyranny" and "democracy,"[128] of wisdom and consent, proves everywhere to be the character of wise political arrangements.

The laws require a general prelude—an exhortation to honor the various beings which deserve honor in their proper order. Since the rule of laws is an imitation of divine rule, honor must be given first and above everything else to the gods, next to the other superhuman beings, then to the ancestors, then to one's father and mother. Everyone must also honor his soul, but next to the gods. The order of rank between honoring one's soul and honoring one's parents is not made entirely clear. Honoring one's soul means acquiring the various virtues without which no one can be a good citizen. The general exhortation culminates in the proof that the virtuous life is more pleasant than the life of vice. Before the founder of the new colony can begin with the legislation proper, he must take two measures of the utmost importance. In the first place he must effect a kind of purge of the potential citizens: only the right kind of settlers must be admitted to the new colony. Second, the land must be distributed among those admitted to citizenship. There will then be no communism. Whatever advantages communism might have, it is not feasible if the legislator does not himself exercise tyrannical rule,[129] whereas in the present case not even the cooperation of the legislator with a tyrant is contemplated. Nevertheless, the land must remain the property of the whole city; no citizen will be the absolute owner of the land allotted to him. The land will be divided into allotments which must never be changed by selling, buying, or in any

127. *Ibid.*, 722e–723a; cf. 808d–e.
128. Cf. Aristotle, *Politics* 1266a 1–3.
129. Plato, *Laws* 739a–740a.

other way, and this will be achieved if every landowner must leave his entire allotment to a single son; the other sons must try to marry heiresses; to prevent the excess of the male citizen population beyond the number of the originally established allotments, recourse must be had to birth control and in the extreme case to the sending out of colonies. There must not be gold and silver in the city and as little money-making as possible. It is impossible that there should be equality of property, but there ought to be an upper limit to what a citizen can own: the richest citizen must be permitted to own no more than four times what the poorest citizens own, i.e., the allotment of land including house and slaves. It is impossible to disregard the inequality of property in the distribution of political power. The citizen body will be divided into four classes according to the amount of property owned. The land assigned to each citizen must be sufficient to enable him to serve the city in war as a knight or as a hoplite. In other words, citizenship is limited to knights and hoplites. The regime seems to be what Aristotle calls a polity—a democracy limited by a considerable property qualification. But this is not correct, as appears particularly from the laws concerning membership in the Council and election to the Council. The Council is what we would call the executive part of the government; each twelfth of the Council is to govern for a month. The Council is to consist of four equally large groups, the first group being chosen from the highest property class, the second group being chosen from the second highest property class, and so on. All citizens have the same voting power, but whereas all citizens are obliged to vote for councillors from the highest property class, only the citizens of the two highest property classes are obliged to vote for councillors from the lowest property class. These arrangements are obviously meant to favor the wealthy; the regime is meant to be a mean between monarchy and democracy[130] or, more precisely, a mean more

130. *Ibid.,* 756b–e.

oligarchic or aristocratic than a polity. Similar privileges are granted to the wealthy also as regards power in the Assembly and the holding of the most honorable offices. It is, however, not wealth as wealth which is favored: no craftsman or trader, however wealthy, can be a citizen. Only those can be citizens who have the leisure to devote themselves to the practice of citizen virtue.

The most conspicuous part of the legislation proper concerns impiety, which is of course treated within the context of the penal law. The fundamental impiety is atheism, or the denial of the existence of gods. Since a good law will not merely punish crimes or appeal to fear but will also appeal to reason, the Athenian stranger is compelled to demonstrate the existence of gods and, since gods who do not care for men's justice, who do not reward the just and punish the unjust, are not sufficient for the city, he must demonstrate divine providence as well. The *Laws* is the only Platonic work which contains such a demonstration. It is the only Platonic work which begins with "A god." One might say that it is Plato's most pious work, and that it is for this reason that he strikes therein at the root of impiety, i.e., at the opinion that there are no gods. The Athenian stranger takes up the question regarding the gods, although it was not even raised in Crete or in Sparta; it was, however, raised in Athens.[131] Kleinias strongly favors the demonstration recommended by the Athenian on the ground that it would constitute the finest and best prelude to the whole code. The Athenian cannot refute the atheists before he has stated their assertions. It appears that they assert that body is prior to soul or mind, or that soul or mind is derivative from body and, consequently, that nothing is by nature just or unjust, or that all right originates in convention. The refutation of them consists in the proof that soul is prior to body, which proof implies that there is natural right. The punishments for impiety differ according to the different kinds of impiety. It is not clear what

131. *Ibid.*, 886; cf. 891b.

punishment, if any, is inflicted on the atheist who is a just man; he is surely less severely punished than, for instance, the man who practices forensic rhetoric for the sake of gain. Even in cases of the other kinds of impiety, capital punishment will be extremely rare. We mention these facts because their insufficient consideration might induce ignorant people to scold Plato for his alleged lack of liberalism. We do not here describe such people as ignorant because they believe that liberalism calls for unqualified toleration of the teaching of all opinions however dangerous or degrading. We call them ignorant because they do not see how extraordinarily liberal Plato is according to their own standards, which cannot possibly be "absolute." The standards generally recognized in Plato's time are best illustrated by the practice of Athens, a city highly renowned for her liberality and gentleness. In Athens Socrates was punished with death because he was held not to believe in the existence of the gods worshipped by the city of Athens —of gods whose existence was known only from hearsay. In the city of the *Laws* the belief in gods is demanded only to the extent to which it is supported by demonstration; and in addition, those who are not convinced by the demonstration, but are just men, will not be condemned to death.

The stability of the order sketched by the Athenian stranger seems to be guaranteed as far as the stability of any political order can be: it is guaranteed by obedience on the part of the large majority of citizens to wise laws which are as unchangeable as possible, by an obedience that results chiefly from education to virtue, from the formation of character. Still, laws are only second best: no law can be as wise as the decision of a truly wise man on the spot. Provision must therefore be made for, as it were, infinite progress in improving the laws in the interest of increasing improvement of the political order, as well as of counteracting the decay of the laws. Legislation must then be an unending process; at each time there must be living legislators. Laws should be changed only with the utmost caution, only in the case of universally admitted necessity. The later legislators must aim at the same commanding end as the original legislator: the excellence of the souls of the members of the city.[132] To prevent change of laws, intercourse of the citizens with foreigners must be closely supervised. No citizen shall go abroad for a private purpose. But citizens of high reputation and more than fifty years old who desire to see how other men live, and especially to converse with outstanding men from whom they can learn something about the improvement of the laws, are encouraged to do so.[133] Yet all these and similar measures do not suffice for the salvation of the laws and the regime; the firm foundation is still lacking. That firm foundation can only be supplied by a Nocturnal Council consisting of the most outstanding old citizens and select younger citizens of thirty years and older. The Nocturnal Council is to be for the city what the mind is for the human individual. To perform its function its members must possess above everything else the most adequate knowledge possible of the single end at which all political action directly or indirectly aims. This end is virtue. Virtue is meant to be one, yet it is also many; there are four kinds of virtue, and at least two of them—wisdom and courage (or spiritedness)—are radically different from one another.[134] How then can there be a single end of the city? The Nocturnal Council cannot perform its function if it cannot answer this question, or, more generally and perhaps more precisely stated, the Nocturnal Council must include at least some men who know what the virtues themselves are or who know the ideas of the various virtues as well as what unites them, so that all together can justly be called "virtue" in the singular: is "virtue," the single end of the city, one or a whole or both or something else? They also must know, as far as is hu-

132. *Ibid.,* 769a–771a, 772a–d, 875c–d.
133. *Ibid.,* 949e ff.
134. *Ibid.,* 963e.

manly possible, the truth about the gods. Solid reverence for the gods arises only from knowledge of the soul as well as of the movements of the stars. Only men who combine this knowledge with the popular or vulgar virtues can be adequate rulers of the city: one ought to hand over the city for rule to the Nocturnal Council if it comes into being. Plato brings the regime of the *Laws* around by degrees to the regime of the *Republic*.[135] Having arrived at the end of the *Laws,* we must return to the beginning of the *Republic*.

135. Aristotle, *Politics* 1265a 1–4.

Part Three

Editor's Note: The first two parts of this essay were published in *Modern Judaism* 1 (1981): 17–45 and represent an edited version of two of three lectures Leo Strauss delivered at the Hillel House, University of Chicago, in November 1952. Part three, the third lecture, was published as "The Mutual Influence of Theology and Philosophy" in *The Independent Journal of Philosophy* 3 (1979): 111–18. The text of the original lecture was edited slightly to bring it into line with a published Hebrew translation (in *Iyyun. Hebrew Philosophical Quarterly* 5, no. 1 January 1954). In the few places where the English text departs from the Hebrew translation, the English reading has been included but set off in brackets. All three parts are reprinted here with permission.

Progress or Return?

The Contemporary Crisis
in Western Civilization

I

The title of this lecture indicates that progress has become a problem—that it could seem as if progress has led us to the brink of an abyss, and it is therefore necessary to consider alternatives to it. For example, to stop where we are or else, if this should be impossible, to return. Return is the translation for the Hebrew word *t'shuvah*. *T'shuvah* has an ordinary and an emphatic meaning. Its emphatic meaning is rendered in English by "repentance." Repentance is return, meaning the return from the wrong way to the right one. This implies that we were once on the right way before we turned to the wrong way. Originally we were on the right way; deviation or sin or imperfection is not original. Man is originally at home in his father's house. He becomes a stranger through estrangement, through sinful estrangement. Repentance, return, is homecoming.

I remind you of a few verses from the first chapter of *Isaiah*. "How is the faithful city become a harlot. It was full of judgment, righteousness lodged in it. But now murderers. Therefore, saith the Lord . . . I will restore thy judges as at first and thy councillors as at the beginning. Afterwards thou shalt be called the city of righteousness, the faithful city." Repentance is return; redemption is restoration. A perfect beginning—the faithful city—is followed by defection, decline, sin, and this is followed by a perfect end. But the perfect end is the restoration of the perfect beginning. The faithful city at the beginning and at the end. At the beginning, men did not roam a forest left to themselves, unprotected and unguided. The beginning is the Garden of Eden. Perfection results in the beginning—in the beginning of time, the oldest time. Hence perfection is sought derivatively in the old time—in the father, the father of fathers, the patriarchs. The patriarchs are the divine chariot which Ezekiel had seen in his vision. The great time—the classic time—is in the past. First the period of the desert; later the period of the temple. The life of the Jew is the life of recollection. It is at the same time a life of anticipation, of hope, but the hope for redemption is restoration—*restituto in integro. Jeremiah* 30: "Their children shall be as aforetime." Redemption consists in the return of the youngest, the most remote from the past, the most future ones, so to speak, to the pristine condition. The past is superior to the present. This thought is, then, perfectly compatible with hope for the future. But does the hope for redemption—the expectation of the Messiah —not assign a much higher place to the future than to the past, however venerable?

This is not unqualifiedly true. According to the most accepted view, the Messiah is inferior to Moses. The messianic age will witness the restoration of the full practice of the Torah, part of which was discontinued owing to the destruction of the Temple. Belief in the Torah was always the way in Judaism, whereas messianism frequently became dormant. For example, as I learn from Gershom Scholem, cabbalism prior to the sixteenth century concentrated upon the beginning; it was only with Isaac Luria that cabbalism began to concentrate upon the future—upon the end. Yet even here, the last age became as important as the first. It did not become more important. Furthermore

(I quote Scholem), "by inclination and habit, Luria was decidedly conservative. This tendency is well expressed in persistent attempts to relate what he had to say to older authorities. For Luria, salvation means actually nothing but restitution, reintegration of the original whole or *tikkun*, to use the Hebrew term. For Luria, the appearance of the Messiah is nothing but the consummation of the continuous process of restoration. The path to the end of all things is also the path to the beginning." Judaism is a concern with return, it is not a concern with progress. Return can easily be expressed in biblical Hebrew; progress cannot. Hebrew renderings of progress seem to be somehow artificial, not to say paradoxic. Even if it were true that messianism bespeaks the predominance of the concern with the future, or of living toward the future, this would not affect in any way the belief in the superiority of the past to the present. The fact that the present is nearer in time to the final redemption than is the past does not mean, of course, that the present is superior in piety or wisdom to the past, especially to the classic past. Today, the word *t'shuvah* has acquired a still more emphatic meaning. Today, *t'shuvah* sometimes means, not a return which takes place within Judaism, but a return to Judaism on the part of many Jews who, or whose fathers, had broken with Judaism as a whole. That abandonment of Judaism—that break with Judaism—did not understand itself, of course, as a defection or desertion, as leaving the right way; nor did it understand itself as a return to a truth which the Jewish tradition in its turn had deserted; nor even merely a turn to something superior. It understood itself as progress. It granted to the Jewish tradition, as it were, that Judaism is old, very old, whereas it itself had no past of which it could boast. But it regarded this very fact, the antiquity of Judaism, as a proof of its own superiority and of Judaism's inadequacy. For it questioned the very premise underlying the notion of return, that premise being the perfect character of the beginning and of the olden times.

It assumed that the beginning is most imperfect and that perfection can be found only in the end. So much so that the movement from the beginning toward the end is in principle a progress from radical imperfection toward perfection. From this point of view, age did not have any claim whatsoever to veneration. Antiquity rather deserved contempt or possibly contempt mitigated by pity.

Let us try to clarify this issue somewhat more fully by contrasting the life characterized by the idea of return with the life characterized by the idea of progress. When the prophets call their people to account, they do not limit themselves to accusing them of this or that particular crime or sin. They recognize the root of all particular crimes in the fact that the people have forsaken their God. They accuse their people of rebellion. Originally, in the past, they were faithful or loyal; now they are in a state of rebellion. In the future they will return, and God will restore them to their original place. The primary, original, initial, is loyalty; unfaithfulness, infidelity, is secondary. The very notion of unfaithfulness or infidelity presupposes that fidelity or loyalty is primary. The perfect character of the origin is a condition of sin—of the thought of sin. Man who understands himself in this way longs for the perfection of the origin, or of the classic past. He suffers from the present; he hopes for the future.

Progressive man, on the other hand, looks back to a most imperfect beginning. The beginning is barbarism, stupidity, rudeness, extreme scarcity. He does not feel that he has lost something of great, not to say infinite, importance; he has lost only his chains. He does not suffer from the recollection of the past. Looking back to the past, he is proud of his achievements; he is certain of the superiority of the present to the past. He is not satisfied with the present; he looks to future progress. But he does not merely hope or pray for a better future; he thinks that he can bring it about by his own effort. Seeking perfection in a future which is in no sense the beginning or the restoration of the beginning, he lives unqualifiedly toward the future. The life which understands itself as a life of loyalty or faithfulness appears to him as backward, as being under the spell of old prejudices. What the others call rebellion, he calls revolution or liberation. To the polarity faithfulness-rebellion, he opposes the polarity prejudice-freedom.

To repeat, the return to Judaism succeeds a break with Judaism which eventually, or from the beginning, understood itself as a progress beyond Judaism. That break was effected in a classic manner by a solitary man—Spinoza. Spinoza denied the truth of Judaism—Judaism, which includes, of course, the Bible, is a set of prejudices and superstitious practices of the ancient tribes. Spinoza found in this mass of heterogeneous lore some elements of truth, but he did not consider this as peculiar to Judaism. He found the same elements of truth in paganism as well. Spinoza was excommunicated by the Jewish community in Amsterdam. He ceased to regard himself as a Jew. He has sometimes been accused of having been hostile to Judaism and to Jews. I do not find that he was more opposed to Judaism than to Christianity, for example, and I do not find that he was hostile to Jews. He acquired a strange, or perhaps not so strange, neutrality in regard to the secular conflict between Judaism and Christianity. Looking at the Jews and the Jewish fate from this neutral point of view, he even made some suggestions as to the redemption of the Jews. One suggestion is almost explicit. After having asserted that the Jews have not been elected in any other sense than that in which the Canaanites too had been elected earlier, and that therefore the Jews have not been elected for eternity, he tries to show that their survival after the loss of the land can be explained in a perfectly natural manner. In this context, he makes the following remark: "If the foundations of their religion did not effeminate their minds, I would absolutely believe that they might again restore their state, under auspicious circumstances, considering the fact that human things are mutable." Which means the hope for divine redemption is altogether baseless. The sufferings of the exiles are altogether meaningless. There is no guarantee whatsoever that these sufferings will ever cease. But the first condition for entertaining any reasonable hope for the end of the exile is that the Jews should get rid of the foundations of their religion, that is to say, of the spirit of Judaism. For that spirit, Spinoza thought, is adverse to warlike enterprise and to the energy of government. As far as I know, this is the earliest suggestion of a purely political solution to the Jewish problem. The substitution of a purely political solution for the miracle of redemption toward which men can contribute, if at all, only by a life of piety. It is the first inkling of unqualifiedly political Zionism. But Spinoza intimated still another solution. In his *Theologico-Political Treatise*, he sketches the outline of what he regarded as a decent society. That society, as described by him, can be characterized as a liberal democracy. Incidentally, Spinoza may be said to be the first philosopher who advocated liberal democracy. Spinoza still regarded it as necessary to underwrite liberal democracy with a public religion or a state religion. Now it is very remarkable that that religion, that state religion, which is emphatically not a religion of reason, is neither Christian nor Jewish. It is neutral in regard to the differences between Judaism and Christianity. Furthermore, Spinoza claims to have proved, on the basis of the Bible, that the Mosaic law was binding only for the period of the Jewish commonwealth. If one considers these two facts, first, that the state religion is neutral in regard to the differences between Judaism and Christianity, and second, that the Mosaic law is no longer binding, one is entitled to say that Spinoza laid the foundation for another purely political solution of the Jewish problem. In fact, for the alternative to political Zionism and the solution known as assimilationism.

In Spinoza's liberal democracy, Jews do not have to become baptized in order to acquire full citizen rights. It is sufficient if they accept the extremely latitudinarian state religion and they may then forget about the Mosaic law. In this neutral atmosphere, the sufferings of the exiles could be expected to wither away. Spinoza has merely intimated the two classical alternatives which followed from the radical break with Judaism. The practical consequences were fully developed in the course of the nineteenth century. But when they were exposed to the test of practice, they led into certain difficulties.

On the premise of assimilationism, Jewish suffering—suffering for Judaism—becomes meaningless. That suffering is merely the residue of a benighted past, a residue which will cease in proportion as mankind makes further progress. But the results were somewhat disappointing. The decrease of the power of Christianity did not bring about the expected decrease of anti-Jewish feeling. Even where legal equality of the Jews became a fact, it contrasted all the more strongly with the social inequality which continued. In a number of countries, legal inequality and the cruder forms of social inequality gave way to subtler forms of social inequality, but the social inequality did not for this reason become less of a hardship. On the contrary, sensitivity increased with social ascent. Our ancestors had been immune to hatred and contempt because it merely proved to them the election of Israel. The uprooted assimilated Jew had nothing to oppose to hatred and contempt except his naked self. Full social equality proved to require the complete disappearance of the Jews as Jews—a proposition which is impracticable, if for no other reason, than at least for the perfectly sufficient one of simple self-respect. Why should we, who have a heroic past behind and within us, which is not second to that of any other group anywhere on earth, deny or forget that past? That past which is all the more heroic, one could say, since its chief characters are not the glitter and trappings of martial glory and of cultural splendor, although it does not lack even these. Assimilation proved to require inner enslavement as the price of external freedom. Or, to put it somewhat differently, assimilationism seemed to land the Jews into the bog of Philistinism, of shallow satisfaction with the most unsatisfactory present. A most inglorious end for a people which had been led out of the house of bondage into the desert with careful avoidance of the land of the Philistines, although, to quote, "and it came to pass when Pharaoh had let the people go, that God led them not through the way of the land of the Philistines, although that was near." It is always near. Once progress was indeed achieved, hatred of the Jews could no longer present itself among educated or half-educated people as hatred of the Jews. It had to disguise itself as anti-Semitism, a term invented by some bashful German or French pedant of the nineteenth century. It is certainly a most improper term. The shock administered by the continued existence of social inequality and by the emergence of anti-Semitism, especially in Germany and France, proved to be a fair warning for what was going to happen in Germany, especially between 1933 to 1945.

Those European Jews who realized that assimilation was no solution to the Jewish problem and looked out for another purely human or political solution turned to political Zionism. But political Zionism led to difficulties of its own. The basic idea underlying purely political Zionism was not Zionist at all. It could have been satisfied by a Jewish state anywhere on earth. Political Zionism was already a concession to the Jewish tradition. Those who were seeking a solution of the Jewish problem other than the disappearance of the Jews had to accept not only the territory hallowed by Jewish tradition but its language, Hebrew, as well. They were forced to accept, furthermore, Jewish culture. Cultural Zionism became a very powerful rival of political Zionism. But the heritage to which cultural Zionism had recourse rebelled against being interpreted in terms of culture or civilization, meaning, as an autonomous product of the genius of the Jewish people. That culture or civilization had its core in the Torah, and the Torah presents itself as given by God, not created by Israel. Thus the attempts to solve the Jewish problem by purely human means ended in failure. The knot which was not tied by man could not be untied by man. I do not believe that the American experience forces us to qualify these statements. It is very far from me to minimize the difference between a nation conceived in liberty and dedicated to the proposition that all men are created equal, and the nations of the old world, which certainly were not conceived in liberty. I share the hope in America and the faith in America, but I am compelled to add that that faith and that hope cannot be of the same character as that faith and that hope which a Jew has in regard to Judaism and which the Christian has in regard to Christianity. No one claims that the faith in America and the hope for America is based on explicit divine premises.

The attempt to solve the Jewish problem has failed because of the overwhelming power of the past. The experience of that power by a generation which had become forgetful of that power is part of what is sometimes called the discovery of history. The discovery was made in the nineteenth century. As a discovery, it consisted in the realization of something which was not realized previously: that the acceptance of the past or the return to the Jewish tradition is something radically different from a mere continuation of that tradition. It is quite true that Jewish life in the past was almost always more than a continuation of a tradition. Very great changes within that tradition have taken place in the course of the centuries. But it is also true that the change which we are witnessing today and which all of us are participating in is, in one way or the other, qualitatively different from all previous changes within Judaism.

Let me try to clarify that difference. Those who today return to Judaism do not assert that, say, Spinoza was altogether wrong. They accept at least the principle of that biblical criticism which was regarded as the major offense of Spinoza. Generally speaking, those who today return to Judaism admit that modern rationalism, to use this vague term, had a number of important insights which cannot be thrown overboard and which were alien to the Jewish tradition. Therefore, they modify the Jewish tradition consciously. You only have to contrast that with the procedure of Maimonides in the twelfth century, who when introducing Aristotelian philosophy into Judaism, had to assume that he was merely recovering Israel's own lost inheritance. These present-day Jews who return to the tradition try to do in the element of reflection what traditionally was done unconsciously or naively. Their attitude is historical rather than traditional. They study the thought of the past as thought of the past and therefore as not necessarily binding on the present generation as it stands. But still what they are doing is meant to be a return—that is to say, the acceptance of something which was equally accepted by the Jewish tradition. Thus the question arises as to the relative importance of these two elements: the new element and the unchanged element, the new element being the fact that present-day Judaism is forced to be what has been called "post-critical." Are we wiser than our ancestors in the decisive respect or only in a subordinate respect? In the first case, we still would have to claim that we have made decisive progress. But if the insights implied in the "post-critical" character of present-day Judaism are only of a subordinate character, the movement which we are witnessing can justly claim to be a return. Now this movement of return would not have had the effect which it had, but for the fact that not only among Jews but throughout the Western world more generally, progress has become a matter of doubt. The term "progress" in its full and emphatic meaning has practically disappeared from serious literature. People speak less and less of "progress" and more and more of "change." They no longer claim to know that we are moving in the right direction. Not progress, but the 'belief' in progress or the 'idea' of progress as a social or historical phenomenon, is a major theme for the present-day student of society. A generation or so ago, the most famous study on this subject was entitled *The Idea of Progress*. Its opposite number in present-day literature is entitled *The Belief in Progress*. The substitution of belief for idea is in itself worthy of note. Now to understand the crisis of the belief in progress, we must first clarify the content of that belief.

What is progress? Now progress, in the emphatic sense, presupposes that there is something which is simply good, or the end, as the goal of progress. Progress is change in the direction of the end. But this is only the necessary, not the sufficient, condition of the idea of progress. A sign of this is the notion of the Golden Age which also presupposes a notion of the simply good but that simply good, that end, is here located in the beginning. The end of man, the simply good, must be understood in a specific manner if it is to become the basis of the idea of progress. I suggest that the end of man must be understood primarily as perfection of the understanding in such a manner that the perfection of the understanding is somehow akin to the arts and crafts. It has always been controversial whether man's beginning was perfect or imperfect, but both parties to the controversy admitted that the arts and the crafts and certainly their perfection do not belong to man's beginning. Therefore, to decide the question, regardless of the perfection or imperfection of man's beginning, depends upon how the question of the value of the arts and crafts is decided. At any rate, the idea of progress presupposes that there is the simply good life and that the beginning of life is radically imperfect. Accordingly, we find in Greek science or philosophy a full consciousness of progress: in the first place, of progress achieved and its inevitable concomitant, looking down on the inferiority or the weakness of the ancients; and as regards future progress, Aristotle himself noted: "In the art of medicine, there is no limit to the pursuit of health, and in the other arts there is no limit to the pursuit of their several ends. For they aim at accomplishing their ends to the uttermost." The possibility of infinite progress, at least in certain respects, is here stated. Yet *the* idea of progress is different from the Greek conception of progress. What is the relative importance of fulfillment, on the one hand, and future progress on the other? The most elaborate statements on progress seemed to occur in Lucretius and Seneca, where the possibility of infinite progress in the sciences and arts is clearly stated. Yet Lucretius was an Epicurean, and Seneca was a Stoic, which means they both presupposed that the fundamental issue has been settled already, either by Epicurus or by the Stoa. No future progress then in the decisive respect is envisioned. Generally speaking, it seems that in classical thought the decisive questions were thought to have been answered as far as they can be answered. The only exception of which I know is Plato, who held that the fulfillment proper, namely full wisdom, is not possible but only quest for wisdom, which in Greek means philosophy. He also insisted that there are no assignable limits to that quest for wisdom, and therefore it follows from Plato's notion that indefinite progress is possible in principle.

Hitherto I have spoken of intellectual progress. What about social progress? Are they parallel? The idea that they are necessarily parallel or that intellectual progress is accompanied in principle by social progress was known to the classics. We find there the idea that the art of legislation, which is the overarching social art, progresses like any other art. Yet Aristotle, who reports this doctrine, questions this solution, and he notes the radical difference between laws and arts or intellectual pursuits. More generally stated, or more simply stated, he notes the radical difference between the requirements of social life and the requirements of intellectual life. The paramount requirement of society is stability, as distinguished from progress. If I summarize this point, in the classical conception of progress, it is clearly admitted that infinite intellectual progress in secondary matters is theoretically possible. But we must add immediately, there is no practical possibility for that, for according to the one school, the visible universe is of finite duration; it has come into being and will perish again. And, according to the other view, which held that the visible universe is eternal, they asserted, especially Aristotle, that there are periodic cataclysms which will destroy all earlier civilization. Hence, eternal recurrence of the same progressive process, followed by decay and destruction.

Now what is lacking in the classical conception as compared to the modern? I see two points. First, there is lacking the notion of a guaranteed parallelism between intellectual and social progress, and secondly, there is no necessary end of the progressive process through telluric or cosmic catastrophes. As to the first point—the guaranteed parallelism between social and intellectual progress—in the classical statements about progress the emphasis is upon intellectual progress rather than on social progress. The basic idea can be stated as follows: science or philosophy is the preserve of a small minority, of those who have good natures, as they called it, who are gifted, as we say. Their progress, the progress of this tiny minority, does not necessarily affect society at large—far from it. It was this thought which was radically challenged in the seventeenth century, the beginning of modern philosophy and with the introduction of the crucial notion of the idea of method. Method brings about the levelling of the natural differences of the mind, and methods can be learned in principle by everyone. Only discovery remains the preserve of the few. But the acquisition of the results of the discovery and especially of the discovery of methods, is open to all. And there was a very simple proof: mathematical problems which formerly could not be solved by the greatest mathematical geniuses are now solved by high-school boys; the level of intelligence—that was the conclusion—has enormously been raised; and since this is possible, there is a necessary parallelism between intellectual and social progress.

As for the second point—the guarantee of an infinite future on earth not interrupted by telluric catastrophes—we find this thought fully developed in the eighteenth century. The human race had a beginning but no end, and it began about seven thousand years ago—you see that man did not accept the biblical chronology. Hence, since mankind is only seven thousand years old, it is still in its infancy. An infinite future is open, and look what we have achieved in this short span—compared with infinity—of seven thousand years. The decisive point is then this: there is a beginning and no end. Obviously the argument presupposes a beginning; otherwise you cannot figure out this infinite progress. The origin of this idea—a beginning but no end—could perhaps be found in Plato's dialogue *Timaeus*, if one takes that literally. Yet Plato certainly admitted regular telluric catastrophes. The source, I think, has to be found in a certain interpretation of the Bible, which we find, for example, in Maimonides, where you have the beginning—the creation—and no end, and cataclysms are excluded, not by natural necessity, but by the covenant of God with Noah. Yet precisely on the basis of the Bible, the beginning cannot be imperfect. Moreover, such additional important notions as the power of sin and of the need for greater redemption counter the effect of the notion of progress necessarily. Then again, in the Bible the core of the process from the beginning to the end is not progress. There is a classic past, whether we seek it at Mount Sinai or in the patriarchs or wherever else. Furthermore, and quite obviously, the core of the process as presented in the Bible is not intellectual-scientific development. The availability of infinite time for infinite progress appears, then, to be guaranteed by a document of revelation which condemns the other crucial elements of the idea of progress. Progress in the full and emphatic sense of the term is a hybrid notion.

This difficulty explains why the idea of progress underwent a radical modification in the nineteenth century. I quote one specimen: "Truth can no longer be found in a collection of fixed dogmatic propositions but only in the process of knowing, which process ascends from the lower to ever higher stages. All those stages are only perishable phases in the endless development from the lower to the higher. There is no final absolute truth and no final absolute stage of the development. Nothing is imperishable except the uninterrupted process of the coming and perishing, of the endless ascent from the lower to the higher. We do not have to consider here the question as to whether this view agrees with the present state of natural science, for at present natural science predicts a possible end to the existence of the earth and a certain end to the inhabitability of the earth. Natural science therefore assumes today that human history consists not only of an ascending, but also of a descending, process. However this may be, we are certainly still rather remote from the point where decline begins to set in." That statement was made by Friedrich Engels, the friend and co-worker of Karl Marx. Here we see infinite progress proper is abandoned, but the grave consequences of that are evaded by a wholly incomprehensible and unjustifiable "never mind." This more recent form of the belief in progress is based on the decision just to forget about the end, to forget about eternity.

The contemporary crisis of Western civilization may be said to be identical with the climactic crisis of the idea of progress in the full and emphatic sense of the term. I repeat, that idea consists of the following elements: the development of human thought as a whole is a progressive development, certainly the emergence of modern thought since the seventeenth century marks an unqualified progress beyond all earlier thought. There is a fundamental and necessary parallelism between intellectual and social progress. There are no assignable limits to intellectual and social progress. Infinite intellectual and social progress is actually possible. Once mankind has reached a certain stage of development, there exists a solid floor beneath which man can no longer sink. All these points have become questionable, I believe, to all of us. To mention only one point, perhaps the most massive one, the idea of progress was bound up with the notion of the conquest of nature, of man making himself the master and owner of nature for the purpose of relieving man's estate. The means for that goal was a new science. We all know of the enormous successes of the new science and of the technology which is based on it, and we all can witness the enormous increase of man's power. Modern man is a giant in comparison to earlier man. But we have also to note that there is no corresponding increase in wisdom and goodness. Modern man is a giant of whom we do not know whether he is better or worse than earlier man. More than that, this development of modern science culminated in the view that man is not able to distinguish in a responsible manner between good and evil—the famous value judgment. Nothing can be said responsibly about the right use of that immense power. Modern man is a blind giant. The doubt of progress led to a crisis of Western civilization as a whole, because in the course of the nineteenth century, the old distinction between good and bad, or good and evil, had been progressively replaced by the distinction between progressive and reactionary. No simple, inflexible, eternal distinction between good and bad could give assurance to those who had learned to take their bearings only by the distinction between progressive and reactionary, as soon as these people had become doubtful of progress.

The substitution of the distinction between progressive and reactionary for the distinction between good and bad is another aspect of the discovery of history, to which I referred before. The discovery of history, to state this very simply, is identical with the substitution of the past or the future for the eternal—the substitution of the temporal for the eternal. Now to understand this crisis of Western civilization, one cannot leave it at understanding the problematic character of the idea of progress, for the idea of progress is only a part, or an aspect, of a larger whole, of what we shall not hesitate to call modernity. What is modernity? A hard question which cannot be discussed in detail here. However, I would like to offer one or two somewhat rambling considerations. First, one might remember the decisive steps which led up to the contemporary crisis of Western civilization, and to those who are familiar with these things I must apologize for the superficiality of what is now offered in brief; but I think it is important to recall these things nevertheless. Therefore regard this as a stenogram, not as an analysis.

Western civilization has two roots: the Bible and Greek philosophy. Let us begin by looking at the first of these elements, the Bible, the biblical element. Modern rationalism rejected biblical theology and replaced it by such things as deism, pantheism, atheism. But in this process, biblical morality was in a way preserved. Goodness was still believed to consist in something like justice, benevolence, love, or charity; and modern rationalism has generated a tendency to believe that this biblical morality is better preserved if it is divorced from biblical theology. Now this was, of course, more visible in the nineteenth century than it is today; it is no longer so visible today because one crucial event happened around 1870–1880: the appearance of Nietzsche. Nietzsche's criticism can be reduced to one proposition: modern man has been trying to preserve biblical morality while abandoning biblical faith. That is impossible. If the biblical faith goes, biblical morality must go too, and a radically different morality must be accepted. The word which Nietzsche used is "the will to power." Nietzsche meant it in a very subtle and noble manner, yet the crude and ignoble way in which it was later understood is not altogether independent of the radical change of orientation he suggested.

As for the other major component of Western civilization, the classical element, that is the idea of philosophy or science, that too began to change. In the seventeenth century, a new philosophy and a new science began to emerge. They made the same claims as all earlier philosophy and science had done, but the result of this seventeenth century revolution produced something which had never existed before—the emergence of Science with a capital "S." Originally the attempt had been to replace traditional philosophy and science by a new philosophy and a new science; but in the course of a few generations it appeared that only a part of the new philosophy and science was successful and, indeed, amazingly successful. No one could question these developments, e.g., Newton. But only a part of the new science or philosophy was successful, and then the great distinction between philosophy and science, which we are all familiar with, came into being. Science is the successful part of modern philosophy or science, and philosophy is the unsuccessful part—the rump. Science is therefore higher in dignity than philosophy. The consequence, which you know, is the depreciation of all knowledge which is not scientific in this peculiar sense. Science becomes the authority for philosophy in a way perfectly comparable to the way in which theology was the authority for philosophy in the middle ages. Science is *the* perfection of man's natural understanding of the world. But then, certain things took place in the nineteenth century, e.g., the discovery of non-Euclidean geometry and its use in physics, which made it clear that science cannot be described adequately as the perfection of man's natural understanding of the world, but rather as a radical modification of man's natural understanding of the world. In other words, science is based on certain fundamental hypotheses which, being hypotheses, are not absolutely necessary and which always remain hypothetical. The consequence was again drawn most clearly by Nietzsche: science is only one interpretation of the world among many. It has certain advantages, but that of course does not give it any ultimately superior cognitive status. The last consequence stated by some men in our age is as you know: modern science is in no way superior to Greek science, as little as modern poetry is superior to Greek poetry. In other words, even science with its enormous prestige—a prestige higher than any other power in the modern world—is also a kind of giant with feet of clay, if you consider its foundations. As a consequence of this chain of scientific development the notion of a rational morality, the heritage of Greek philosophy, has, to repeat myself, lost its standing completely; all choices are, it is argued, ultimately nonrational or irrational.

II

The immediate cause of the decline of the belief in progress can perhaps be stated as follows: the idea of progress in the modern sense implies that once man has reached a certain level, intellectual and social or moral, there exists a firm level of being below which he cannot sink. This contention, however, is empirically refuted by the incredible barbarization which we have been so unfortunate as to witness in our century. We can say that the idea of progress, in the full and emphatic sense of the term, is based on wholly unwarranted hopes. You can see this even in many critics of the idea of progress. One of the most famous critics of the idea of progress, prior to the First World War, was the Frenchman, Georges Sorel, who wrote a book, *The Delusions of Progress*. But strangely, Sorel declared that the decline of the Western world was impossible because of the vitality of the Western tradition. I think that we have all now become sufficiently sober to admit that whatever may be wrong in Spengler—and there are many things wrong in Spengler—that the very title, in the English translation especially, of the work is more sober, more reasonable, than these hopes which lasted so long.

This barbarization which we have witnessed and which we continue to witness is not altogether accidental. The intention of the modern development was, of course, to bring about a higher civilization, a civilization which would surpass all earlier civilizations. Yet the effect of the modern development was different. What has taken place in the modern period has been a gradual corrosion and destruction of the heritage of Western civilization. The soul of the modern development, one may say, is a peculiar "realism," the notion that moral principles and the appeal to moral principles—preaching, sermonizing—is ineffectual and therefore that one has to seek a substitute for moral principles which would be much more efficacious than ineffectual preaching. Such substitutes were found, for example, in institutions or in economics, and perhaps the most important substitute is what was called "the historical process," meaning that the historical process is, in a way, a much more important guarantee for the actualization of the good life than what the individual could or would do through his own efforts. This change shows itself, as already noted, in the change of general language, namely, in the substitution of the distinction between progressive and reactionary for the distinction between good and bad. The implication being that we have to choose and to do what is conducive to progress, what is in agreement with the historical trends, and it is indecent or immoral to be squeamish in such adaptations. Once it became clear, however, that historical trends are absolutely ambiguous and therefore cannot serve as a standard or, in other words, that to jump on the bandwagon or the wave of the future is not more reasonable than to resist those trends, no standard whatever was left. The facts, understood as historical processes, indeed do not teach us anything regarding values, and the consequence of the abandonment of moral principle proper was that value judgments have no objective support whatsoever. To spell this out with the necessary clarity—although one knows this from the study

of the social sciences—the values of barbarism and cannibalism are as defensible as those of civilization.

I have spoken of modernity as of something definite and
hence, knowable. An analysis of this phenomenon is out of
the question here, as goes without saying. Instead I would
like briefly to enumerate those characteristic elements of
modernity which are particularly striking, at least to me.
But I must make one observation in order to protect myself against gross misunderstanding. Modern phenomenon
is not characterized by the fact that it is located, say, between 1600 and 1952, because premodern traditions of
course survived and survive. And more than that, throughout the modern period, there has been a constant movement against this modern trend. From the very beginning
—one phenomenon which is very well known, perhaps un-
duly well-known—is the quarrel between the ancients and
moderns at the end of the seventeenth century, which in
its most well-known form was concerned with the relatively
unimportant question of whether the French drama of the
seventeenth century was really comparable to the classical
drama. The real quarrel between the ancients and moderns did not concern the drama, of course, but concerned
modern science and philosophy. But there was a resistance
to that from the very beginning: the greatest man in English letters who represented this is Swift; but then you
have it again very strongly in German classicism in the second half of the eighteenth century; and then indeed in the
nineteenth century this movement, this counter-move-
ment, was completely pushed to the wall as a great intellectual movement. But in a way, of course, the tradition still
persisted. So having made clear that by modernity I do not
mean something which is simply chronological, let me now
indicate what I think are the most striking elements of
modernity in a purely enumerative fashion without attempting an analysis.

The first characteristic feature of modern thought as
modern thought, one can say, is its anthropocentric char-

acter. Although apparently contradicted by the fact that modern science with its Copernicanism is much more radically anti-anthropocentric than earlier thought, a closer study shows that this is not true. When I speak of the anthropocentric character of modern thought, I contrast it with the theocentric character of biblical and medieval thought and the cosmocentric character of classical thought. You see this most clearly if you look at modern philosophy, modern philosophy which, while it does not have the general authority which modern science has, is nevertheless a kind of conscience or consciousness of modern science. One has only to look at the titles of the most famous books of modern philosophy to see that philosophy is, or tends to become, analysis of the human mind. You could also see this same trait easily, but that would be too laborious, by looking at what philosophic disciplines emerged in modern times that were unknown to earlier philosophy—all parts of the philosophy of man or of the human mind. The underlying idea, which shows itself not in all places clearly but in some places very clearly, is that all truths or all meaning, all order, all beauty, originate in the thinking subject, in human thought, in man. Some famous formulations: "We know only what we make"—Hobbes. "Understanding prescribes nature its laws"—Kant. "I have discovered a spontaneity little known previously of the monads of the thoughts"—Leibnitz. To give you a very simple popular example, certain human pursuits which were formerly called imitative arts are now called creative arts. One must not forget that even the atheistic, materialistic thinkers of classical antiquity took it for granted that man is subject to something higher than himself, e.g., the whole cosmic order, and that man is not the origin of all meaning.

Connnected with this anthropocentric character is a radical change of moral orientation, which we see with particular clarity in the fact of the emergence of the concept of rights in the precise form in which it was developed in modern social thought. Generally speaking, pre-modern thought put the emphasis on duty, and rights, as far as they were mentioned at all, were understood only as derivative from duties and subservient to the fulfillment of duties. In modern times, we find the tendency, again not always expressed with the greatest clarity but definitely traceable, to assign the primary place to rights and to regard the duties as secondary if, of course, very important. This is connected with another fact that in the crucial period of the seventeenth century, where the change becomes most visible, it is understood that the basic right coincides with a passion. The passions are in a way emancipated, because in the traditional notion, the passion is subordinate to the action, and the action means virtue. The change which we can observe throughout the seventeenth century in all the most famous revolutionary thinkers is that virtue itself is now understood as a passion. In other words, a notion that virtue is a controlling, refraining, regulating, ordering attitude towards passion—think of the image in Plato's *Phaedrus*, the horses and the charioteer— is given up when virtue itself is understood as a passion. This leads to another change which becomes manifest only at a somewhat later age, namely, that freedom gradually takes the place of virtue; so that in much present-day thought you find that—of course, freedom is not the same as license, that goes without saying—but that the distinction between freedom and license takes on a different meaning, a radically different meaning. The good life does not consist, as it did according to the earlier notion, in compliance with a pattern antedating the human will, but consists primarily in originating the pattern itself. The good life does not consist of both a "what" and a "how," but only of a "how." To state it somewhat differently, and again repeating that I am only enumerating, man has no nature to speak of. He makes himself what he is; man's very humanity is acquired. That is granted, I think, in many quarters; that is what is absolutely stable are certain so-called biological characteristics and perhaps some very elementary psychological characteristics, the character of perception, etc. But all interesting things are not modelled on a pattern antedating human action but are a product of human activity itself. Man's very humanity is acquired.

And this leads me to the third point, which became fully clear only in the nineteenth century, and which is already a kind of corrective of this radical emancipation of man from the superhuman. It became ever more clear that man's freedom is inseparable from a radical dependence. Yet this dependence was understood as itself a product of human freedom, and the name for that is history. The so-called discovery of history consists in the realization, or in the alleged realization, that man's freedom is radically limited by his earlier use of his freedom, and not by his nature or by the whole order of nature or creation. This element is, I think, increasing in importance. So much so that today one tends to say that the specific character of modern thought is "history," a notion which is in this form, of course, wholly alien to classical thought or to any premodern thought or biblical thought as well, naturally. If I had the time I would try to show that precisely in this so-called historicization of modern thought the problem of modernity becomes most visible from a technical point of view, and a technical point of view has a peculiarly convincing character, at least to a certain type of person. So I leave it at that.

The crisis of modernity on which we have been reflecting leads to the suggestion that we should return. But return to what? Obviously, to Western civilization in its premodern integrity, to the principles of Western civilization. Yet there is a difficulty here, because Western civilization consists of two elements, has two roots, which are in radical disagreement with each other. We may call these elements, as I have done elsewhere, Jerusalem, and Athens or, to speak in non-metaphorical language, the Bible and Greek philosophy. This radical disagreement today is frequently played down, and this playing down has a certain superficial justification, for the whole history of the West presents itself at first glance as an attempt to harmonize or to synthesize the Bible and Greek philosophy. But a closer study shows that what happened and has been happening in the West for many centuries, is not a harmonization but an attempt at harmonization. These attempts at harmonization were doomed to failure for the following reason: each of these two roots of the Western world sets forth one thing as the one thing needful, and the one thing needful proclaimed by the Bible is incompatible, as it is understood by the Bible, with the one thing needful proclaimed by Greek philosophy, as it is understood by Greek philosophy. To put it very simply and therefore somewhat crudely, the one thing needful according to Greek philosophy is the life of autonomous understanding. The one thing needful as spoken by the Bible is the life of obedient love. The harmonizations and synthesizations are possible because Greek philosophy can *use* obedient love in a subservient function and the Bible can *use* philosophy as a handmaid; but what is so used in each case rebels against such use, and therefore the conflict is really a radical one. Yet this very disagreement presupposes some agreement. In fact, every disagreement we may say, presupposes some agreement, because people must disagree about something and must agree as to the importance of that something. But in this case the agreement is deeper than this purely formal one.

Now what then is the area of agreement between Greek philosophy and the Bible? Negatively we can say, and one could easily enlarge on this position, that there is a perfect agreement between the Bible and Greek philosophy in opposition to those elements of modernity which were described above. They are rejected explicitly or implicitly by both the Bible and Greek philosophy. But this agreement is, of course, only an implicit one, and we should rather look at the agreement as it appeared directly in the text.

One can say, and it is not misleading to say so, that the Bible and Greek philosophy agree in regard to what we may call, and we do call in fact, morality. They agree, if I may say so, regarding the importance of morality, regarding the content of morality, and regarding its ultimate insufficiency. They differ as regards that "x" which supplements or completes morality, or, which is only another way of putting it, they disagree as regards the basis of morality.

I will give you first a brief statement, a reminder rather, of the agreement. Now some people assert that there is a radical and unqualified opposition between biblical morality and philosophic morality. If one heard certain people speak, one would believe that the Greek philosophers did nothing but preach pederasty, whereas Moses did nothing but curb pederasty. Now these people must have limited themselves to a most perfunctory reading of a part of Plato's *Banquet* or of the beginning of the *Charmides*, but they cannot have read the only work in which Plato set forth specific prescriptions for human society, namely, Plato's *Laws*; and what Plato's *Laws* say about this subject agrees fully with what Moses says. Those theologians who identified the second table of the Decalogue as the Christians call it with the natural law of Greek philosophy, were well-advised. It is as obvious to Aristotle as it is to Moses that murder, theft, adultery, etc., are unqualifiedly bad. Greek philosophy and the Bible agree as to this, that the proper framework of morality is the patriarchal family, which is, or tends to be, monogamous, and which forms the cell of a society in which the free adult males, and especially the old ones, predominate. Whatever the Bible and philosophy may tell us about the nobility of certain women, in principle both insist upon the superiority of the male sex. The Bible traces Adam's Fall to Eve's temptation. Plato traces the fall of the best social order to the covetousness of a woman. Consisting of free men, the society praised by the Bible and Greek philosophy refuses to worship any human being. I do not have to quote the Bible for I read it in a Greek author who says: "You worship no human being as your Lord, but only the gods," and he expresses an almost biblical abhorrence of human beings who claim divine honors. Bible and Greek philosophy agree in assigning the highest place among the virtues, not to courage or manliness, but to justice. And by justice both understand primarily, obedience to the law. The law that requires man's full obedience is in both cases not merely civil, penal, and constitutional law, but moral and religious law as well. It is, in biblical language, the guidance, the Torah, for the whole life of man. In the words of the Bible, "It is your life," or "It is the tree of life for those who cling to it"; and in the words of Plato, "The law effects the blessedness of those who obey it." Its comprehensiveness can be expressed, as Aristotle does it, by saying, "What the law does not command, it forbids"; and substantially that is the biblical view as well, as is shown by such commandments as "Thou shall eat and be full and be fruitful and multiply." Obedience to a law of this kind is more than ordinary obedience; it is humility. No wonder that the greatest prophet of the Bible as well as the most law-abiding among the Greeks are praised for their humility. Law and justice, thus understood, are divine law and divine justice. The rule of law is fundamentally the rule of God, theocracy. Man's obedience and disobedience to the law is the object of divine retribution. What Plato says in the tenth book of the *Laws* about man's inability to escape from divine retribution is almost literally identical with certain verses of *Amos* and the Hundred-and-thirty-ninth Psalm. In this context, one may even mention, and without apology I think, the kinship between the monotheism of the Bible and the monotheism toward which Greek philosophy is tending, and the kinship between the first chapter of *Genesis* and Plato's *Timaeus*. But the Bible and Greek philosophy agree not merely regarding the place which they assign to justice, the connection between justice and law, the character of law, and divine retribution. They also agree regarding the problem of justice, the difficulty created by the misery of the just and the prospering of the wicked. One cannot read Plato's description in the second book of the *Republic* of the perfectly just man who suffers what would be the just fate of the most unjust man without being reminded of Isaiah's description of him who has done no violence, neither was any deceit in his mouth, yet who was oppressed and afflicted and brought as a lamb to the slaughter. And just as Plato's *Republic* ends with restoring all kinds of prosperity to the just, the book of *Job* ends with the restoration to the just Job of everything he had temporarily lost.

Now in the course of these extremely summary remarks, I have tacitly replaced morality by justice, understanding by justice obedience to the divine law. This notion, the divine law, it seems to me is the common ground between the Bible and Greek philosophy. And here I use a term which is certainly easily translatable into Greek as well as into biblical Hebrew. But I must be more precise. The common ground between the Bible and Greek philosophy is the problem of divine law. They solve that problem in a diametrically opposed manner.

Before I speak of the root of their difference, I would like to illustrate the fundamental antagonism between the bible and philosophy by enumerating some of its consequences. I have indicated the place of justice in both Bible and Greek philosophy. We may take Aristotle's *Ethics* as the most perfect or certainly the most accessible presentation of philosophic ethics. Now Aristotle's *Ethics* has two foci, not one: one is justice, the other, however, is magnanimity or noble pride. Both justice and magnanimity comprise all other virtues, as Aristotle says, but in different ways. Justice comprises all other virtues in so far as the actions flowing from them relate to other men; magnanimity, however, comprises all other virtues in so far as they enhance the man himself. Now there is a close kinship between Aristotle's justice and biblical justice, but Aristotle's magnanimity, which means a man's habitual claiming for himself great honors while he deserves these honors, is alien to the Bible. Biblical humility excludes magnanimity in the Greek sense. There is a close relation between the magnanimous man and the perfect gentleman. There occur a few, very few, gentlemen and ladies in the Bible—I hope that this remark is not understood as a criticism of the Bible. There is Saul, who disobeys a divine command and by so doing does the noble thing—he spared his brother, King Agag, and destroys only what is vile and refuse. For this he was rejected by God and Agag was hewn to pieces by the prophet Samuel before the Lord. Instead of Saul, God elected David, who did a lot of things a gentleman would not do, who was one of the greatest sinners, but at the same time one of the greatest repenters, who ever lived. There is a gentleman Jonathan who was too noble to compete with his friend David for kingship in Israel. There is a lady Michal, the wife of David, who saw David leaping and dancing before the Lord, and she despised him in her heart and ridiculed him for having shamelessly compromised his royal dignity by leaping and dancing before the riffraff, but she was punished by God with sterility. I need not dwell on the obvious connection between the biblical rejection of the concept of a "gentleman" and the biblical insistence on man's duties to the poor. The Greek philosophers were very far from being vulgar worshippers of wealth—must I say so?—Socrates lived in thousand-fold poverty, as he himself says, and he failed to see why a horse can be good without having money whereas man cannot. But they held that as far as the general run of man is concerned, virtue presupposes a reasonable economic underpinning. The Bible, on the other hand, uses poor and pious or just as synonymous terms. Compared with the Bible, Greek philosophy is heartless in this as well as in other respects. Magnanimity presupposes a man's conviction of his own worth. It presupposes that man is capable of being virtuous, thanks to his own efforts. If this condition is fulfilled, consciousness of one's shortcomings or failings or sins is something which is below the good man. Again I quote Aristotle, [the] "Sense of shame," which is such consciousness of human failing, "befits young men who cannot yet be fully virtuous, but not men of mature age who are free not to do the wrong thing in the first place." Or to quote the re- mark made by one twentieth century gentleman about an- other, "Disgrace was impossible because of his character and behavior." The Greek philosophers differed as to whether man can become fully virtuous, but if some deny this possibility, as Socrates does, he merely replaces his self-satisfaction, the self-admiration of the virtuous man, by the self-satisfaction or self-admiration of him who steadily progresses in virtue. He does not imply, as far as the happy few are concerned, that they should be contrite, repentant, or express a sense of guilt. Man's guilt was indeed the guiding theme to tragedy. Hence Plato rejects tragedy from his best city. (I do not say that is the whole story; that is only a part of the story as you see from the fact that tragedy is replaced by songs praising the virtuous. And ac- cording to Aristotle, the tragic hero is necessarily an aver- age man, not a man of the highest order.) However, it should be noted that tragedy is composed and performed for the benefit of the multitude. Its function is to arouse the passions of fear and pity while at the same time purg- ing them.

Now fear and pity are precisely the passions which are necessarily connected with the feeling of guilt. When I be- come guilty, when I become aware of my being guilty, I have at once the feeling of pity toward him whom I have hurt or ruined and the feeling of fear of him who avenges my crime. Humanly speaking, the unity of fear and pity combined with the phenomenon of guilt might seem to be the root of religion. God, the king or the judge, is the ob- ject of fear; and God, the father of all men, makes all men brothers, and thus hallows pity. According to Aristotle, without these feelings which have to be purged by tragedy, the better type of man is liberated from all morbidity and thus can turn wholeheartedly to noble action. Greek philosophy has frequently been blamed for the absence from it of that ruthless examination of one's intentions which is the consequence of the biblical demand for purity of the heart. "Know thyself" means for the Greeks, know what it means to be a human being, know what is the place of man in the universe, examine your opinions and prejudices, rather than "Search your heart." This philosophic lack of depth, as it is called, can consistently be maintained only if God is assumed not to be concerned with man's goodness or if man's goodness is assumed to be entirely his own affair. The Bible and Greek philosophy agree indeed as regards the importance of morality or justice and as to the insufficiency of morality, but they disagree as to what completes morality. According to the Greek philosophers, as already noted, it is understanding or contemplation. Now this necessarily tends to weaken the majesty of the moral demands, whereas humility, a sense of guilt, repentance, and faith in divine mercy, which complete morality according to the Bible, necessarily strengthen the majesty of the moral demands. A sign of this is the fact that contemplation is essentially a trans- or asocial possibility, whereas obedience and faith are essentially related to the community of the faithful. To quote the Jewish medieval thinker, Yehuda Halevi, "The wisdom of the Greeks has most beautiful blossoms, but no fruits," with 'fruits' here meaning actions. That asocial perfection which is contemplation normally presupposes a political community, the city, which accordingly is considered by the philosophers as fundamentally good, and the same is true of the arts, without whose services, and even model, political life and philosophic life are not possible. According to the Bible, however, the first founder of a city was the first murderer, and his descendents were the first inventors of the arts. Not the city, not civilization, but the desert, is the place in which the biblical God reveals himself. Not the farmer Cain, but the shepherd Abel, finds favor in the eyes of the biblical God.

The force of the moral demand is weakened in Greek philosophy because in Greek philosophy this demand is not backed up by divine promises. According to Plato, for example, evil will never cease on earth, whereas according to the Bible the end of days will bring perfect redemption. Hence the philosopher lives in a state above fear and trembling as well as above hope, and the beginning of his wisdom is not as in the Bible the fear of God, but rather the sense of wonder; whereas biblical man lives in fear and trembling as well as in hope. This leads to a peculiar serenity in the philosopher which I would like to illustrate here by only one example which I think is not wholly accidental. The prophet Nathan seriously and ruthlessly rebukes King David for having committed one murder and one act of adultery. I contrast that with the way in which a Greek poet-philosopher playfully and elegantly tries to convince a Greek tyrant who has committed an untold number of murders and other crimes, that he would derive greater pleasure if he would have been more reasonable. Now let me leave it with these examples, which naturally are to a certain extent arbitrary, but I think not misleading. I think I can illustrate the difference also as follows by two characteristic events or accounts. Contrast the account of the *Akedah*—the binding of Isaac—in the story of Abraham. There the crucial point is that Abraham obeys an unintelligible command, the command being unintelligible because he has been promised that his name would be called through Isaac and in the descendants of Isaac, and now he is asked to slaughter that son. Yet, Abraham obeys the command unhesitatingly. The only analogy in Greek philosophy of which I can think would be the example of Socrates who is, or believes at least that he has been, commanded by Apollo to something, and yet the action consists not in unhesitating obedience, but in examining an unintelligible saying of Apollo.

Now after these illustrations, what is the difference? These principles were clarified, particularly in the medieval discussion, in the heyday of theological discussion; Maimonides especially, in the *Guide for the Perplexed*, is probably the greatest analyst of this fundamental difference. The issue as he stated it was as follows: philosophy teaches the eternity of the world, and the Bible teaches the creation out of nothing. This conflict must be rightly understood, because Maimonides is primarily thinking of Aristotle, who taught the eternity of the visible universe. But if you enlarge that and apply it not only to this cosmos, to this visible universe in which we live now, but to any cosmos or chaos which might ever exist, certainly Greek philosophy teaches the eternity of cosmos or chaos; whereas the Bible teaches creation, implying creation out of nothing. The root of the matter, however, is that only the Bible teaches divine omnipotence, and the thought of divine omnipotence is absolutely incompatible with Greek philosophy in any form. And I think one can even trace that back to the very beginnings of Greek literature—though technically much beyond philosophy—to the passage in the *Odyssey*, where Hermes shows Odysseus a certain herb which he could use for protecting himself and his fellows against Circe. Now in this context, the gods can do everything, the gods are omnipotent one can say, but it is very interesting what this concept means in this context. Why are the gods omnipotent? Because they know the natures of all things, which means, of course, they are not omnipotent. They know the natures of things which are wholly independent of them and through that knowledge they are capable of using all things properly. In all Greek thought, we find in one form or the other an impersonal necessity higher than any personal being; whereas in the Bible the first cause is, as people say now, a person. This is connected with the fact that the concern of God with man is absolutely, if we may say so, essential to the biblical God; whereas that concern is, to put it very mildly, a problem for every Greek philosopher. Stated somewhat differently, what is now called religious experience is underlined in the Bible and is understood by the Bible as genuine experience; whereas from the point of view of the Greek philosophers, this religious experience is a questionable interpretation—I take the example of Plato—a questionable interpretation of experiences of the soul as an all-pervasive principle.

We must try as far as it is possible to understand this antagonism. It can well be questioned whether what I am going to say can in truth be called an attempt at understanding, and so you can take it as a kind of illustration from the point of view of, say, social science. In order to clarify this antagonism, it is proposed that we go back to the common stratum between Bible and Greek philosophy, to the most elementary stratum, a stratum which is common, or can be assumed to be common, to all men. How can we find that? I think it is easier to start from philosophy for the simple reason that the question which I raise here is a scientific or philosophic question. We have to move in the element of conceptual thought, as it is called, and that is of course the element of Greek philosophy. With a view to this fact, I would like to state the issue more precisely. What distinguishes the Bible from Greek philosophy is the fact that Greek philosophy is based on this premise: that there is such a thing as nature, or natures—a notion which has no equivalent in biblical thought. It should be noted that there is no Hebrew-biblical term for nature, the Hebrew word being derived very indirectly from a Greek word which is an equivalent of nature in Greek, *character, teva* in Hebrew. So the issue from this point of view would be this: we have to go back behind that discovery or invention of nature. We have to try to discern what we may call the pre-philosophical equivalent of nature, and by starting from that, perhaps we can arrive at a purely historical understanding of the antagonism we are analyzing. Let me add, parenthetically, another point.

Philosophy is the quest for principles, meaning—and let us be quite literal—for the beginnings, for the first things. This is, of course, something common to philosophy and myth, and I would suggest for the time being that philosophy, as distinguished from myth, comes into being when the quest for the beginnings is understood in the light of the idea of nature.

Now what is the pre-philosophic equivalent of nature? I think we can find the answer to this question in such notions as 'custom' or 'ways.' This answer occurred to me, very simply, as a result of reading Maimonides, who knew the true roots of which I speak very well indeed. In the beginning of his great legal work, the *Mishneh Torah*, in the first section, the "Hilchot Yesodei ha-Torah," "Laws Regarding the Foundations of the Torah," Chapter Four, he speaks of the four elements. Before he introduces the term nature, he speaks first of the custom or way—the custom of fire, and the way of earth, and somewhat later refers to the nature of water. And this insight goes, I think, to the root of the problem. The rubrics 'custom' or 'way' are biblical notions and are, of course, also to be found in Greek sources. Moreover, I would assume, until the contrary has been proven, that these ideas are really universal ones. People in all times and places have observed that things behave in a regular manner; that they have customs of behaving and ways of behaving. Take, for example, a biblical expression, *derech nashim*, the way of women, menstruation, or in Greek an expression such as *boskaematon dikei*, the custom of beasts, meaning the same as the nature of beasts. Or again, in biblical Hebrew, the word *mishpat* means the custom or the law of a thing as reflected in its regular behavior. In this context it is clear that no distinction is made between the custom of dogs and the custom of the Philistines, for example: a Philistine regularly behaves in his way and the dog regularly behaves in his way. You can also take lions and Hebrews, if you think I employ only poor examples. So things have regular behavior, customs or ways. I have also learnt from a Hindu student that the Hindu term *dharma*, which is usually translated as "religion," means custom or way, and can refer to such things as the custom or way of iron, of trees, and of what not. And since the custom or way of human beings is, of course, the Hindu religion, it means derivatively, if most importantly, what is according to religion.

If we now assume that this idea of the 'way' is really the pre-philosophical equivalent of nature, we have immediately to add this very obvious observation: that there is one way, among the many ways, which is particularly important, and that is the way of the group to which one belongs: "our way." Now our way is, of course, the right way. And why is it right? The answer: because it is old and because it is one's own, or to use the beautiful expression of Edmund Burke, because it is "home-bred and prescriptive." We can bring it altogether under the term "ancestral." Hence the original notion is that the ancestral is identical with the good. The good is necessarily ancestral which implies, since man was always a thinking being, that the ancestors were superior. If this were not the case in what sense would the ancestral be good? The ancestors are superior, and therefore the ancestors must be understood, if this notion is fully thought through, as gods or sons of gods, or pupils of gods. In other words, it is necessary to consider the 'right way' as the divine law, *theos nomos.* Whether this conclusion is always reached is, of course, uninteresting to us, because we admit the possibility that sometimes people do not think with sufficient penetration; but in those places where they did they arrived at this understanding.

Unfortunately, the divine law, the *theos nomos*, to use the Greek image, leads to *two* fundamental alternatives: one is the character of Greek philosophy; the other is the character of the Bible. Now why is this problematic? The answer is all too familiar, i.e., the variety of divine laws. We find everywhere such orders claiming to be divine, and these orders are not only different from each other—that would not technically be a difficulty, because different gods could have assigned different codes to different tribes—but they contradict each other. In every code of this kind, there are some elements which claim to be universal. For example, one only has to read Herodotus to get very beautiful examples of conflicting claims: one tribe burned the dead and the other buried them. Now the alternative burial custom was not only looked upon as a different folk-more, a different cultural pattern, but as an abomination. So we may say that different laws contradict each other, and they contradict each other especially regarding what they say about the first things, because no early code, written or unwritten, is thinkable without a preamble which explains the obligations involved and which provides an account of the first things. Given this variety and this contradictory character of the various allegedly divine codes, it becomes necessary to transcend this whole dimension, to find one's bearings independently of the ancestral, or to realize that the ancestral and the good are two fundamentally different things despite occasional coincidences between them.

There is, too, the basic question of how to find one's bearings in the cosmos. The Greek answer fundamentally is this: we have to discover the first things on the basis of inquiry, that everyone knows. We can note two implications of what inquiry means here: in the first place, seeing with one's own eyes as distinguished from hearsay, to observe for oneself; and secondly, the notion of inquiry presupposes the realization of the fundamental difference between human production and the production of things which are not man-made, so that no conclusion from human production to the production of non-man-made things is possible except if it is first established by demonstration that the visible universe has been made by thinking beings. This implication, I think, is decisive: it was on the basis of the principles of Greek philosophy that what later became known as demonstrations of the existence of

God or gods came into being. This is absolutely necessary, and that is true not only in Aristotle, but in Plato as well, as you see, for example, from the tenth book of the *Laws*. An ascent from sense perception and reasoning on sense data, an ascent indeed guided, according to Plato and Aristotle, by certain notions, leads upwards and everything depends on the solidity of the ascending process, on the demonstration. Because the quest for the beginning, for the first things, becomes now philosophic or scientific analysis of the cosmos, the place of the divine law in the traditional sense of the term, where it is a code traced to a personal God, is replaced by a natural order which may even be called, as it was later to be called, a natural law—or at any rate, to use a wider term, a natural morality. So the divine law, in the real and strict sense of the term, is only the starting point, the absolutely essential starting point, for Greek philosophy, but it is abandoned in the process. And if it is accepted by Greek philosophy, it is accepted only politically, meaning, for the education of the many, and not as something which stands independently.

To understand the biblical notion in the sense of understanding to which I refer, one can say this: the Bible, biblical thought, clings to this notion that there is one particular divine law; but it contends that this particular divine law is the only one which is truly divine law. All these other codes are, in their claim to divine origin, fraudulent. They are figments of man. Since, however, one code is accepted, then no possibility of independent questioning arises and is meant to arise. Now what then is it that distinguishes the biblical solution from the mythical solution? I think it is this: that the author or authors of the Bible were aware of the problem of the variety of the divine law. In other words, they realized, and I am now speaking not as a theologian but as a historian, they realized what are the absolutely necessary conditions if one particular law should be *the* divine law. How has one to conceive of the whole if one particular, and therefore contingent, law of one particular contingent tribe is to be the divine law? The answer is: it must be a personal God; the first cause must be God; He must be omnipotent, not controlled and not controllable. But to be knowable means to be controllable, and therefore He must not be knowable in the strict sense of the term. Thus in the language of later thought, of already Graecified thought, God's essence is not knowable; as the Bible says, one cannot see God's face. But this is not radical enough, and the divine name given in *Exodus*, which literally translated means, "I shall be what I shall be," is the most radical formulation of that. It is just the opposite of the Greek notion of essence, where it means the being is what it is and was and will be. . . . But here the core, one could say, is inaccessible, it is absolutely free: God is what he shall be. It is a free God, unpredictable. Why then can man trust Him? Answer: only because of the covenant. God has freely bound himself, but all trust depends on trust in God's word, in God's promise; there is no necessary and therefore intelligible relation; and, needless to say, this covenant is not a free covenant, freely entered into by originally independent partners; it is a covenant which, according to the Bible, God commanded man to perform.

To complete this extremely sketchy picture by a few points, I would like to say this. There is no doubt that the Greek philosophers of the classical period did not know the Bible, and it is, I think, generally admitted that the authors of the Bible did not know the Greek philosophers. But the extraordinary fact is that if one studies both the Greek philosophers and the Bible a little more carefully, one sees that in both sources of Western thought the alternative was, if I may say so, divined. Even in Aristotle you will find passages where he speaks of certain very crude notions in Greece which pointed fundamentally to what we know in the Bible in a more developed form, e.g., the notion that maybe it is bad to devote oneself to the philosophical rebellion against God.

By way of comparison now consider the perfect agreement as to the decisive biblical message between the first account of creation and the second account of creation, the second account of creation which culminates in the story of the Fall. It is the same notion which underlies the account of the first chapter of the depreciation of heaven and the prohibition against the eating of the fruit of the tree of knowledge of good and evil. Because the knowledge of good and evil means, of course, not one special branch of knowledge, as is shown by the fact that in God's knowing of the created things, they always end, "And He saw that it was good." The completed thing, the complete knowledge of the completed thing, is knowledge of the good, the notion being that the desire for, striving for, knowledge is forbidden. Man is not meant to be a theoretical, a knowing, a contemplating being; man is meant to live in childlike obedience. Needless to say, this notion was modified in various ways in the later tradition, but it seems to me that the fundamental thought was preserved, if we disregard some marginal developments.

What then is the principle underlying the seemingly changed attitude of later times? I think we can understand this from the Bible itself. You recall that the story of the Fall is followed by the account of Cain and later on by the genealogy of Cain, where the city and the arts are assigned to this undesirable branch of mankind; and yet later on we find that there is a very different attitude toward the city and arts: think of the holy city of Jerusalem, and of the arts which Bezalel used in adorning the Temple, etc. I think we find the clearest discussion of this issue later on, in the discussion of kingship, of the institution of human kingship in Israel, in the first book of *Samuel*, where we see what the general trend of the biblical solution is. Fundamentally, the institution of human kingship is bad—it is a kind of rebellion against God, as is the *polis* and the arts and knowledge. But then it becomes possible by divine dispensation that these things, which originate in human rebellion, become dedicated to the service of God, and thus become holy. And I think that this is the biblical solution to the problem of human knowledge: human knowledge if it is dedicated to the service of God, and only then, can be good, and perhaps, in that sense, it is even necessary. But without that dedication it is a rebellion. Man was *given* understanding in order to understand God's commands. He could not be freely obedient if he did not have understanding. But at the same time this very fact allows man to emancipate the understanding from the service, from the subservient function for which it was meant, and this emancipation is the origin of philosophy or science from the biblical point of view. And so the antagonism between them. Even if you take later versions as your model, e.g., so-called Jewish medieval philosophy, you will still find that this difficulty is very noticeable.

However this may be, it seems to me that this antagonism must be considered by us in action. That is to say: it seems to me that the core, the nerve of Western intellectual history, Western spiritual history, one could almost say, is the conflict between the biblical and the philosophic notions of the good life. This was a conflict which showed itself primarily, of course, in arguments—arguments advanced by theologians on behalf of the biblical point of view, and by philosophers on behalf of the philosophic point of view. There are many reasons why this is important but I would like to emphasize only one: it seems to me that this unresolved conflict is the secret of the vitality of Western civilization.

III

1.

When we attempt to return to the roots of Western civilization, we observe soon that Western civilization has two roots which are in conflict with each other, the biblical and

the Greek philosophic, and this is to begin with a very dis-
concerting observation. Yet this realization has also something reassuring and comforting. The very life of Western
civilization is the life between two codes, a fundamental
tension. There is therefore no reason inherent in the
Western civilization itself, in its fundamental constitution,
why it should give up life. But this comforting thought is
justified only if we live that life, if we live that conflict, that
is. No one can be both a philosopher and a theologian or,
for that matter, a third which is beyond the conflict between philosophy and theology, or a synthesis of both. But
every one of us can be and ought to be either the one or
the other, the philosopher open to the challenge of theology or the theologian open to the challenge of philosophy.

There is a fundamental conflict or disagreement between the Bible and Greek philosophy. This fundamental
conflict is blurred to a certain extent by the close similarity
in points. There are, for example, certain philosophies
which come seemingly close to the biblical teaching—think
of philosophic teachings which are monotheistic, which
speak of the love of God and of man, which even admit
prayer, etc. And so the difference becomes sometimes almost invisible. But we recognize the difference immediately if we make this observation. For a philosopher or philosophy there can never be an absolute sacredness of a
particular or contingent event. This particular or contingent is called, since the eighteenth century, the historical.
Therefore people have come to say that revealed religion
means historical religion, as distinguished from natural religion, and that philosophers could have a natural religion,
and furthermore, that there is an essential superiority of
the historical to the natural. As a consequence of this interpretation of the particular and contingent as historical,
it came to be held, and that is very frequently held today,
that the Bible is in an emphatic sense historical, that the
Bible, as it were, discovered history (or the biblical authors), whereas philosophy as philosophy is essentially non-

historical. This view is underlying much of present-day interpretation of biblical thought. What is called existentialism is really only a more elaborate form of this interpretation. I do not believe that this approach is very helpful for the understanding of the Bible, at least as far as its basic parts are concerned; and as an explanation, I will suggest here only one consideration: that these present-day concepts, such as History with a capital "H," are very late concepts, very derivative, and by this very fact not as capable of unlocking to us early thought, thought which is in no way derivative, but at the beginning of a tradition.

One can begin to describe the fundamental disagreement between the Bible and Greek philosophy, and doing that from a purely historical point of view, from the fact that we observe first a broad agreement between the Bible and Greek philosophy regarding both morality and the insufficiency of morality; the disagreement concerns that "x" which completes morality. According to Greek philosophy, that "x" is *theoria*, contemplation, and the biblical completion we may call, I think without creating any misleading understanding, piety, the need for divine mercy or redemption, obedient love. To be more precise (the term morality itself is one of these derivative terms which are not quite adequate for the understanding of earlier thought), we may replace the term morality by the term justice, a term common to both sources; and justice means primarily obedience to law, and law in the full and comprehensive sense, divine law. Going even back behind that, we suggest as a starting point of the whole moral development of mankind, if we may say so, a primeval identification of the good with the ancestral. Out of this primeval equation which we still understand, of which we still make use in actual life, the notion of a divine law necessarily arose. And then in a further step, the problem of divine law: the original notion of a divine law or divine code implies that there is a large variety of them. The very variety and, more specifically, the contradiction between the various divine codes makes the idea of a divine law in the simple and primary sense of the term radically problematic.

There are two diametrically opposed solutions to this problem possible, the one is the philosophic and the other is the biblical solution. The philosophic solution we may describe in the following terms: The philosophers transcend the dimension of divine codes altogether, the whole dimension of piety and of pious obedience to a pre-given code. Instead they embark on a free quest for the beginnings, for the first things, for the principles. And they assume that on the basis of the knowledge of first principles, of the first principles, of the beginnings, it will be possible to determine what is by nature good, as distinguished from what is good merely by convention. This quest for the beginnings proceeds through sense perception, reasoning, and what they called *noesis*, which is literally translated by "understanding" or "intellect," and which we can perhaps translate a litle bit more cautiously by "awareness," an awareness with the mind's eye as distinguished from sensible awareness. But while this awareness has certainly its biblical equivalent and even its mystical equivalent, this equivalent in the philosophic context is never divorced from sense perception and reasoning based on sense perception. In other words, philosophy never becomes oblivious of its kinship with the arts and crafts, with the knowledge used by the artisan and with this humble but solid kind of knowledge.

Now turning to the biblical alternative, here the basic premise is that one particular divine code is accepted as truly divine; that one particular code of one particular tribe is the divine code. But the divine character of all other allegedly divine codes is simply denied, and this implies a radical rejection of mythology. This rejection of mythology is also characteristic of the primary impulse of philosophy, but the biblical rejection of mythology proceeds in the opposite direction as philosophy does. To give some meaning to the term mythology which I am here forced to use, I would say that mythology is characterized by the conflict between gods and impersonal powers behind the gods. What is in Greek sometimes called *moira*, for example. Now philosophy replaces this impersonal fate, as we might say, by nature and intelligible necessity. The Bible, on the other hand, conceives of God as the cause of everything else, impersonal necessities included. The biblical solution then stands or falls by the belief in God's omnipotence. The notion of omnipotence requires, of course, monotheism, because if you have more than one God clearly none of them can be omnipotent. Only the biblical authors, we may say, understand what omnipotence really means, because only if God is omnipotent can one particular code be the absolute code. But an omnipotent God who is in principle perfectly knowable to man is in a way subject to man, in so far as knowledge is in a way power. Therefore a truly omnipotent God must be a mysterious God, and that is, as you know, the teaching of the Bible. Man cannot see the face of God, and especially the divine name, "I shall be that I shall be," means it is never possible in any present to know that, what God shall be. But if man has no hold whatever over the biblical God, how can there be any link between man and God? The biblical answer is the covenant, a free and mysterious action of love on the part of God, and the corresponding attitude on the part of man is trust, or faith, which is radically different from theoretical certainty. The biblical God is known in a humanly relevant sense only by his actions, by his revelations. The book, the Bible, is the account of what God has done and what he has promised. It is not speculation about God. In the Bible, as we would say, men tell about God's actions and promises on the basis of their experience of God. This experience and not reasoning based on sense perception, is the root of biblical wisdom.

This radical difference between the Bible and Greek philosophy shows itself also in the literary character of the Bible, on the one hand, and of Greek philosophic books, on the other. The works of the Greek philosophers are really books, works, works of one man, who begins at what he regards as the necessary beginning, either the beginning simply or the best beginning for leading up people to what he regards as the truth. And this one man–one book, was characteristic of Greek thought from the very beginning: Homer. But the Bible is fundamentally, as is today generally held, a compilation of sources, which means the Bible continues already a tradition with a minimum of changes, and therefore the famous difficulties with which the biblical scholars are concerned. The decisive point, I think, is this: here is no beginning made by an individual, no beginning made by man, ultimately. There is a kinship between this art of writing and the favored form of writing, favored in the Jewish tradition, namely, the commentary, always referring back to something earlier. Man does not begin.

In my analysis I presupposed that the equation of the good with the ancestral is the primeval equation. That may be so in chronological terms, but one cannot leave it at that, of course, because the question arises, why should this be so, what evidence does this equation have? That is a very long question, and I do not propose to answer it now. I would only refer to a Greek myth according to which *Mnemosyne*, memory, is the mother of the muses, meaning the mother of wisdom. In other words, primarily the good, the true, however you might call it, can be known only as the old because prior to the emergence of wisdom memory occupied the place of wisdom. Ultimately, I think, one would have to go back to a fundamental dualism in man in order to understand this conflict between the Bible and Greek philosophy, to the dualism of deed and speech, of action and thought—a dualism which necessarily poses the question as to the primacy of either—and one can say that Greek philosophy asserts the primacy of thought, of speech, whereas the Bible asserts the primacy of deed. That is, I know very well, open to misunderstandings, but permit me to leave it at this for the moment.

2.

Now we are at any rate confronted with the fact that there is a radical opposition between Bible and philosophy, and this opposition has given rise to a secular conflict from the very beginning. This conflict is characteristic of the West, the West in the wider sense of the term including even the whole Mediterranean basin, of course. It seems to me that this conflict is the secret of the vitality of the West. I would venture to say that as long as there will be a Western civilization there will be theologians who will suspect the philosophers and philosophers who will be annoyed or feel annoyed by the theologians. But, as the saying goes, we have to accept our fate, and it is not the worst fate which men could imagine. We have this radical opposition: the Bible refuses to be integrated into a philosophical framework, just as philosophy refuses to be integrated into a biblical framework. As for this biblical refusal, there is the often-made remark, that the god of Aristotle is not the God of Abraham, Isaac, and Jacob, and therefore any attempt to integrate the biblical understanding into philosophic understanding means to abandon that which is meant by the God of Abraham, Isaac, and Jacob. As for philosophy, that is perhaps a little bit obscured by a number of facts and therefore we must dwell upon it for a moment. The obscuration, I believe, is ultimately due to the fact that in the discussions regarding the relation of theology and philosophy, philosophy is identified with the completed philosophic system, in the Middle Ages, of course, primarily with Aristotle—by which I do not mean to say that Aristotle has a system, although it is sometimes believed that he had—but certainly with Hegel in modern times. That is, of course, one very special form of philosophy: it is not the primary and necessary form of philosophy. I have to explain that.

In a medieval work, the *Kuzari*, by Yehuda Halevi, we find this statement: "Socrates says to the people, 'I do not reject your divine wisdom, I simply do not understand it.

My wisdom is merely human wisdom.' " Now in the mouth of Socrates, as in this apophthegm, human wisdom means imperfect wisdom or quest for wisdom, that is to say, philosophy. Since he realizes the imperfection of human wisdom, it is hard to understand why he does not go from there to divine wisdom. The reason implied in this text is this: as a philosopher, he refuses assent to anything which is not evident to him, and revelation is for him not more than an unevident, unproven possibility. Confronted with an unproven possibility, he does not reject, he merely suspends judgment. But here a great difficulty arises which one can state as follows: it is impossible to suspend judgment regarding matters of utmost urgency, regarding matters of life and death. Now the question of revelation is evidently of utmost urgency. If there is revelation, unbelief in revelation or disobedience to revelation is fatal. Suspense of judgment regarding revelation would then seem to be impossible. The philosopher who refuses to assent to revelation because it is not evident therewith rejects revelation. But this rejection is unwarranted if revelation is not disproved. Which means to say that the philosopher, when confronted with revelation, seems to be compelled to contradict the very idea of philosophy by rejecting without sufficient grounds. How can we understand that? The philosophic reply can be stated as follows: the question of utmost urgency, the question which does not permit suspense, is the question of how one should live. Now this question is settled for Socrates by the fact that he is a philosopher. As a philosopher, he knows that we are ignorant of the most important things. The ignorance, the evident fact of this ignorance, evidently proves that quest for knowledge of the most important things is the most important thing for us. Philosophy is then evidently the right way of life. This is in addition, according to him, confirmed by the fact that he finds his happiness in acquiring the highest possible degree of clarity which he can acquire. He sees no necessity whatever to assent to something which is not evident to him. And if he is told that his disobedience to revelation might be fatal, he raises the question, what does fatal mean? In the extreme case, it would be eternal damnation. Now the philosophers of the past were absolutely certain that an all-wise God would not punish with eternal damnation or with anything else such human beings as are seeking the truth or clarity. We must consider later on whether this reply is quite sufficient. At any rate, philosophy is meant, and that is the decisive point, not as a set of propositions, a teaching, or even a system, but as a way of life, a life animated by a peculiar passion, the philosophic desire or *eros*, not as an instrument or a department of human self-realization. Philosophy understood as an instrument or as a department is, of course, compatible with every thought of life, and therefore also with the biblical way of life. But this is no longer philosophy in the original sense of the term. This has been greatly obscured, I believe, by the Western development, because philosophy was certainly in the Christian Middle Ages deprived of its character as a way of life and became just a very important compartment.

I must therefore try to restate why, according to the original notion of philosophy, philosophy is necessarily a way of life and not a mere discipline, if even the highest discipline. I must explain, in other words, why philosophy cannot possibly lead up to the insight that another way of life apart from the philosophic one is the right one. Philosophy is quest for knowledge regarding the whole. Being essentially quest and being not able ever to become wisdom, as distinguished from philosophy, the problems are always more evident than the solutions. All solutions are questionable. Now the right of way of life cannot be fully established except by an understanding of the nature of man, and the nature of man cannot be fully clarified except by an understanding of the nature of the whole. Therefore, the right way of life cannot be established metaphysically except by a completed metaphysics, and therefore the right way of life remains questionable. But the very uncertainty of all solutions, the very ignorance regarding the most important things, makes quest for knowledge the most important thing, and therefore a life devoted to it, the right way of life. So philosophy in its original and full sense is then certainly incompatible with the biblical way of life. Philosophy and Bible are the alternatives or the antagonists in the drama of the human soul. Each of the two antagonists claims to know or to hold the truth, the decisive truth, the truth regarding the right way of life. But there can be only one truth: hence, conflict between these claims and necessarily conflict among thinking beings; and that means inevitably argument. Each of the two opponents has tried since millenia to refute the other. This effort is continuing in our day, and in fact it is taking on a new intensity after some decades of indifference.

3.

Now I have to say a few words about the present-day argument. The present-day argument in favor of philosophy, we can say, is practically non-existent because of the disintegration of philosophy. I have spoken on a former occasion of the distinction between philosophy and science as understood today, a distinction which necessarily leads to a discrediting of philosophy. The contrast between the lack of results in philosophy and the enormous success of the sciences brings this about. Science is the only intellectual pursuit which today successfully can claim to be the perfection of the human understanding. Science is neutral in regard to revelation. Philosophy has become uncertain of itself. Just one quotation, a statement of one of the most famous present-day philosophers: "Belief in revelation is true, but not true for the philosopher. Rejection of revelation is true for the philosopher, but not true for the believer." Let us turn to the more promising present-day argument in favor of revelation. I shall not waste words on the most popular argument which is taken from the needs of present-day civilization, the present-day crisis, which would simply amount to this: that we need today, in order to compete with communism, revelation as a myth. Now this argument is either stupid or blasphemous. Needless to say, we find similar arguments also within Zionism, and I think this whole argument has been disposed of in advance a long time ago by Dostoievsky in *The Possessed*.

Now the serious argument in favor of revelation can be stated as follows: there is no objective evidence whatever in favor of revelation, which means there is no shred of evidence in favor of revelation except, first, the experience, the personal experience, of man's encounter with God, and secondly, the negative proof of the inadequacy of any non-believing position. Now as to the first point—there is no objective evidence in favor of revelation except the experience of one's encounter with God—a difficulty arises. Namely, what is the relation of this personal experience to the experience expressed in the Bible? It becomes necessary to distinguish between what the prophets experience, what we may call the call of God or the presence of God, and what they said, and this latter would have to be called, as it is today called by all non-orthodox theologians, a human interpretation of God's action. It is no longer God's action itself. The human interpretation cannot be authoritative. But the question arises, is not every specific meaning attached to God's call or to God's presence a human interpretation? For example, the encounter with God will be interpreted in radically different manners by the Jew on the one hand, and by the Christian on the other, to say nothing of the Muslim and others. Yet only one interpretation can be the true one. There is therefore a need for argument between the various believers in revelation, an argument which cannot help but to allude somehow to objectivity. As for the second point—the negative proof of the inadequacy of any non-believing position—that is usually very strong in so far as it shows the inadequacy of modern progressivism, optimism, or cynicism, and to that extent I regard it as absolutely convincing.

But that is not the decisive difficulty. The decisive difficulty concerns classical philosophy, and here the discussions, as far as I know them, do not come to grips with the real difficulty. To mention only one point, it is said that classical philosophy is based on a kind of delusion which can be proved to be a delusion. Classical philosophy is said to be based on the unwarranted belief that the whole is intelligible. Now this is a very long question. Permit me here to limit myself to say that the prototype of the philosopher in the classical sense was Socrates, who knew that he knew nothing, who therewith admitted that the whole is not intelligible, who merely wondered whether by saying that the whole is not intelligible we do not admit to have some understanding of the whole. For of something of which we know absolutely nothing, we could of course not say anything, and that is the meaning, it seems to me, of what is so erroneously translated by the intelligible, that man as man necessarily has an awareness of the whole. Let me only conclude this point. As far as I know, the present-day arguments in favor of revelation against philosophy are based on an inadequate understanding of classical philosophy.

Now, to find our bearings, let us return to a more elementary stratum of the conflict. What is truly significant in the present-day argument will then become clearer, and we shall understand also the reasons for the withdrawal from objectivity in the argument in favor of revelation in present-day theology. The typical older view regarding revelation and reason is today accepted fully only by the Catholic Church and by Orthodox Jews and orthodox Protestants. I speak of course only of the Jewish version. The question is, how do we know that the *Torah* is from Sinai or the word of the living God? The traditional Jewish answer is primarily that our fathers have told us, and they knew it from their fathers, an uninterrupted chain of reliable tradition, going back to Mount Sinai. If the question is answered in this form, it becomes inevitable to wonder, is the tradition reliable? I will mention only one specimen from the earlier discussion. At the begining of his legal code, Maimonides gives the chain of tradition from Moses down to Talmudic times, and there occurs the figure of Ahijah the Shilonite who is said to have received the Torah from King David and also is introduced as a contemporary of Moses, who had received the Torah from Moses. Now, whatever Maimonides may have meant by the insertion of this Talmudic story, from our point of view it would be an indication of the fact that this chain of the tradition, especially in its earlier parts, contains what today is called "mythical," that is to say, unhistorical elements. I shall not dwell on the very well-known discrepancies in the Bible. The question, who wrote the Pentateuch, was traditionally answered, as a matter of course, by Moses, so much so that when Spinoza questioned the Mosaic origin of the Torah it was assumed that he denied its divine origin. Who wrote the Pentateuch, Moses himself, or men who knew of the revelation only from hearsay or indirectly? The details are of no interest to us here; we have to consider the principle.

Is an historical proof of the fact of revelation possible? An historical proof of the fact of revelation would be comparable to the historical proof of the fact, say, of the assassination of Caesar by Brutus and Cassius. That is demonstrably impossible. In the case of historical facts proper, or historical facts in the ordinary sense of the term, there is always evidence by impartial observers or by witnesses belonging to both parties. For example, here, friends and enemies of Caesar. In the case of revelation, there are no impartial observers. All witnesses are adherents and all transmitters were believers. Furthermore, there are no pseudo-assassinations or pseudo-wars, but there are pseudo-revelations and pseudo-prophets. The historical proof presupposes, therefore, criteria for distinguishing between genuine and spurious revelation. We know the biblical criterion, at least the decisive one in our context: a prophet cannot be a genuine prophet if he contradicts the preceding classic revelations, the Mosaic revelation. Therefore the question is, how to establish the classic revelation?

The usual traditional answer was, "miracles." But here the difficulty arises in this form: miracles as miracles are not demonstrable. In the first place, a miracle as a miracle is a fact of which we do not know the natural causes, but our ignorance of the cause of a given phenomenon does not entitle us to say it cannot have been produced by any natural cause but only supernaturally. Our ignorance of the power of nature—that is Spinoza's phrasing of the argument—our ignorance of the power of nature disqualifies us from ever having recourse to supernatural causation. Now this argument in this form is not quite adequate for the following reasons: because while our knowledge of the power of nature is certainly very limited, of certain things we know, or at least men like Spinoza believed to know, that they are impossible by nature. I mention only the resurrection of a dead man, to take the strongest example, which Spinoza would admit could never have taken place naturally. Therefore the argument taken from the ignorance of the power of nature is supplemented by the following argument: that it might be possible theoretically to establish in given cases that a certain phenomenon is miraculous, but it so happens that all these events regarding which this claim is made are known only as reported, and many things are reported which have never happened. More precisely, all miracles which are important, certainly to the Jew and even to the Protestant (the case of Catholicism is different), took place in a pre-scientific age. No miracle was performed in the presence of first-rate physicists, etc. Therefore, for these reasons, many people today say, and that was also said by certain famous theologians of the past, that miracles presuppose faith; they are not meant to establish faith. But whether this is sufficient, whether this is in accordance with the biblical view of miracles, is a question. To begin with, one could make this objection:

that if you take the story of the prophet Elijah on Carmel, you see that the issue between God and Baal is decided by an objective occurrence, equally acceptable to the sense perception of believers as well as unbelievers.

The second ordinary traditional argument in favor of revelation is the fulfillment of prophecies. But I need not tell you that this again is open to very great difficulties. In the first place, we have the ambiguity of prophecies, and even in cases like unambiguous prophecies—for example, the prophecy of Cyrus in the fortieth chapter of *Isaiah*, that is today generally taken to be a prophecy after the event, the reasoning being that such a prophecy would be a miracle if established; but it is known only as reported and therefore the question of historical criticism of the sources comes in.

Much more impressive is the other line of the argument which proves revelation by the intrinsic quality of revelation. The revealed law is the best of all laws. Now this, however, means that the revealed law agrees with the rational standard of the best law; but if this is the case, is then the allegedly revealed law not in fact the product of reason, of human reason, the work of Moses and not of God? Yet the revealed law, while it never contradicts reason, has an excess over reason; it is supra-rational, and therefore it cannot be the product of reason. That is a very famous argument, but again we have to wonder what does supra-rational mean? The supra has to be proved and it cannot be proved. What unassisted reason sees is only a non-rational element, an element which, while not contradicting reason, is not in itself supported by reason. From the point of view of reason, it is an indifferent possibility: possibly true, possibly false, or possibly good, possibly bad. It would cease to be indifferent if it were proved to be true or good, which means if it were true or good according to natural reason. But again, if this were the case, it would appear to be the product of reason, of human reason. Let me try to state this in more general terms. The revealed law is either fully rational—in that case it is a product of reason—or it is not fully rational—in that case it may as well be the product of human unreason as of divine super-reason. Still more generally, revelation is either a brute fact, to which nothing in purely human experience corresponds—in that case it is an oddity of no human importance—or it is a meaningful fact, a fact required by human experience to solve the fundamental problems of man—in that case it may very well be the product of reason, of the human attempt to solve the problem of human life. It would then appear that it is impossible for reason, for philosophy, to assent to revelation as revelation. Moreover, the intrinsic qualities of the revealed law are not regarded as decisive by the revealed law itself. Revealed law puts the emphasis not on the universal, but on the contingent, and this leads to the difficulties which I have indicated before.

Let us turn now to the other side of the picture; these things are, of course, implied in all present-day secularism. Now all these and similar arguments prove no more than that unassisted human reason is invincibly ignorant of divine revelation. They do not prove the impossibility of revelation. Let us assume that revelation is a fact, if a fact not accessible to unassisted reason, and that it is meant to be inaccessible to unassisted reason. For if there were certain knowledge, there would be no need for faith, for trust, for true obedience, for free surrender to God. In that case, the whole refutation of the alleged rejection of the alleged objective historical proofs of revelation would be utterly irrelevant. Let me take this simple example of Elijah on Carmel: were the believers in Baal, whom Elijah or God convinced, impartial scientific observers? In a famous essay, Francis Bacon made a distinction between idolators and atheists and said that the miracles are meant only for the conviction, not of atheists, but of idolators, meaning of people who in principle admit the possibility of divine action. These men were fearing and trembling, not beyond hope or fear like philosophers. Not theology, but philosophy, begs the question. Philosophy demands that revelation should establish its claim before the tribunal of human reason, but revelation as such refuses to acknowledge that tribunal. In other words, philosophy recognizes only such experiences as can be had by all men at all times in broad daylight. But God has said or decided that he wants to dwell in mist. Philosophy is victorious as long as it limits itself to repelling the attack which theologians make on philosophy with the weapons of philosophy. But philosophy in its turn suffers a defeat as soon as it starts an offensive of its own, as soon as it tries to refute, not the necessarily inadequate proofs of revelation, but revelation itself.

4.

Now there is today, I believe, still a very common view, common to nineteenth and twentieth century freethinkers, that modern science and historical criticism have refuted revelation. Now I would say that they have not even refuted the most fundamentalistic orthodoxy. Let us look at that. There is the famous example which played such a role still in the nineteenth century and, for those of us who come from conservative or orthodox backgrounds, in our own lives. The age of the earth is much greater than the biblical reports assume, but it is obviously a very defective argument. The refutation presupposes that everything happens naturally; but this is denied by the Bible. The Bible speaks of creation; creation is a miracle, the miracle. All the evidence supplied by geology, paleontology, etc., is valid against the Bible only on the premise that no miracle intervened. The freethinking argument is really based on poor thinking. It begs the question. Similarly, textual criticism—the inconsistencies, repetitions, and other apparent deficiencies of the biblical text: if the text is divinely inspired, all those things mean something entirely different from what they would mean if we were entitled to assume that the Bible is a merely human book. Then they are just deficiencies, but otherwise they are secrets.

Historical criticism presupposes unbelief in verbal inspiration. The attack, the famous and very effective attack by science and historical criticism on revelation is based on the dogmatic exclusion of the possibility of miracles and of verbal inspiration. I shall limit myself to miracles, because verbal inspiration itself is one miracle. Now this attack, which underlies all the scientific and historical argments, would be defensible if we knew that miracles are impossible. Then we would indeed be able to draw all these conclusions. But what does that mean? We would have to be in possession of either a proof of the non-existence of an omnipotent God, who alone could do miracles, or of a proof that miracles are incompatible with the nature of God. I see no alternative to that. Now the first alternative—a proof of the non-existence of an omnipotent God—would presuppose that we have perfect knowledge of the whole, so as it were we know all the corners, there is no place for an omnipotent God. In other words, the presupposition is a completed system. We have the solution to all riddles. And then I think we may dismiss this possibility as absurd. The second alternative—namely, that miracles are incompatible with the nature of God—would presuppose human knowledge of the nature of God: in traditional language, natural theology. Indeed the basis, the forgotten basis, of modern free thought, is natural theology. When the decisive battles were waged, not in the nineteenth century, but in the eighteenth and seventeenth, the attempted refutation of miracles, etc., were based on an alleged knowledge of the nature of God—natural theology is the technical name for that.

Let us sketch the general character of this argument. God is the most perfect being. This is what all men mean by God, regardless of whether He exists or not. Now the philosophers claim that they can prove the incompatiblity of revelation and of any other miracle with divine perfection. That is a long story, not only in the seventeenth and eighteenth centuries but of course also in the Middle Ages.

I will try to sketch this argument by going back to its human roots. Fundamentally, the philosophic argument in natural theology is based on an analogy from human perfection. God is the most perfect being. But we know empirically perfection only in the form of human perfection, and human perfection is taken to be represented by the wise man or by the highest human approximation to the wise man. For example, just as the wise man does not inflict infinite punishment on erring human beings, God, still more perfect, would do it even less. A wise man does not do silly or purposeless things, but to use the miracle of verbal inspiration, for example, in order to tell a prophet the name of a pagan king who is going to rule centuries later, would be silly. I mean that is the argument underlying these things or something of this kind. To this I would answer as follows: God's perfection implies that he is incomprehensible. God's ways may seem to be foolish to man; this does not mean that they are foolish. Natural theology would have to get rid, in other words, of God's incomprehensibility in order to refute revelation, and that it never did.

There was one man who tried to force the issue by denying the incomprehensibility of God's essence, and that man was Spinoza. [May I say this in passing that I have leaned very heavily in my analysis of these things on Spinoza.] One can learn much from Spinoza, who is the most extreme, certainly of the modern critics of revelation, not necessarily in his thought but certainly in the expression of his thought. I like to quote the remark of Hobbes, you know, a notoriously bold man, who said that he had not dared to write as boldly as Spinoza. Now Spinoza says, "We have adequate knowledge of the essence of God," and if we have that, God is clearly fully comprehensible. What Spinoza called the adequate knowledge of the essence of God led to the consequence that miracles of any kind are impossible. But what about Spinoza's adequate knowledge of the essence of God? Let us consider that for one moment, because it is really not a singular and accidental case. [Many of you will have seen Spinoza's *Ethics*, his exposition of that knowledge.] Spinoza's *Ethics* begins, as you know, with certain definitions. Now these definitions are in themselves absolutely arbitrary, especially the famous definition of substance: substance is what is by itself and is conceived by itself. Once you admit that, everything else follows from that; there are no miracles possible then. But since the definitions are arbitrary, the conclusions are arbitrary. The basic definitions are, however, not arbitrary if we view them with regard to their function. Spinoza defines by these definitions the conditions which must be fulfilled if the whole is to be fully intelligible. But they do not prove that these conditions are in fact fulfilled—that depends on the success of Spinoza's venture. The proof lies in the success. If Spinoza is capable of giving a clear and distinct account of everything, then we are confronted with this situation. We have a clear and distinct account of the whole, and, on the other hand, we have obscure accounts of the whole, one of whom would be the biblical account. And then every sane person would prefer the clear and distinct account to the obscure account. That is, I think, the real proof which Spinoza wants to give. But is Spinoza's account of the whole clear and distinct? Those of you who have ever tried their hands, for example, at his analysis of the emotions, would not be so certain of that. But more than that, even if it is clear and distinct, is it necessarily true? Is its clarity and distinctness not due to the fact that Spinoza abstracts from those elements of the whole which are not clear and distinct and which can never be rendered clear and distinct? Now fundamentally, Spinoza's procedure is that of modern science according to its original conception—to make the universe a completely clear and distinct, a completely mathematizable unit.

Let me sum this up: the historical refutation of revelation [—and I say here that this is not changed if you take revelation in the most fundamentalist meaning of the term

—] presupposes natural theology because the historical refutation always presupposes the impossibility of miracles,
and the impossibility of miracles is ultimately guaranteed
only by knowledge of God. Now a natural theology which
fills this bill presupposes in its turn a proof that God's nature is comprehensible, and this in its turn requires completion of the true system of the true or adequate account
of the whole. Since such a true or adequate, as distinguished from a merely clear and distinct, account of the
whole, is certainly not available, philosophy has never refuted revelation. Nor, to come back to what I said before,
has revelation, or rather theology, ever refuted philosophy. For from the point of view of philosophy, revelation
is only a possibility; and secondly, man, in spite of what the
theologians say, can live as a philosopher, that is to say, un-
tragically. It seems to me that all these attempts, made, for
example, by Pascal and by others, to prove that the life of
philosophy is fundamentally miserable, presuppose faith; it
is not acceptable and possible as a refutation of philosophy.
Generally stated, I would say that all alleged refutations of
revelation presuppose unbelief in revelation, and all alleged refutations of philosophy presuppose already faith in
revelation. There seems to be no ground common to both,
and therefore superior to both.

If one can say colloquially, the philosophers have never
refuted revelation and the theologians have never refuted
philosophy, that would sound plausible, considering the
enormous difficulty of the problem from any point of view.
And to that extent we may be said to have said something
very trivial; but to show that it is not quite trivial, I submit
to you this consideration in conclusion. And here when I
use the term philosophy, I use it in the common and vague
sense of the term where it includes any rational orientation
in the world, including science and what have you, common sense. If this is so, philosophy must admit the possibility of revelation. Now that means that philosophy itself is
possibly not the right way of life. It is not necessarily the

right way of life, not evidently the right way of life, because this possibility of revelation exists. But what then
does the choice of philosophy mean under these conditions? In this case, the choice of philosophy is based on
faith. In other words, the quest for evident knowledge
rests itself on an unevident premise. And it seems to me
that this difficulty underlies all present-day philosophizing
and that it is this difficulty which is at the bottom of what
in the social sciences is called the value problem: that philosophy or science, however you might call it, is incapable
of giving an evident account of its own necessity. I do not
think I have to prove that showing the practical usefulness
of science, natural and social science, does not of course
prove its necessity at all. I mean I shall not speak of the
great successes of the social sciences, because they are not
so impressive; but as for the great successes of the natural
sciences, we in the age of the hydrogen bomb have the
question completely open again whether this effort is really
reasonable with a view to its practical usefulness. That is of
course not the most important reason theoretically, but
one which has practically played a great role.

What Is Liberal Education?

Liberal education is education in culture or toward culture. The finished product of a liberal education is a cultured human being. "Culture" (*cultura*) means primarily agriculture: the cultivation of the soil and its products, taking care of the soil, improving the soil in accordance with its nature. "Culture" means derivatively and today chiefly the cultivation of the mind, the taking care and improving of the native faculties of the mind in accordance with the nature of the mind. Just as the soil needs cultivators of the soil, the mind needs teachers. But teachers are not as easy to come by as farmers. The teachers themselves are pupils and must be pupils. But there cannot be an infinite regress: ultimately there must be teachers who are not in turn pupils. Those teachers who are not in turn pupils are the great minds or, in order to avoid any ambiguity in a matter of such importance, the greatest minds. Such men are extremely rare. We are not likely to meet any of them in any classroom. We are not likely to meet any of them anywhere. It is a piece of good luck if there is a single one alive in one's time. For all practical purposes, pupils, of whatever degree of proficiency, have access to the teachers who are not in turn pupils, to the greatest minds, only through the great books. Liberal education will then consist in studying with the proper care the great books which the greatest minds have left behind—a study in which the more experienced pupils assist the less experienced pupils, including the beginners.

This is not an easy task, as would appear if we were to consider the formula which I have just mentioned. That formula requires a long commentary. Many lives have been spent and may still be spent in writing such commentaries. For instance, what is meant by the remark that the great books should be studied "with the proper care"? At present I mention only one difficulty which is obvious to everyone among you: the greatest minds do not all tell us the same things regarding the most important themes; the community of the greatest minds is rent by discord and even by various kinds of discord. Whatever further consequences this may entail, it certainly entails the consequence that liberal education cannot be simply indoctrination. I mention yet another difficulty. "Liberal education is education in culture." In what culture? Our answer is: culture in the sense of the Western tradition. Yet Western culture is only one among many cultures. By limiting ourselves to Western culture, do we not condemn liberal education to a kind of parochialism, and is not parochialism incompatible with the liberalism, the generosity, the openmindedness, of liberal education? Our notion of liberal education does not seem to fit an age which is aware of the fact that there is not *the* culture of *the* human mind, but a variety of cultures. Obviously, culture if susceptible of being used in the plural is not quite the same thing as culture which is a *singulare tantum*, which can be used only in the singular. Culture is now no longer, as people say, an absolute, but has become relative. It is not easy to say what culture susceptible of being used in the plural means. As a consequence of this obscurity people have suggested, explicitly or implicitly, that culture is any pattern of conduct common to any human group. Hence we do not hesitate to speak of the culture of suburbia or of the cultures of juvenile gangs, both nondelinquent and delinquent. In other words, every human being outside of lunatic asylums is a cultured human being, for he participates in a culture. At the frontiers of research there arises the question as to whether there are not cultures also of inmates of lunatic asylums. If we contrast the present-day usage of "culture" with the original meaning, it is as if someone would say that the cultivation of a garden may consist of the garden's being littered with empty tin cans and whisky bottles and used papers of various descriptions thrown around the garden at random. Having arrived at this point, we realize that we have lost our way somehow. Let us then make a fresh start by raising the question: what can liberal education mean here and now?

Liberal education is literate education of a certain kind: some sort of education in letters or through letters. There is no need to make a case for literacy; every voter knows that modern democracy stands or falls by literacy. In order to understand this need we must reflect on modern democracy. what is modern democracy? It was once said that democracy is the regime that stands or falls by virtue: a democracy is a regime in which all or most adults are men of virtue, and since virtue seems to require wisdom, a regime in which all or most adults are virtuous and wise, or the society in which all or most adults have developed their reason to a high degree, or *the* rational society. Democracy, in a word, is meant to be an aristocracy which has broadened into a universal aristocracy. Prior to the emergence of modern democracy some doubts were felt whether democracy thus understood is possible. As one of the two greatest minds among the theorists of democracy put it, "If there were a people consisting of gods, it would rule itself democratically. A government of such perfection is not suitable for human beings." This still and small voice has by now become a high-powered loud-speaker.

There exists a whole science—the science which I among thousands profess to teach, political science—which so to speak has no other theme than the contrast between the original conception of democracy, or what one may call the ideal of democracy, and democracy as it is. According to an extreme view, which is the predominant view in the profession, the ideal of democracy was a sheer delusion, and the only thing which matters is the behavior of democracies and the behavior of men in democracies. Modern democracy, so far from being universal aristocracy, would be mass rule were it not for the fact that the mass cannot rule, but is ruled by elites, that is, groupings of men who for whatever reason are on top or have a fair chance to arrive at the top; one of the most important virtues required for the smooth working of democracy, as far as the mass is concerned, is said to be electoral apathy, viz., lack of public spirit; not indeed the salt of the earth, but the salt of modern democracy are those citizens who read nothing except the sports page and the comic section. Democracy is then not indeed mass rule, but mass culture. A mass culture is a culture which can be appropriated by the meanest capacities without any intellectual and moral effort whatsoever and at a very low monetary price. But even a mass culture and precisely a mass culture requires a constant supply of what are called new ideas, which are the products of what are called creative minds: even singing commercials lose their appeal if they are not varied from time to time. But democracy, even if it is only regarded as the hard shell which protects the soft mass culture, requires in the long run qualities of an entirely different kind: qualities of dedication, of concentration, of breadth, and of depth. Thus we understand most easily what liberal education means here and now. Liberal education is the counterpoison to mass culture, to the corroding effects of mass culture, to its inherent tendency to produce nothing but "specialists without spirit or vision and voluptuaries without heart." Liberal education is the ladder by which we try to ascend from mass democracy to democracy as originally meant. Liberal education is the necessary endeavor to found an aristocracy within democratic mass society. Liberal education reminds those members of a mass democracy who have ears to hear, of human greatness.

Someone might say that this notion of liberal education is merely political, that it dogmatically assumes the goodness of modern democracy. Can we not turn our backs on modern society? Can we not return to nature, to the life of preliterate tribes? Are we not crushed, nauseated, degraded by the mass of printed material, the graveyards of so many beautiful and majestic forests? It is not sufficient to say that this is mere romanticism, that we today cannot return to nature: may not coming generations, after a man-wrought cataclysm, be compelled to live in illiterate tribes? Will our thoughts concerning thermonuclear wars not be affected by such prospects? Certain it is that the horrors of mass culture (which include guided tours to integer nature) render intelligible the longing for a return to nature. An illiterate society at its best is a society ruled by age-old ancestral custom which it traces to original founders, gods, or sons of gods or pupils of gods; since there are no letters in such a society, the late heirs cannot be in direct contact with the original founders; they cannot know whether the fathers or grandfathers have not deviated from what the original founders meant, or have not defaced the divine message by merely human additions or subtractions; hence an illiterate society cannot consistently act on its principle that the best is the oldest. Only letters which have come down from the founders can make it possible for the founders to speak directly to the latest heirs. It is then self-contradictory to wish to return to illiteracy. We are compelled to live with books. But life is too short to live with any but the greatest books. In this respect as well in some others, we do well to take as our model that one among the greatest minds who because of his common sense is *the* mediator between us and the greatest minds. Socrates never wrote a book, but he read books. Let me quote a statement of Socrates which says almost everything that has to be said on our subject, with the noble simplicity and quiet greatness of the ancients. "Just as others are pleased by a good horse or dog or bird, I myself am pleased to an even higher degree by good friends. . . . And the treasures of the wise men of old which they left behind by writing them in books, I unfold and go through them together with my friends, and if we see something good, we pick it out and regard it as a great gain if we thus become useful to one another." The man who reports this utterance adds the remark: "When I heard this, it seemed to me both that Socrates was blessed and that he was leading those listening to him toward perfect gentlemanship." This report is defective since it does not tell us anything as to what Socrates did regarding those passages in the books of the wise men of old of which he did not know whether they were good. From another report we learn that Euripides once gave Socrates the writing of Heraclitus and then asked him for his opinion about that writing. Socrates said: "What I have understood is great and noble; I believe this is also true of what I have not understood; but one surely needs for understanding that writing some special sort of a diver."

Education to perfect gentlemanship, to human excellence, liberal education consists in reminding oneself of human excellence, of human greatness. In what way, by what means does liberal education remind us of human greatness? We cannot think highly enough of what liberal education is meant to be. We have heard Plato's suggestion that education in the highest sense is philosophy. Philosophy is quest for wisdom or quest for knowledge regarding the most important, the highest, or the most comprehensive things; such knowledge, he suggested, is virtue and is happiness. But wisdom is inaccessible to man, and hence virtue and happiness will always be imperfect. In spite of this, the philosopher, who, as such, is not simply wise, is declared to be the only true king; he is declared to possess all the excellences of which man's mind is capable, to the highest degree. From this we must draw the conclusion that we cannot be philosophers—that we cannot acquire the highest form of education. We must not be deceived by the fact that we meet many people who say that they are philosophers. For those people employ a loose expression which is perhaps necessitated by administrative convenience. Often they mean merely that they are members of philosophy departments. And it is as absurd to expect members of philosophy departments to be philosophers as it is to expect members of art departments to be artists. We cannot be philosophers, but we can love philosophy; we can try to philosophize. This philosophizing consists at any rate primarily and in a way chiefly in listening to the conversation between the great philosophers or, more generally and more cautiously, between the greatest minds, and therefore in studying the great books. The greatest minds to whom we ought to listen are by no means exclusively the greatest minds of the West. It is merely an unfortunate necessity which prevents us from listening to the greatest minds of India and of China: we do not understand their languages, and we cannot learn all languages.

To repeat: liberal education consists in listening to the conversation among the greatest minds. But here we are confronted with the overwhelming difficulty that this conversation does not take place without our help—that in fact we must bring about that conversation. The greatest minds utter monologues. We must transform their monologues into a dialogue, their "side by side" into a "together." The greatest minds utter monologues even when they write dialogues. When we look at the Platonic dialogues, we observe that there is never a dialogue among minds of the highest order: all Platonic dialogues are dialogues between a superior man and men inferior to him. Plato apparently felt that one could not write a dialogue between two men of the highest order. We must then do something which the greatest minds were unable to do. Let us face this difficulty—a difficulty so great that it seems to condemn liberal education as an absurdity. Since the

greatest minds contradict one another regarding the most
important matters, they compel us to judge of their monologues; we cannot take on trust what any one of them says.
On the other hand, we cannot but notice that we are not
competent to be judges.

This state of things is concealed from us by a number of
facile delusions. We somehow believe that our point of
view is superior, higher than those of the greatest minds—
either because our point of view is that of our time, and
our time, being later than the time of the greatest minds,
can be presumed to be superior to their times; or else because we believe that each of the greatest minds was right
from his point of view but not, as he claims, simply right:
we know that there cannot be *the* simply true substantive
view, but only a simply true formal view; that formal view
consists in the insight that every comprehensive view is relative to a specific perspective, or that all comprehensive
views are mutually exclusive and none can be simply true.
The facile delusions which conceal from us our true situation all amount to this: that we are, or can be, wiser than
the wisest men of the past. We are thus induced to play the
part, not of attentive and docile listeners, but of impre-
sarios or lion tamers. Yet we must face our awesome situation, created by the necessity that we try to be more than
attentive and docile listeners, namely, judges, and yet we
are not competent to be judges. As it seems to me, the
cause of this situation is that we have lost all simply authoritative traditions in which we could trust, the *nomos* which
gave us authoritative guidance, because our immediate
teachers and teachers' teachers believed in the possibility
of a simply rational society. Each of us here is compelled to
find his bearings by his own powers, however defective
they may be.

We have no comfort other than that inherent in this activity. Philosophy, we have learned, must be on its guard
against the wish to be edifying—philosophy can only be intrinsically edifying. We cannot exert our understanding

without from time to time understanding something of importance; and this act of understanding may be accompanied by the awareness of our understanding, by the understanding of understanding, by *noesis noeseos*, and this is so high, so pure, so noble an experience that Aristotle could ascribe it to his God. This experience is entirely independent of whether what we understand primarily is pleasing or displeasing, fair or ugly. It leads us to realize that all evils are in a sense necessary if there is to be understanding. It enables us to accept all evils which befall us and which may well break our hearts in the spirit of good citizens of the city of God. By becoming aware of the dignity of the mind, we realize the true ground of the dignity of man and therewith the goodness of the world, whether we understand it as created or as uncreated, which is the home of man because it is the home of the human mind.

Liberal education, which consists in the constant intercourse with the greatest minds, is a training in the highest form of modesty, not to say of humility. It is at the same time a training in boldness: it demands from us the complete break with the noise, the rush, the thoughtlessness, the cheapness of the Vanity Fair of the intellectuals as well as of their enemies. It demands from us the boldness implied in the resolve to regard the accepted views as mere opinions, or to regard the average opinions as extreme opinions which are at least as likely to be wrong as the most strange or the least popular opinions. Liberal education is liberation from vulgarity. The Greeks had a beautiful word for "vulgarity"; they called it *apeirokalia*, lack of experience in things beautiful. Liberal education supplies us with experience in things beautiful.

Liberal Education
and Responsibility

When I was approached by The Fund for Adult Education with the suggestion that I prepare an essay on liberal
education and responsibility, my first reaction was not one
of delight. While I am in many ways dependent on the
administration of education and hence on the organiza-
tions serving education, I looked at these things, if I
looked at them, with that awe which arises from both grat-
itude and apprehension mixed with ignorance. I thought
that it was my job, my responsibility, to do my best in the
classroom, in conversations with students wholly regardless
of whether they are registered or not, and last but not
least in my study at home. I own that education is in a
sense the subject matter of my teaching and my research.
But I am almost solely concerned with the goal or end of
education at its best or highest—of the education of the
perfect prince, as it were—and very little with its conditions and its how. The most important conditions, it seems
to me, are the qualities of the educator and of the human
being who is to be educated; in the case of the highest
form of education those conditions are very rarely fulfilled,
and one cannot do anything to produce them; the only
things we can do regarding them are not to interfere with

their interplay and to prevent such interference. As for the how, one knows it once one knows what education is meant to do to a human being or once one knows the end of education. Certainly, there are some rules of thumb. Almost every year I meet once with the older students of my department in order to discuss with them how to teach political theory in college. Once on such an occasion a student asked me whether I could not give him a general rule regarding teaching. I replied: "Always assume that there is one silent student in your class who is by far superior to you in head and in heart." I meant by this: do not have too high an opinion of your importance, and have the highest opinion of your duty, your responsibility.

There was another reason why I was somewhat bewildered when I first began to prepare this essay. That reason has to do with the word "responsibility." For clearly, liberal education and responsibility are not identical. They may not be separable from each other. Before one could discuss their relation, one would have to know what each of them is. As for the word "responsibility," it is now in common use, and I myself have used it from time to time, for instance a very short while ago. In the sense in which it is now frequently used, it is a neologism. It is, I believe, the fashionable substitute for such words as "duty," "conscience," or "virtue." We frequently say of a man that he is a responsible man, where people of former generations would have said that he is a just man or a conscientious man or a virtuous man. Primarily, a man is responsible if he can be held accountable for what he does—for example, for a murder; being responsible is so far from being the same as being virtuous that it is merely the condition for being either virtuous or vicious. By substituting responsibility for virtue, we prove to be much more easily satisfied than our forefathers, or, more precisely perhaps, we assume that by being responsible one is already virtuous or that no vicious man is responsible for his viciousness. There is a kinship between "responsibility" thus understood and "decency" as sometimes used by the British: if a man ruins himself in order to save a complete stranger, the stranger, if British, is supposed to thank him by saying, "It was rather decent of you." We seem to loathe the grand old words and perhaps also the things which they indicate and to prefer more subdued expressions out of delicacy or because they are more businesslike. However this may be, my misgivings were caused by my awareness of my ignorance as to what the substitution of responsibility for duty and for virtue means.

I certainly felt that I was particularly ill-prepared to address professional educators on the subject "Education and Responsibility." But then I learnt to my relief that I was merely expected to explain two sentences occurring in my speech "What is Liberal Education?" The sentences run as follows: "Liberal education is the ladder by which we try to ascend from mass democracy to democracy as originally meant. Liberal education is the necessary endeavor to found an aristocracy within democratic mass society."

To begin at the beginning, the word "liberal" had at the beginning, just as it has now, a political meaning, but its original political meaning is almost the opposite of its present political meaning. Originally a liberal man was a man who behaved in a manner becoming a free man, as distinguished from a slave. "Liberality" referred then to slavery and presupposed it. A slave is a human being who lives for another human being, his master; he has in a sense no life of his own: he has no time for himself. The master, on the other hand, has all his time for himself, that is, for the pursuits becoming him: politics and philosophy. Yet there are very many free men who are almost like slaves since they have very little time for themselves, because they have to work for their livelihood and to rest so that they can work the next day. Those free men without leisure are the poor, the majority of citizens. The truly free man who can live in a manner becoming a free man is the man of leisure, the gentleman who must possess some wealth—but wealth of a certain kind: a kind of wealth the administration of which, to say nothing of its acquisition, does not take up much of his time, but can be taken care of through his supervising of properly trained supervisors; the gentleman will be a gentleman farmer and not a merchant or entrepreneur. Yet if he spends much of his time in the country he will not be available sufficiently for the pursuits becoming him; he must therefore live in town. His way of life will be at the mercy of those of his fellow citizens who are not gentlemen, if he and his like do not rule: the way of life of the gentlemen is not secure if they are not the unquestioned rulers of their city, if the regime of their city is not aristocratic.

One becomes a gentleman by education, by liberal education. The Greek word for education is derived from the Greek word for child: education in general, and therefore liberal education in particular, is, then, to say the least, primarily not adult education. The Greek word for education is akin to the Greek word for play, and the activity of the gentlemen is emphatically earnest; in fact, the gentlemen are "the earnest ones." They are earnest because they are concerned with the most weighty matters, with the only things which deserve to be taken seriously for their own sake, with the good order of the soul and of the city. The education of the potential gentlemen is the playful anticipation of the life of gentlemen. It consists above all in the formation of character and of taste. The fountains of that education are the poets. It is hardly necessary to say that the gentleman is in need of skills. To say nothing of reading, writing, counting, reckoning, wrestling, throwing of spears, and horsemanship, he must possess the skill of administering well and nobly the affairs of his household and the affairs of his city by deed and by speech. He acquires that skill by his familiar intercourse with older or more experienced gentlemen, preferably with elder statesmen, by receiving instruction from paid teachers in the art of speaking, by reading histories and books of travel, by meditating on the works of the poets, and, of course, by taking part in political life. All this requires leisure on the part of the youths as well as on the part of their elders; it is the preserve of a certain kind of wealthy people.

This fact gives rise to the question of the justice of a society which in the best case would be ruled by gentlemen ruling in their own right. Just government is government which rules in the interest of the whole society, and not merely of a part. The gentlemen are therefore under an obligation to show to themselves and to others that their rule is best for everyone in the city or for the city as a whole. But justice requires that equal men be treated equally, and there is no good reason for thinking that the gentlemen are by nature superior to the vulgar. The gentlemen are indeed superior to the vulgar by their breeding, but the large majority of men are by nature capable of the same breeding if they are caught young, in their cradles; only the accident of birth decides whether a given individual has a chance of becoming a gentleman or will necessarily become a villain; hence aristocracy is unjust. The gentlemen replied as follows: the city as a whole is much too poor to enable everyone to bring up his sons so that they can become gentlemen; if you insist that the social order should correspond with tolerable strictness to the natural order—that is, that men who are more or less equal by nature should also be equal socially or by convention—you will merely bring about a state of universal drabness. But only on the ground of a narrow conception of justice, owing its evidence to the power of the ignoble passion of envy, must one prefer a flat building which is everywhere equally drab to a structure which from a broad base of drabness rises to a narrow plateau of distinction and of grace and therefore gives some grace and some distinction to its very base. There must then be a few who are wealthy and well born and many who are poor and of obscure origin. Yet there seems to be no good reason why this family is elected to gentility and that family is condemned to indistinctness; that selection seems to be arbitrary, to say the least. It would indeed be foolish to deny that old wealth sometimes has its forgotten origins in crime. But it is more noble to believe, and probably also truer, that the old families are the descendants from the first settlers and from leaders in war or counsel; and it is certainly just that one be grateful.

Gentlemen may rule without being rulers in their own right; they may rule on the basis of popular election. This arrangement was regarded as unsatisfactory for the following reason. It would mean that the gentlemen are, strictly speaking, responsible to the common people—that the higher is responsible to the lower—and this would appear to be against nature. The gentlemen regard virtue as choiceworthy for its own sake, whereas the others praise virtue as a means for acquiring wealth and honor. The gentlemen and the others disagree, then, as regards the end of man or the highest good; they disagree regarding first principles. Hence they cannot have genuinely common deliberations.[1] The gentlemen cannot possibly give a sufficient or intelligible account of their way of life to the others. While being responsible to themselves for the well-being of the vulgar, they cannot be responsible to the vulgar.

But even if one rests satisfied with a less exacting notion of the rule of gentlemen, the principle indicated necessarily leads one to reject democracy. Roughly speaking, democracy is the regime in which the majority of adult free males living in a city rules, but only a minority of them are educated. The principle of democracy is therefore not virtue, but freedom as the right of every citizen to live as he likes. Democracy is rejected because it is as such the rule of the uneducated. One illustration must here suffice. The sophist Protagoras came to the democratic city of Athens in order to educate human beings, or to teach for pay the art of administering well the affairs of one's household and

1. Cf. *Crito* 49d 2–5.

of the city by deed and by speech—the political art. Since in a democracy everyone is supposed to possess the political art somehow, yet the majority, lacking equipment, cannot have acquired that art through education, Protagoras must assume that the citizens received that art through something like a divine gift, albeit a gift which becomes effective only through human punishments and rewards: the true political art, the art which enables a man not only to obey the laws but to frame laws, is acquired by education, by the highest form of education, which is necessarily the preserve of those who can pay for it.

To sum up, liberal education in the original sense not only fosters civic responsibility: it is even required for the exercise of civic responsibility. By being what they are, the gentlemen are meant to set the tone of society in the most direct, the least ambiguous, and the most unquestionable way: by ruling it in broad daylight.

It is necessary to take a further step away from our opinions in order to understand our opinions. The pursuits becoming the gentleman are said to be politics and philosophy. Philosophy can be understood loosely or strictly. If understood loosely, it is the same as what is now called intellectual interests. If understood strictly, it means quest for the truth about the most weighty matters or for the comprehensive truth or for the truth about the whole or for the science of the whole. When comparing politics to philosophy strictly understood, one realizes that philosophy is of higher rank than politics. Politics is the pursuit of certain ends; decent politics is the decent pursuit of decent ends. The responsible and clear distinction between ends which are decent and ends which are not is in a way presupposed by politics. It surely transcends politics. For everything which comes into being through human action and is therefore perishable or corruptible presupposes incorruptible and unchangeable things—for instance, the natural order of the human soul—with a view to which we can distinguish between right and wrong actions.

In the light of philosophy, liberal education takes on a new meaning: liberal education, especially education in the liberal arts, comes to sight as a preparation for philosophy. This means that philosophy transcends gentlemanship. The gentleman as gentleman accepts on trust certain most weighty things which for the philosopher are the themes of investigation and of questioning. Hence the gentleman's virtue is not entirely the same as the philosopher's virtue. A sign of this difference is the fact that whereas the gentleman must be wealthy in order to do his proper work, the philosopher may be poor. Socrates lived in tenthousandfold poverty. Once he saw many people following a horse and looking at it, and he heard some of them conversing much about it. In his surprise he approached the groom with the question whether the horse was rich. The groom looked at him as if he were not only grossly ignorant but not even sane: "How can a horse have any property?" At that Socrates understandably recovered, for he thus learned that it is lawful for a horse which is a pauper to become good provided it possesses a naturally good soul: it may then be lawful for Socrates to become a good man in spite of his poverty. Since it is not necessary for the philosopher to be wealthy, he does not need the entirely lawful arts by which one defends one's property, for example, forensically; nor does he have to develop the habit of self-assertion in this or other respects—a habit which necessarily enters into the gentleman's virtue. Despite these differences, the gentleman's virtue is a reflection of the philosopher's virtue; one may say it is its political reflection.

This is the ultimate justification of the rule of gentlemen. The rule of the gentlemen is only a reflection of the rule of the philosophers, who are understood to be the men best by nature and best by education. Given the fact that philosophy is more evidently quest for wisdom than possession of wisdom, the education of the philosopher never ceases as long as he lives; it is the adult education par excellence. For, to say nothing of other things, the highest kind of knowledge which a man may have acquired can never be simply at his disposal as other kinds of knowledge can; it is in constant need of being acquired again from the start. This leads to the following consequence. In the case of the gentleman, one can make a simple distinction between the playful education of the potential gentleman and the earnest work of the gentleman proper. In the case of the philosopher this simple distinction between the playful and the serious no longer holds, not in spite of the fact that his sole concern is with the weightiest matters, but because of it. For this reason alone, to say nothing of others, the rule of philosophers proves to be impossible. This leads to the difficulty that the philosophers will be ruled by the gentlemen, that is, by their inferiors.

One can solve this difficulty by assuming that the philosophers are not as such a constituent part of the city. In other words, the only teachers who are as such a constituent part of the city are the priests. The end of the city is then not the same as the end of philosophy. If the gentlemen represent the city at its best, one must say that the end of the gentleman is not the same as the end of the philosopher. What was observed regarding the gentleman in his relation to the vulgar applies even more to the philosopher in his relation to the gentlemen and a fortiori to all other nonphilosophers: the philosopher and the nonphilosophers cannot have genuinely common deliberations. There is a fundamental disproportion between philosophy and the city. In political things it is a sound rule to let sleeping dogs lie or to prefer the established to the nonestablished or to recognize the right of the first occupier. Philosophy stands or falls by its intransigent disregard of this rule and of anything which reminds of it. Philosophy can then live only side by side with the city. As Plato put it in the *Republic*, only in a city in which the philosophers rule and in which they therefore owe their training in philosophy to the city is it just that the philosopher be compelled to engage in political activity; in all other cities—

that is, in all actual cities—the philosopher does not owe
his highest gift of human origin to the city and therefore is
not under an obligation to do the work of the city. In entire agreement with this, Plato suggests in his *Crito*, where
he avoids the very term "philosophy," that the philosopher
owes indeed very much to the city and therefore he is
obliged to obey at least passively even the unjust laws of
the city and to die at the behest of the city. Yet he is not
obliged to engage in political activity. The philosopher as
philosopher is responsible to the city only to the extent
that by doing his own work, by his own well-being, he contributes to the well-being of the city: philosophy has necessarily a humanizing or civilizing effect. The city needs philosophy, but only mediately or indirectly, not to say in a
diluted form. Plato has presented this state of things by
comparing the city to a cave from which only a rough and
steep ascent leads to the light of the sun: the city as city is
more closed to philosophy than open to it.

The classics had no delusions regarding the probability
of a genuine aristocracy's ever becoming actual. For all
practical purposes they were satisfied with a regime in
which the gentlemen share power with the people in such
a way that the people elect the magistrates and the council
from among the gentlemen and demand an account of
them at the end of their term of office. A variation of this
thought is the notion of the mixed regime, in which the
gentlemen form the senate and the senate occupies the key
position between the popular assembly and an elected or
hereditary monarch as head of the armed forces of society.
There is a direct connection between the notion of the
mixed regime and modern republicanism. Lest this be misunderstood, one must immediately stress the important
differences between the modern doctrine and its classic
original. The modern doctrine starts from the natural
equality of all men, and it leads therefore to the assertion
that sovereignty belongs to the people; yet it understands
that sovereignty in such a way as to guarantee the natural

rights of each; it achieves this result by distinguishing between the sovereign and the government and by demanding that the fundamental governmental powers be separated from one another. The spring of this regime was held to be the desire of each to improve his material conditions. Accordingly the commercial and industrial elite, rather than the landed gentry, predominated.

The fully developed doctrine required that one man have one vote, that the voting be secret, and that the right to vote be not abridged on account of poverty, religion, or race. Governmental actions, on the other hand, are to be open to public inspection to the highest degree possible, for government is only the representative of the people and responsible to the people. The responsibility of the people, of the electors, does not permit of legal definition and is therefore the most obvious crux of modern republicanism. In the earlier stages the solution was sought in the religious education of the people, in the education, based on the Bible, of everyone to regard himself as responsible for his actions and for his thoughts to a God who would judge him, for, in the words of Locke, rational ethics proper is as much beyond the capacities of "day laborers and tradesmen, and spinsters and dairy maids" as is mathematics. On the other hand, the same authority advises the gentlemen of England to set their sons upon Puffendorf's *Natural Right* "wherein (they) will be instructed in the natural rights of men, and the origin and foundation of society, and the duties resulting from thence." Locke's *Some Thoughts Concerning Education* is addressed to the gentlemen, rather than to "those of the meaner sort," for if the gentlemen "are by their education once set right, they will quickly bring all the rest into order." For, we may suppose, the gentlemen are those called upon to act as representatives of the people, and they are to be prepared for this calling by a liberal education which is, above all, an education in "good breeding." Locke takes his models from the ancient Romans and Greeks, and the liberal education which he recommends consists to some extent in acquiring an easy familiarity with classical literature: "Latin I look upon as absolutely necessary to a gentleman."[2]

Not a few points which Locke meant are brought out clearly in the *Federalist Papers*. These writings reveal their connection with the classics simply enough by presenting themselves as the work of one Publius. This eminently sober work considers chiefly that diversity and inequality in the faculties of men which shows itself in the acquisition of property, but it is very far from being blind to the difference between business and government. According to Alexander Hamilton, the mechanics and manufacturers "know that the merchant is their natural patron and friend," their natural representative, for the merchant possesses "those acquired endowments without which, in a deliberative assembly, the greatest natural abilities are for the most part useless." Similarly, the wealthier landlords are the natural representatives of the landed interest. The natural arbiter between the landed and the moneyed interests will be "the man of the learned professions," for "the learned professions . . . truly form no distinct interest in society" and therefore are more likely than others to think of "the general interests of the society." It is true that in order to become a representative of the people, it sometimes suffices that one practice "with success the vicious arts by which elections are too often carried," but these deplorable cases are the exception, the rule being that the representatives will be respectable landlords, merchants, and members of the learned professions. If the electorate is not depraved, there is a fair chance that it will elect as its representatives for deliberation as well as for execution those among the three groups of men "who possess most wisdom to discern, and most virtue to pursue, the common

2. Ep. Ded., pp. 93–94, 164, 186.

good of the society," or those who are most outstanding by "merits and talents," by "ability and virtue."[3]

Under the most favorable conditions, the men who will hold the balance of power will then be the men of the learned professions. In the best case, Hamilton's republic will be ruled by the men of the learned professions. This reminds one of the rule of the philosophers, but only reminds one of it. Will the men of the learned professions at least be men of liberal education? It is probable that the men of the learned professions will chiefly be lawyers. No one ever had a greater respect for law and hence for lawyers than Edmund Burke: "God forbid I should insinuate anything derogatory to that profession, which is another priesthood, administrating the rites of sacred justice." Yet he felt compelled to describe the preponderance of lawyers in the national counsels as "mischievous." "Law . . . is, in my opinion, one of the first and noblest of human sciences; a science which does more to quicken and invigorate the understanding, than all the other kinds of learning put together; but it is not apt, except in persons very happily born, to open and to liberalize the mind exactly in the same proportion." For to speak "legally and constitutionally" is not the same as to speak "prudently." "Legislators ought to do what lawyers cannot; for they have no other rules to bind them, but the great principles of reason and equity, and the general sense of mankind."[4] The liberalization of the mind obviously requires understanding of "the great principles of reason and equity," which for Burke are the same thing as the natural law.

But it is not necessary to dwell on this particular shortcoming from which representative government might suffer. Two generations after Burke, John Stuart Mill took up the question concerning the relation of representative government and liberal education. One does not exagger-

3. Nos. 10, 35, 36, 55, 57, 62, 68.
4. *The Works of Edmund Burke* (Bohn Standard Library), I 407, II 7, 317–318, V 295.

ate too much by saying that he took up these two subjects in entire separation from each other. His *Inaugural Address at St. Andrews* deals with liberal education as "the education of all who are not obliged by their circumstances to discontinue their scholastic studies at a very early age," not to say the education of "the favorites of nature and fortune." That speech contains a number of observations which will require our consideration and reconsideration. Mill traces the "superiority" of classical literature "for purposes of education" to the fact that that literature transmits to us "the wisdom of life": "In cultivating . . . the ancient languages as our best literary education, we are all the while laying an admirable foundation for ethical and philosophical culture." Even more admirable than "the substance" is "the form" of treatment: "It must be remembered that they had more time and that they wrote chiefly for a select class possessed of leisure," whereas we "write in a hurry for people who read in a hurry." The classics used "the right words in the right places" or, which means the same thing, they were not "prolix."[5] But liberal education has very little effect on the "miscellaneous assembly" which is the legal sovereign and which is frequently ruled by men who have no qualification for legislation except "a fluent tongue, and a faculty of getting elected by a constituency." To secure "the intellectual qualifications desirable in representatives," Mill thought, there is no other mode than proportional representation as devised by Hare and Fawcett, a scheme which in his opinion is of "perfect feasibility" and possesses "transcendent advantages."

> The natural tendency of representative government, as of modern civilization, is toward collective mediocrity: and this tendency is increased by all reductions and extensions of the franchise, their effect being to place the principal power in

5. James and John Stuart Mill, *On Education*, ed. by F.A. Cavenagh (Cambridge: University Press, 1931), pp. 151–157.

the hands of classes more and more below the highest level of instruction in the community. . . . It is an admitted fact that in the American democracy, which is constructed on this faulty model, the highly-cultivated members of the community, except such of them as are willing to sacrifice their own opinions and modes of judgment, and become the servile mouthpieces of their inferiors in knowledge, do not ever offer themselves for Congress or State legislatures, so certain is it that they would have no chance of being returned. Had a plan like Mr. Hare's by good fortune suggested itself to the enlightened and patriotic founders of the American Republic, the Federal and State Assemblies would have contained many of those distinguished men, and democracy would have been spared its greatest reproach and one of its most formidable evils.

Only proportional representation which guarantees or at least does not exclude the proper representation of the best part of society in the government will transform "the falsely called democracies which now prevail, and from which the current idea of democracy is exclusively derived" into "the only true type of democracy," into democracy as originally meant.

For reasons which are not all bad, Mill's remedy has come to be regarded as insufficient, not to say worthless. Perhaps it was a certain awareness of this which induced him to look for relief in another part of the body politic. From the fact that the representative assemblies are not necessarily "a selection of the greatest political minds of the country," he drew the conclusion that for "the skilled legislation and administration" one must secure "under strict responsibility to the nation, the acquired knowledge and practiced intelligence of a specially trained and experienced Few."[6] Mill appears to suggest that with the growth and maturity of democracy, the institutional seat of public-spirited intelligence could and should be sought in the high and middle echelons of the appointed officials. This

6. *Considerations on Representative Government* (London: Routledge, s.d.), pp. 93, 95, 101–102, 133–140, 155.

hope presupposes that the bureaucracy can be transformed into a civil service properly so called, the specific difference between the bureaucrat and the civil servant being that the civil servant is a liberally educated man whose liberal education affects him decisively in the performance of his duties.

Permit me to summarize the preceding argument. In the light of the original conception of modern republicanism, our present predicament appears to be caused by the decay of religious education of the people and by the decay of liberal education of the representatives of the people. By the decay of religious education I mean more than the fact that a very large part of the people no longer receive any religious education, although it is not necessary on the present occasion to think beyond that fact. The question as to whether religious education can be restored to its pristine power by the means at our disposal is beyond the scope of this year's Arden House Institute. Still, I cannot help stating to you these questions: Is our present concern with liberal education of adults, our present expectation from such liberal education, not due to the void created by the decay of religious education? Is such liberal education meant to peform the function formerly performed by religious education? Can liberal education perform that function? It is certainly easier to discuss the other side of our predicament—the predicament caused by the decay of liberal education of the governors. Following Mill's suggestion, we would have to consider whether and to what extent the education of the future civil servants can and should be improved, or in other words whether the present form of their education is liberal education in a tolerably strict sense. If it is not, one would have to raise the broader question whether the present colleges and universities supply such a liberal education and whether they can be reformed. It is more modest, more pertinent, and more practical to give thought to some necessary reforms of the teaching in the Departments of Political Science and perhaps also in the Law Schools. The changes I have in mind are less in the subjects taught than in the emphasis and in the approach: whatever broadens and deepens the understanding should be more encouraged than what in the best case cannot as such produce more than narrow and unprincipled efficiency.

No one, I trust, will misunderstand the preceding remarks so as to impute to me the ridiculous assertion that education has ceased to be a public or political power. One must say, however, that a new type of education or a new orientation of education has come to predominate. Just as liberal education in its original sense was supported by classical philosophy, so the new education derives its support, if not its being, from modern philosophy. According to classical philosophy the end of the philosophers is radically different from the end or ends actually pursued by the nonphilosphers. Modern philosophy comes into being when the end of philosophy is identified with the end which is capable of being actually pursued by all men. More precisely, philosophy is now asserted to be essentially subservient to the end which is capable of being actually pursued by all men. We have suggested that the ultimate justification for the distinction between gentlemen and nongentlemen is the distinction between philosophers and nonphilosophers. If this is true, it follows that by causing the purpose of the philosophers, or more generally the purpose which essentially transcends society, to collapse into the purpose of the nonphilosophers, one causes the purpose of the gentlemen to collapse into the purpose of the nongentlemen. In this respect, the modern conception of philosophy is fundamentally democratic. The end of philosophy is now no longer what one may call disinterested contemplation of the eternal, but the relief of man's estate. Philosophy thus understood could be presented with some plausibility as inspired by biblical charity, and accordingly philosophy in the classic sense could be disparaged as pagan and as sustained by sinful pride. One may doubt whether the claim to biblical inspiration was justified and even whether it was always raised in entire sincerity. However this may be, it is conducive to greater clarity, and at the same time in agreement with the spirit of the modern conception, to say that the moderns opposed a "realistic," earthly, not to say pedestrian conception to the "idealistic," heavenly, not to say visionary conception of the classics. Philosophy or science was no longer an end in itself, but in the service of human power, of a power to be used for making human life longer, healthier, and more abundant. The economy of scarcity, which is the tacit presupposition of all earlier social thought, was to be replaced by an economy of plenty. The radical distinction between science and manual labor was to be replaced by the smooth co-operation of the scientist and the engineer. According to the original conception, the men in control of this stupendous enterprise were the philosopher-scientists. Everything was to be done by them for the people, but, as it were, nothing by the people. For the people were, to begin with, rather distrustful of the new gifts from the new sort of sorcerers, for they remembered the commandment, "Thou shalt not suffer a sorcerer to live." In order to become the willing recipients of the new gifts, the people had to be enlightened. This enlightenment is the core of the new education. It is the same as the diffusion or popularization of the new science. The addresses of the popularized science were in the first stage countesses and duchesses, rather than spinsters and dairymaids, and popularized science often surpassed science proper in elegance and charm of diction. But the first step entailed all the further steps which were taken in due order. The enlightenment was destined to become universal enlightenment. It appeared that the difference of natural gifts did not have the importance which the tradition had ascribed to it; method proved to be the great equalizer of naturally unequal minds. While invention or discovery continued to remain the preserve of the few, the results could be transmitted to all. The leaders in this great enterprise did not rely entirely on the effects of formal education for weaning men away from concern with the bliss of the next world to work for happiness in this. What study did not do, and perhaps could not do, trade did: immensely facilitated and encouraged by the new inventions and discoveries, trade which unites all peoples, took precedence over religion, which divides the peoples.

But what was to be done to moral education? The identification of the end of the gentlemen with the end of the nongentlemen meant that the understanding of virtue as choiceworthy for its own sake gave way to an instrumental understanding of virtue: honesty is nothing but the best policy, the policy most conducive to commodious living or comfortable self-preservation. Virtue took on a narrow meaning, with the final result that the word "virtue" fell into desuetude. There was no longer a need for a genuine conversion from the premoral if not immoral concern with worldly goods to the concern with the goodness of the soul, only for the calculating transition from unenlightened to enlightened self-interest. Yet even this was not entirely necessary. It was thought that at least the majority of men will act sensibly and well if the alternative will be made unprofitable by the right kind of institution, political and economic. The devising of the right kind of institutions and their implementation came to be regarded as more important than the formation of character by liberal education.

Yet let us not for one moment forget the other side of the picture. It is a demand of justice that there should be a reasonable correspondence between the social hierarchy and the natural hierarchy. The lack of such a correspondence in the old scheme was defended by the fundamental fact of scarcity. With the increasing abundance it became increasingly possible to see and to admit the element of hypocrisy which had entered into the traditional notion of aristocracy; the existing aristocracies proved to be oligarchies, rather than aristocracies. In other words it became increasingly easy to argue from the premise that natural inequality has very little to do with social inequality, that practically or politically speaking one may safely assume that all men are by nature equal, that all men have the same natural rights, provided one uses this rule of thumb as the major premise for reaching the conclusion that everyone should be given the same opportunity as everyone else: natural inequality has its rightful place in the use, nonuse, or abuse of opportunity in the race as distinguished from at the start. Thus it became possible to abolish many injustices or at least many things which had become injustices. Thus was ushered in the age of tolerance. Humanity, which was formerly rather the virtue appropriate in one's dealings with one's inferiors—with the underdog—became the crowning virtue. Goodness became identical with compassion.

Originally the philosopher-scientist was thought to be in control of the progressive enterprise. Since he had no power, he had to work through the princes. The control was then in fact in the hands of the princes, if of enlightened princes. But with the progress of enlightenment, the tutelage of the princes was no longer needed. Power could be entrusted to the people. It is true that the people did not always listen to the philosopher-scientists. But apart from the fact that the same was true of princes, society came to take on such a character that it was more and more compelled to listen to the philosopher-scientists if it desired to survive. Still there remained a lag between the enlightenment coming from above and the way in which the people exercised its freedom. One may even speak of a race: will the people come into full possession of its freedom before it has become enlightened, and if so, what will it do with its freedom and even with the imperfect enlightenment which it will already have received? An apparent solution was found through an apparent revolt against the enlightenment and through a genuine revolt against enlightened despotism. It was said that every man has the right to political freedom, to being a member of the sovereign, by virtue of the dignity which every man has as man —the dignity of a moral being. The only thing which can be held to be unqualifiedly good is not the contemplation of the eternal, not the cultivation of the mind, to say nothing of good breeding, but a good intention, and of good intentions everyone is as capable as everyone else, wholly independently of education. Accordingly, the uneducated could even appear to have an advantage over the educated: the voice of nature or ɔf the moral law speaks in them perhaps more clearly and nore decidedly than in the sophisticated who may have scɔhisticated away their conscience. This belief is not the only starting point and perhaps not the best starting point, but it is for us now the most convenient starting point for understanding the assertion which was made at that moment: the assertion that virtue is the principle of democracy and only of democracy. One conclusion from this assertion was Jacobin terror which punished not only actions and speeches but intentions as well. Another conclusion was that one must respect every man merely because he is a man, regardless of how he uses his will or his freedom, and this respect must be implemented by full political rights for everyone who is not technically criminal or insane, regardless of whether he is mature for the exercise of those rights or not. That reasoning reminds one of a reasoning which was immortalized by Locke's criticism and which led to the conclusion that one may indeed behead a tyrannical king, but only with reverence for that king. It remains then at the race between the political freedom below and the enlightenment coming from above.

Hitherto I have spoken of the philosopher-scientist. That is to say, I have pretended that the original conception, the seventeenth-century conception, has retained its force. But in the meantime philosophy and science have become divorced: a philosopher need not be a scientist, and a scientist need not be a philosopher. Only the title

Ph.D. is left as a reminder of the past. Of the two hence-forth divorced faculties of the mind, science has acquired supremacy; science is the only authority in our age of which one can say that it enjoys universal recognition. This science has no longer any essential connection with wisdom. It is a mere accident if a scientist, even a great scientist, happens to be a wise man politically or privately. Instead of the fruitful and ennobling tension between religious education and liberal education, we now see the tension between the ethos of democracy and the ethos of technocracy. During the last seventy years, it has become increasingly the accepted opinion that there is no possibility of scientific, and hence rational knowledge of "values," that is, the science or reason is incompetent to distinguish between good and evil ends. It would be unfair to deny that, thanks to the survival of utilitarian habits, scientists in general and social scientists in particular still take it for granted in many cases that health, a reasonably long life, and prosperity are good things and that science must find means for securing or procuring them. But these ends can no longer claim the evidence which they once possessed; they appear now to be posited by certain desires which are not "objectively" superior to the opposite desires. Since science is then unable to justify the ends for which it seeks the means, it is in practice compelled to satisfy the ends which are sought by its customers, by the society to which the individual scientist happens to belong and hence in many cases by the mass. We must disregard here the older traditions which fortunately still retain some of their former power; we must disregard them because their power is more and more corroded as time goes on. If we look then only at what is peculiar to our age or characteristic of our age, we see hardly more than the interplay of mass taste with high-grade but strictly speaking unprincipled efficiency. The technicians are, if not responsible, at any rate responsive to the demands of the mass; but a mass as mass cannot be responsible to anyone or to anything for anything. It is in this situation that we here, and others in the country, raise the question concerning liberal education and responsibility.

In this situation the insufficiently educated are bound to have an unreasonably strong influence on education—on the determination of both the ends and the means of education. Furthermore, the very progress of science leads to an ever increasing specialization, with the result that a man's respectability becomes dependent on his being a specialist. Scientific education is in danger of losing its value for the broadening and the deepening of the human being. The only universal science which is possible on this basis—logic or methodology—becomes itself an affair of and for technicians. The remedy for specialization is therefore sought in a new kind of universalism—a universalism which has been rendered almost inevitable by the extension of our spatial and temporal horizons. We are trying to expel the narrowness of specialization by the superficiality of such things as general civilization courses or by what has aptly been compared to the unending cinema, as distinguished from a picture gallery, of the history of all nations in all respects: economic, scientific, artistic, religious, and political. The gigantic spectacle thus provided is in the best case exciting and entertaining; it is not instructive and educating. A hundred pages—no, ten pages—of Herodotus introduce us immeasurably better into the mysterious unity of oneness and variety in human things than many volumes written in the spirit predominant in our age. Besides, human excellence or virtue can no longer be regarded as the perfection of human nature toward which man is by nature inclined or which is the goal of his eros. Since "values" are regarded as in fact conventional, the place of moral education is taken by conditioning, or more precisely by conditioning through symbols verbal and other, or by adjustment to the society in question.

What then are the prospects for liberal education within mass democracy? What are the prospects for the liberally educated to become again a power in democracy? We are not permitted to be flatterers of democracy precisely because we are friends and allies of democracy. While we are not permitted to remain silent on the dangers to which democracy exposes itself as well as human excellence, we cannot forget the obvious fact that by giving freedom to all, democracy also gives freedom to those who care for human excellence. No one prevents us from cultivating our garden or from setting up outposts which may come to be regarded by many citizens as salutary to the republic and as deserving of giving to it its tone. Needless to say, the utmost exertion is the necessary, although by no means the sufficient, condition for success. For "men can always hope and never need to give up, in whatever fortune and in whatever travail they find themselves." We are indeed compelled to be specialists, but we can try to specialize in the most weighty matters or, to speak more simply and more nobly, in the one thing needful. As matters stand, we can expect more immediate help from the humanities rightly understood than from the sciences, from the spirit of perceptivity and delicacy than from the spirit of geometry. If I am not mistaken, this is the reason why liberal education is now becoming almost synonymous with the reading in common of the Great Books. No better beginning could have been made.

We must not expect that liberal education can ever become universal education. It will always remain the obligation and the privilege of a minority. Nor can we expect that the liberally educated will become a political power in their own right. For we cannot expect that liberal education will lead all who benefit from it to understand their civic responsibility in the same way or to agree politically. Karl Marx, the father of communism, and Friedrich Nietzsche, the stepgrandfather of fascism, were liberally educated on a level to which we cannot even hope to aspire. But perhaps one can say that their grandiose failures make it easier for us who have experienced those failures to understand again the old saying that wisdom cannot be separated from moderation and hence to understand that wisdom requires unhesitating loyalty to a decent constitution and even to the cause of constitutionalism. Moderation will protect us against the twin dangers of visionary expectations from politics and unmanly contempt for politics. Thus it may again become true that all liberally educated men will be politically moderate men. It is in this way that the liberally educated may again receive a hearing even in the market place.

No deliberation about remedies for our ills can be of any value if it is not preceded by an honest diagnosis—by a diagnosis falsified neither by unfounded hopes nor by fear of the powers that be. We must realize that we must hope almost against hope. I say this, abstracting entirely from the dangers threatening us at the hands of a barbaric and cruel, narrow-minded and cunning foreign enemy who is kept in check, if he is kept in check, only by the justified fear that whatever would bury us would bury him too. In thinking of remedies we may be compelled to rest satisfied with palliatives. But we must not mistake palliatives for cures. We must remember that liberal education for adults is not merely an act of justice to those who were in their youth deprived through their poverty of an education for which they are fitted by nature. Liberal education of adults must now also compensate for the defects of an education which is liberal only in name or by courtesy. Last but not least, liberal education is concerned with the souls of men and therefore has little or no use for machines. If it becomes a machine or an industry, it becomes undistinguishable from the entertainment industry unless in respect to income and publicity, to tinsel and glamour. But liberal education consists in learning to listen to still and small voices and therefore in becoming deaf to loud-speakers. Liberal education seeks light and therefore shuns the limelight.

Major Works Published by
LEO STRAUSS

1936   The Political Philosophy of Hobbes. (Presently published by the University of Chicago Press.)

1948   On Tyranny: An Interpretation of Xenophon's Hiero. (Present published by the Free Press in a revised and expanded edition.)

1952   Persecution and the Art of Writing. (Presently published by the University of Chicago Press.)

1953   Natural Right and History. (Original and Presently published by the University of Chicago Press.)

1958   Thoughts on Machiavelli. (Presently published by the University of Chicago Press.)

1959   What Is Political Philosophy? and Other Studies. (Presently published by the University of Chicago Press.)

1964   The City and Man. (Presently published by the University of Chicago Press.)

1966   Socrates and Aristophanes. (Presently published by the University of Chicago Press.)

1968   Liberalixm Ancient and Modern. (Presently published by the University of Chicago Press.)

1970   Xenophon's Socratic Discourse: An Interpretation of the Oeconomicus. (Originally published by the Cornell University Press.)

1972   Xenophon's Socrates. (Originally published by the Cornell University Press.)

1975   The Argument and the Action of Plato's Laws. (Originally and presently published by the University of Chicago Press.)

1983   Studies in Platonic Political Philosophy. (Originally and presently published by the University of Chicago Press.)

Index

Abraham, 280
Absolute moment, 119
Adeimantos, 168, 179, 192, 197, 198, 206, 211
Anti-Semitism, 256
Apology of Socrates (Plato), 30–31, 228
Aquinas, Thomas, 5
Aristocracy, 225, 339; universal, democracy as, 313, 314
Aristotle, xix, xxiii, 4, 31, 35, 52, 70, 75, 78, 113, 160, 165, 190, 225–26, 241, 259–60, 275, 281, 287, 295, 319; actualization of best regime, 84–85; definition of good citizen, 33–34; ethics of, 276–77, 278–79; political science of, 127–32
Assimilationism, Jewish, 254–56
Atheism, 242, 243
Athenian stranger, 26–28, 29, 30, 231–45
Autoemancipation (Pinsker), 7

Bacon, Francis, 304
Behavioralists, 127

Bergbohm, Karl, 100n–101n
Bergson, Henri, 12
Bible: account of creation, 281, 288, 305; agreement with philosophic viewpoint, 273–76, 287–88, 291–92; as compilation of sources, 294; conflict with philosophic viewpoint, 276–86, 289–91, 292–95; and divine law, 276, 284–87, 292–93; as historical, 290–91; idea of progress in, 262; morality of, 265, 274–75, 276–79; obedience to law in, 275; and problem of human knowledge, 288–89; rejection of mythology, 292–93; view of man, 86. *See also* God; Revelation
Burke, Edmund, xxi, 140–41, 284, 333

Cabbalism, 250
Causality, principle of, xv–xvi
Cicero, 217
City. *See* Just city; Regime
Cohen, Hermann, 12